A Survey of Structural Linguistics

THE LANGUAGE LIBRARY

EDITED BY DAVID CRYSTAL

A SURVEY OF
STRUCTURAL LINGUISTICS

GIULIO C. LEPSCHY

ANDRE DEUTSCH

First published 1970 by
Faber and Faber Limited
This edition published 1982 by
André Deutsch Limited
105 Great Russell Street London WC1

Printed in Great Britain by
Billing and Sons Limited
Guildford, London, Oxford, Worcester

ISBN 0 233 97415 6

Distributed in the United States of America and Canada by
Westview Press, 5500 Central Avenue, Boulder, Colorado 80301

For Anna Laura

Contents

🆂🆂🆂🆂🆂🆂

Preface

𑂴𑂴𑂴𑂴𑂴𑂴

This book examines the main trends in structural linguistics. It consists of an introduction in which the main features of structuralism are discussed, and of eight chapters devoted to Saussure, the School of Prague (Trubeckoj), the School of Copenhagen (Hjelmslev), American linguistics (Sapir and Bloomfield), functional linguistics (Jakobson and Martinet), 'structural linguistics' in a more limited sense (the post-Bloomfieldians), transformational grammar (Chomsky), and lastly mathematical linguistics and machine translation.

I have tried to be as comprehensive as possible without letting the book spread over too many pages, and as objective as possible without suppressing my own views. The bibliographical references constitute an essential part of this work, both as sources of what is said in the text, and as a guide for further reading.

In this new edition I have added an Appendix which brings the bibliography up to date, and adds a few observations on recent developments in transformational linguistics, and on Montague grammar.

This work was originally published in Italian,* in a different

*First as two articles, 'Aspetti teorici di alcune correnti della glottologia contemporanea', in *ASNP*, 30, 1961, 187–267 and 34, 1965, 221–95, then as a book, *La linguistica strutturale,* Torino 1966 (latest edition, brought up to date, 1979). I wish to express my debt to Professors T. Bolelli, A. Martinet and L. R. Palmer, who gave me valuable advice in Pisa, Paris and Oxford. I owe many clarifications to discussions with Professor Antonio Lepschy. I am also grateful to friends and colleagues who read parts of the work at various stages and made constructive criticisms. For the first edition published by Faber and Faber, I wish to thank Professor L. R. Palmer who did much to improve the English text. I am grateful to my colleague, Professor David Crystal, who, after the Faber edition went out of print, accepted this updated version in the series he edits for André Deutsch.

11

Preface

version, and was intended for readers who already had a basic training in comparative philology and wanted to be informed about modern linguistic theories. It turned out to be of interest not only to its originally intended public, but also to students of general linguistics, specialists of other disciplines, and lay readers without any prior knowledge of linguistics. That it was well received is indicated by the mostly favourable reviews, by successive updated reprints of the Italian version, and by numerous translations (into French, German, Spanish, Portuguese, and Japanese).

I am pleased to be able to repeat what I wrote in the preface to the first English edition, as I feel that it is still valid now: 'The author hopes that, in spite of the numerous studies of modern linguistics published recently, this English version—specially revised and brought up to date—will not be out of place. There does not seem to be another work with the same range and perspective, nor animated by the same interests.'

Giulio Lepschy
Reading, June 1981.

Abbreviations

🔲🔲🔲🔲🔲

1st Congr. Ling.	Actes du premier congrès international de linguistes à la Haye, du 10–15 avril 1928, Leiden (n.d.)
2nd Congr. Ling.	Actes du deuxième congrès international de linguistes, Genève 25–29 août 1931, Paris 1933
3rd Congr. Ling.	Atti del III Congresso internazionale dei linguisti (Roma 19–26 settembre 1933), Firenze 1935
4th Congr. Ling.	Actes du quatrième congrès international de linguistes tenu à Copenhague du 27 août au 1er septembre 1936, Copenhague 1938
5th Congr. Ling.	(the Congress, planned for 1939 in Brussels, was not held. The following texts were distributed: Réponses au Questionnaire, Bruges (n.d.); Supplément, ib. (n.d.); Rapports, ib. (n.d.); Résumés des communications, ib. (n.d.))
6th Congr. Ling.	Actes du sixième congrès international des linguistes (Paris, juillet 1948), Paris 1949
7th Congr. Ling.	Proceedings of the Seventh International Congress of Linguists, London, 1–6 September 1952, London 1956
8th Congr. Ling.	Proceedings of the Eighth International Congress of Linguists, Oslo 1958

9th Congr. Ling.	Proceedings of the Ninth International Congress of Linguists, Cambridge, Mass., August 27–31, 1962, The Hague 1964
1st Congr. Phon.	Proceedings of the International Congress of Phonetic Sciences, Amsterdam, 3–8 July 1932, *ANPE*, 8–9, 1933
2nd Congr. Phon.	Proceedings of the Second International Congress of Phonetic Sciences, London, 22–26 July 1935, Cambridge 1936
3rd Congr. Phon.	Proceedings of the Third International Congress of Phonetic Sciences, Ghent, 18–22 July 1938, Ghent 1939
4th Congr. Phon.	Proceedings of the Fourth International Congress of Phonetic Sciences, Helsinki, 4–9 September 1961, The Hague 1962
5th Congr. Phon.	Proceedings of the Fifth International Congress of Phonetic Sciences, Münster, 16–22 August 1964, Basel 1965
AAWL	Abhandlungen der Akademie der Wissenschaften und der Literatur in Mainz, Geistes- und sozialwissenschaftliche Klasse. Wiesbaden
AGI	Archivio Glottologico Italiano. Firenze
AION–L	Annali, Istituto Universitario Orientale, Sezione linguistica. Napoli
AJPh	American Journal of Philology. Baltimore
AL	Acta Linguistica. Revue internationale de linguistique structurale (from vol. 9, 1965 Acta Linguistica Hafniensia). Copenhague
ALH	Acta Linguistica Academiae Scientiarum Hungaricae. Budapest
AmA	American Anthropologist. Menasha, Wisc.
AnL	Anthropological Linguistics. Bloomington, Ind.

14

Abbreviations

ANPE	Archives néerlandaises de phonétique expérimentale. La Haye
AO	Archiv Orientální. Praha
ArchL	Archivum Linguisticum. A Review of Comparative Philology and General Linguistics. Glasgow
AS	American Speech. New York
ASLU	Acta Societatis Linguisticae Upsaliensis. Uppsala
ASNP	Annali della Scuola Normale Superiore di Pisa. Lettere, storia e filosofia. Pisa
ÅVsLund	Vetenskaps-societeten i Lund, Årsbok. Lund
BIHP	Bulletin of the Institute of History and Philology, Academia Sinica. Taipei
BPTJ	Biuletyn polskiego towarzystwa językoznawczego. Wrocław
BSL	Bulletin de la Société de Linguistique de Paris. Paris
BSOAS	Bulletin of the School of Oriental and African Studies, University of London. London
CAnthr	Current Anthropology. A World Journal of the Sciences of Man. Chicago
CFS	Cahiers Ferdinand de Saussure. Genève
CILP	Conférences de l'Institut de Linguistique, Université de Paris. Paris
ČMF	Časopis pro Moderní Filologii (now PhP). Praha
CW	The Classical Weekly (now The Classical World). New York
Diogène	Diogène. Revue internationale des sciences humaines. Paris

15

Abbreviations

Diogenes	Diogenes. An International Review of Philosophy and Humanistic Studies. Montreal (a parallel edition of the former)
DLZ	Deutsche Literaturzeitung für Kritik der internationalen Wissenschaft. Berlin
ETC.	ETC. A Review of General Semantics. Chicago
FL	Foundations of Language. International Journal of Language and Philosophy. Dordrecht
FM	Le Français Moderne. Paris
GGA	Göttingische Gelehrte Anzeigen. Berlin
GK	Gengo Kenkyū. Tokyo
Homme	L'Homme. Revue française d'anthropologie. Paris
HSPh	Harvard Studies in Classical Philology. Cambridge, Mass.
IF	Indogermanische Forschungen. Zeitschrift für Indogermanistik und allgemeine Sprachwissenschaft. Berlin
IJ	Indogermanisches Jahrbuch. Strassburg
IJAL	International Journal of American Linguistics. Baltimore
ISSJ	International Social Science Journal. Paris
IzvAN	Izvestija Akademii Nauk SSSR, Otdelenie literatury i jazyka. Moskva
JAcS	Journal of the Acoustical Society of America. Lancaster, Pas.
JAOS	Journal of the American Oriental Society. New Haven, Conn.
JCLA	The Journal of the Canadian Linguistic Association. Edmonton, Alberta (now Canadian Journal of Linguistics. Toronto)

JEGP	The Journal of English and Germanic Philology. Urbana, Ill.
JL	Journal of Linguistics. London
JP	Język Polski. Kraków
JPsych	Journal de Psychologie normale et pathologique. Paris
JSL	The Journal of Symbolic Logic. Menasha, Wisc.
KNf	Kwartalnik Neofilologiczny. Warszawa
Kratylos	Kratylos. Wiesbaden
L&S	Language and Speech. Teddington
LbR	Limba Română. București
LeSt	Lingua e Stile (formerly QIGB). Bologna
Lg	Language. Journal of the Linguistic Society of America. Baltimore
LGRP	Literaturblatt für germanische und romanische Philologie. Heilbronn
Lingua	Lingua. International Review of General Linguistics. Amsterdam
Linguistics	Linguistics. An International Review. The Hague
Linguistique	La Linguistique. Revue internationale de linguistique générale. Paris
LL	Language Learning. Ann Arbor
MALinc	Atti della Accademia Nazionale dei Lincei, Memorie della Classe di scienze morali, storiche e filologiche. Serie VIII. Roma
Methodos	Methodos. Linguaggio e cibernetica. Milano
MLF	Modern Language Forum. Los Angeles
MLJ	Modern Language Journal. Ann Arbor
Monatshefte	Monatshefte für deutschen Unterricht. Madison, Wisc.

Abbreviations

MPh	Modern Philology. Chicago
MPhon	Le Maître Phonétique. Organe de l'Association Phonétique Internationale. London
MPiPL	Mašinnyj perevod i prikladnaja lingvistika. Moskva
MSLL	Monograph Series on Languages and Linguistics, Georgetown University. Washington, D.C.
MSpråk	Moderna Språk. Stockholm
MT	Mechanical Translation. Cambridge, Mass.
Nph	Neophilologus. Groningen
NTF	Nordisk Tidsskrift for Filologi. København
NTg	De Nieuwe Taalgids. Groningen
NTS	Norsk Tidsskrift for Sprogvidenskap. Oslo
NTTS	Nordisk Tidsskrift for Tale og Stemme. København
PAPhilosS	Proceedings of the American Philosophical Society. Philadelphia
PF	Prace filologiczne. Warszawa
Phonetica	Phonetica. International Journal of Phonetics. Basel
PhP	Philologica Pragensia (formerly ČMF). Praha
PI	Le parole e le idee. Rivista internazionale di varia cultura. Napoli
PJ	Poradnik Językowy. Warszawa
PK	Problemy kibernetiki. Moskva
PLG	Probleme de lingvistică generală. Bucureşti
PSAM	Proceedings of Symposia in Applied Mathematics, American Mathematical Society. Providence, Rhode Island
QIGB	Quaderni dell'Istituto di Glottologia della Università di Bologna (from 1966 LeSt). Bologna

Abbreviations

RALinc	Atti della Accademia Nazionale dei Lincei, Rendiconti della Classe di scienze morali, storiche e filologiche. Serie VIII. Roma
RBF	Revista Brasileira de Filologia. Rio de Janeiro
RESl	Revue des Études Slaves. Paris
RFV	Russkij Filologičeskij Vestnik. Varšava
RJaŠ	Russkij Jazyk v Škole. Moskva
RJb	Romanistisches Jahrbuch. Hamburg
RL	Ricerche Linguistiche. Bollettino dell'Istituto di Glottologia dell'Università di Roma. Roma
RLaR	Revue des Langues Romanes. Montpellier
RLaV	Revue des Langues Vivantes. Bruxelles
RLing	Revue Roumaine de Linguistique. Bucarest
Romania	Romania. Paris
RomPh	Romance Philology. Berkeley
RPA	Revue de phonétique appliquée. Mons
RPF	Revista Portuguesa de Filologia. Coimbra
RSlav	Ricerche Slavistiche. Roma
SbÖAW	Sitzungsberichte der Österreichischen Akademie der Wissenschaften, Philosophisch-historische Klasse. Wien
SbSAW	Sitzungsberichte der Sächsischen Akademie der Wissenschaften zu Leipzig, Philologisch-historische Klasse. Berlin
SCL	Studii şi Cercetări Lingvistice. Bucureşti
SFFBU	Sborník Prací Filosofické Fakulty Brněnské University. Brno
SIL	Studies in Linguistics. Buffalo, N.Y.
SL	Studia Linguistica. Revue de linguistique générale et comparée. Lund
SlOr	Slavia Orientalis. Warszawa

Abbreviations

SNPh	Studia Neophilologica. A Journal of Germanic and Romanic Philology. Uppsala
SPh	Studies in Philology. Chapel Hill, N.C.
SS	Slovo a Slovesnost. Praha
SSL	Studi e Saggi Linguistici. Supplemento alla Rivista 'L'Italia Dialettale'. Pisa
TA	La Traduction automatique. La Haye
TCLC	Travaux du Cercle Linguistique de Copenhague. Copenhague
TCLP	Travaux du Cercle Linguistique de Prague. Prague
TIL	Travaux de l'Institut de Linguistique. Faculté de Lettres de l'Université de Paris. Paris
TLP	Travaux linguistiques de Prague. Prague
TPhS	Transactions of the Philological Society. Oxford
UCPL	University of California Publications in Linguistics. Berkeley
UZLU	Učenye zapiski Leningradskogo Universiteta. Leningrad.
UZMU	Učenye zapiski Moskovskogo Universiteta. Moskva
VJa	Voprosy Jazykoznanija. Moskva
VMU	Vestnik Moskovskogo Universiteta. Serija VII: Filologija. Moskva
VR	Vox Romanica. Annales Helvetici explorandis linguis Romanicis destinati. Bern
Word	Word. Journal of the Linguistic Circle of New York. New York
WSlJb	Wiener Slavistisches Jahrbuch. Graz
ZPhon	Zeitschrift für Phonetik, Sprachwissenschaft und Kommunikationsforschung. Berlin
ZRPh	Zeitschrift für romanische Philologie. Tübingen

CHAPTER I

Introductory Notions

🐚🐚🐚🐚🐚🐚

1.1 Comparative Grammar

According to a traditional view, particularly widespread in continental Europe, the scientific study of language is identical with historical linguistics; and what is generally meant by historical linguistics is Indo-European comparative grammar, or the study of other linguistic families according to the methods of Indo-European comparative grammar.[1] The implicit or explicit identification of linguistics with the methods used in the historical and comparative study of the earliest stages of Indo-European languages was in part due to the success of this discipline during the nineteenth century in providing proof of the genetic relationships between Indo-European languages and in identifying precise rules (like the much-discussed 'phonetic laws') which govern linguistic change. Such a degree of certainty and exactness was attained that comparative grammar came to be regarded as the linguistic study which is scientific *par excellence*; it was thus contrasted with other fields, both of historical and of linguistic research, in which the same degree of precision had not been reached. Indeed, the foundation of scientific linguistics is attributed not to Herder, the Schlegels, or W. von Humboldt (who had provided Indo-European comparative grammar with its philosophical bases), but to a figure of lesser importance in the history of culture, Franz Bopp; and the development of the discipline is marked by scholars more noted for their technical skill (as Indo-Europeanists) than for their theoretical insight (as general linguists), such as Pott, Schleicher,

21

and the Neo-grammarians. Amongst these we find Brugmann and Delbrück, who offered in their formidable *Grundriss* a survey (now antiquated, but still unsubstituted) which is typically representative of the methods of Indo-European comparative grammar.[2]

The comparative philologist used to distinguish his own work from both normative and descriptive grammar—which he identified as 'practical' pursuits—whereas he regarded his own research as 'scientific' because it was devoted to the history of language, the study of language change. He refused to consider the 'origin of language', as this problem could not be dealt with 'scientifically', but he dwelt on problems of pre-history: in a certain place, at a certain time, there were certain people (but we are not sure exactly which place and time and people) who spoke a language (or a group of similar dialects) of which no texts are preserved (writing was still unknown to the speakers of that language). In time, that language or those dialects became what we call Indo-European languages—of which texts from different ages are preserved—many still being spoken today.

During the nineteenth century comparative philologists were confident that they could 'reconstruct' the original language from which the Indo-European tongues developed: as is well known, A. Schleicher concocted a short story in what he conceived to be Indo-European, with the title 'The sheep and the horses': *avis akvāsas ka*; and not so long ago H. Hirt translated it into what he conceived to be Indo-European: *owis ek'wōses-kʷe*.[3] In our century a more prudent conception has been evolved, according to which the 'starred' or 'asterisked' items ('reconstructed', as they used to be called; i.e. attributed to Indo-European) are not considered as belonging to some real language actually spoken by definite people at a definite time in a definite place, but as a purely algebraic formula which expresses in abbreviated form the 'correspondences' (scientifically established by comparative grammar) between linguistic items belonging to historically documented Indo-European languages. It seems, then, that purely for convenience we choose a written symbol which is similar to, rather than different from, the symbols used in representing the historical items which are 'genetically' related. But as there is no *a priori* limit to the changes which any particular item can undergo, there are cases (like the laryngeals for instance) in which the choice of the written symbol is relatively arbitrary. Thus the symbol *p is not meant to represent an Indo-European voiceless bilabial unaspirated stop (whether it also does not refer to a tense or lax sound is more difficult to state); nor is the symbol *$ə$ meant to represent a laryngeal articulation (presumably one out of several such articulations). The symbol *p simply means that one finds a systematic correspondence, in certain conditions, between Sanskrit *p*, Greek *p*, Latin *p*, Armenian *h*, Gothic *f*, Old Irish Ø, etc. The symbol *$ə$ means that one finds a systematic correspondence between Sanskrit *i*, Greek *a*, Latin *a*, Armenian *a*, Old Slav *o* etc.[4] The relationship between the criteria of phonetic realism and of elegance and simplicity of solution in comparative grammar, and indeed the relationship between comparative grammar and historical reconstruction, have by no means been clarified even today.

1.2 The Crisis in Comparative Grammar

The use of algebraic symbols in asterisked formulae was widespread in the second half of the nineteenth century; and the more cautious attitude towards reconstruction was already clearly expressed at the beginning of the twentieth century by one of the most authoritative comparatists, A. Meillet: 'Indo-European is unknown, and correspondences are the only reality to be studied by the comparatist.' 'One cannot recreate through comparison a language which has disappeared.' 'What the method of comparative grammar provides is not a recreation of Indo-European as it was spoken: *it is a definite system of correspondences between historically documented languages.*'[5] This caution was partly due to the crisis which, in the last decades of the nineteenth century, had destroyed the confidence of the comparatists in the 'blind regularity' of sound change,

23

and thus in the possibility of reconstruction. In particular H. Schuchardt and J. Schmidt[6] had criticized the 'family tree' theory, according to which one started with a single trunk (the Indo-European original language), which in time split into branches, each of which kept splitting into other branches, and so on, culminating in a large number of present-day twigs. And, as with a tree, the branches would always diverge and split into new branches, and never converge and unite in a single branch. Each node at which the split occurred would be characterized by a set of sound laws which gave different results in the two new languages. But, as far as I know, it was never explained just why each split had to be binary, i.e. why a language should become two, rather than several new languages.[7] The comparative method, it was claimed, applied to prehistory the laws which had been tested in the field of history. But in the field of history it is not true that the further back we go in time the fewer languages we find; nor in the field of history do we find any support for the hypothesis of clear-cut binary splits.

Schmidt upheld the 'wave theory': linguistic innovations spread from a centre (like the waves caused by throwing a stone into a pond), and their spread can be marked on a map with an 'isogloss'. At any particular point on the map, at any particular time, a tongue is spoken which is a bundle of isoglosses; but each isogloss may have started in a different centre, and may have a different extension. Thus the presence of the same linguistic innovation x in two different languages A and B (in which presumably x had not originated independently), but not in language C, does not necessarily point to an earlier period in which A and B were not yet separated but constituted a single language D different from C (or from the language which became C). It may instead be due to the penetration of the same isogloss x (originating perhaps in another language E) into A and B, but not into C. This point of view makes the notion of a genealogical tree untenable, and the proper object of study appears to be not the history of any one language, but of particular phonological, grammatical or lexical innovations.

These tenets developed fruitfully with the elaboration of

'linguistic geography' and the production of linguistic atlases. Less profitably, they were in some quarters associated with a form of 'neo-idealist' philosophy, according to which the only linguistic reality is the individual speech act (identified with artistic creation), and any concept used in linguistic study (from 'language' to 'grammar', including of course 'isogloss' or 'the history of a word') is ruled out as a spurious abstraction which has, at best, a practical use as a help for classifying and remembering, but gives no insight into language. 'General linguistics', to paraphrase the title of a book by the main philosophical upholder of this thesis, is identical with 'science of expression' and with 'aesthetics'.[8]

1.3 Structuralism

Out of this crisis of traditional linguistics emerged other approaches to language which, in spite of their considerable differences, have often been associated under the same label as 'structuralist'.[9] These schools of thought have produced an immense literature devoted both to theory and its application to the description and interpretation of specific linguistic facts. In the chapters which follow, the theoretical work inspired by some of these trends will be reviewed. For the moment, by way of introduction, some notions will be touched upon which may constitute a useful framework for the subsequent discussion.

A notion basic to structural linguistics, yet not hitherto sufficiently discussed, is that of *model*. The term is somewhat ambiguous. In various sciences mathematical models are used, in which some aspects of the facts described are represented by certain equations; or else we may have physical models in which the aspects in question are reproduced, usually on a different scale, by some device in the laboratory. Both these kinds of models are used in linguistics: for instance, the first type is employed when algebraic formalism is devised to represent the syntactic functioning of a language; the second when we attempt to make a computer simulate some features of human linguistic behaviour.

In either case the use of a model presupposes an *analogy* between the model itself and some aspects of the phenomenon which is under discussion. The analogy is based on the *abstraction* of those aspects which are *relevant* for the purposes of the discussion from others which are, for those purposes, not relevant. The relevant ones are chosen from those which are common to whole groups of linguistic facts. Any aspect which belongs to one linguistic fact only, and so characterizes it as unique, is, in what we normally call linguistic description, non-relevant; in itself, the sharing of a particular feature between the linguistic fact and its model would detract from the uniqueness of this fact.

A structural description is thus marked by its *abstraction* and *generality*, and does not look for the concrete and the particular, as much of traditional linguistics does, or claims it does. I cannot tackle here the distinction between historical and naturalistic knowledge based, among other things, in discussions of historicism, on the 'individualizing' character of the former, and on the 'generalizing' character of the latter. But it may be noted that scientists whose knowledge is generally thought of as more technical than historical must often solve very 'individual' problems; an engineer, for instance, when planning a building may have to take into account specific conditions of climate, soil etc., which make that particular work individual and different from any other; and he may have to consider all sorts of aspects in his work, such as the colour of the roof, bearing in mind the effects of the rays of the sun, or the height of neighbouring buildings, having regard for norms imposed by a town planning authority. But nobody will say that the engineer has no use for the normal laws of science, which are abstract and general, because the work he is doing is concrete and particular; nor that he ignores 'relevance', because in his work he has to consider aspects which are relevant from *different* angles.

It would be useful to clarify the notion of model in linguistics, not only from a theoretical point of view, but also by considering its origins. Although the explicit discussion of the theory of models is very recent, its implicit use in linguistics is much earlier, and a study would be welcome of its relationship with the use made of models by mathematics, physics and the natural sciences on the one hand, and by historiography and sociology on the other.[10]

The notion of *relevance* must be considered in connexion with the different *functions* of language. Structural linguistics has generally insisted on one *aspect* of the *communicative function* of language: that of transmitting information, on the 'representational' level.

From listening to an utterance like *John rang yesterday* one can gather various kinds of information. One can normally tell whether the speaker was a man, a woman or a child, and perhaps guess the age; it is also possible to ascertain that the utterance had a certain speed, a certain loudness, a certain pitch, and that the voice had certain features such as breathiness, throatiness etc. One also knows that somebody is saying something. But besides all this, and much more information, one gathers that what is (truly or falsely) said is that John rang yesterday. In one sense the features conveying all the former information are *not relevant* from the point of view of the latter information. One can say that, in this sense, the utterance could convey the same information even if the speaker were different, if he used a different speed, loudness and pitch, if his voice were different, and so on. One would say that the utterance was the same—that one would have repetitions of the same utterance—even if these non-relevant features varied. As we have seen, there is *abstraction* of the relevant from the non-relevant aspects. What is common to different repetitions of an utterance is clearly abstract. One would look in vain for concrete physical elements common to all repetitions of an utterance. If we consider writing, we find that (1) '*John rang yesterday*' is physically more similar to (has more in common with) (2) '*John sang yesterday*' than with (3) 'John rang yesterday' or (4) 'JOHN RANG YESTERDAY'. But in spite of this, (1), (3) and (4) are different repetitions of the same message; they convey the same information (i.e. that John rang yesterday), whereas (2) is a different message; it conveys different information (i.e. that

27

John sang yesterday). The same is true in the spoken language: (1) will be more similar to (2), if both are pronounced by the same person, with the same speed, loudness etc., than to other repetitions of (1) pronounced by different voices, at different speeds etc.

One can extend this even further and point out that the sounds of speech can be described at different points along the communication channel. One can examine for instance the speech organs during speech production, the vibrations of the air (the sound waves), or the nervous impulses which transmit the noise from the ear to the brain. These three kinds of phenomena are of course connected (the first causes the second, and the second causes the third), but they are physically very different from each other, and each is physically different from the visual marks used to represent them (say an X-ray film of the speech organs in the first case; a spectrogram, or the soundtrack of a film, or a diagram of the sound waves in the second case, and so on). The sounds which we hear and the letters which we see are also in a sense incommensurable. We can say that what we hear when the word *rang* is pronounced, and what we see when we look at the written word 'rang', are just two physically different repetitions of the same English word which can be uttered or written. But the *sounds*, spoken and heard, and the *marks*, written and seen, have physically little in common (what they have physically in common is shared also by an indefinite number of things which are not repetitions of the English word *rang*). They are different concrete repetitions of the same abstract unit: and if we want a description of this abstract unit, a minute analysis of the sounds or of the letters of *rang* will not provide it.

A comparison is made frequently between linguistic units and chess pieces: the game remains the same whatever the substance and shape of the pieces. These must just be distinguishable one from the other. What each one looks like is hardly important. A comparison with numerical systems can also be suggested. In writing numbers according to the decimal system we use ten figures from 0 to 9 to represent the units; immediately to the left of these the same figures represent tens, and so on with hundreds, thousands etc. Thus the number twenty-seven is written as 27, where '2' represents twice ten units, and '7' seven units. One can use different systems; binary, quinary, duodecimal, and vigesimal systems are all in fact used. The difference between these systems (which offer distinct ways of dealing with the same numbers) can be compared to the difference between grammatical systems or phonemic systems in different languages (which can all be used to talk about the same facts). But differences in *numerical systems* should not be confused with differences in *codification*, i.e. in the way in which our units are manifested. The decimal system and the Roman numerical system are different: 27 corresponds to XXVII. They would still be different even if one used the same figures in both, i.e. Arabic figures in the Roman system (10.10.5.1.1), or Roman letters in the decimal system (II.VII). In using a computer one often has recourse to a decimal numerical system in a binary code which represents each of the ten figures of the decimal system with a four figure string of the symbols 0 and 1 belonging to a binary system: 0 = 0000, 1 = 0001, 2 = 0010, 3 = 0011, etc. Here 27 is represented by 2 = 0010 plus 7 = 0111, i.e. by 00100111. In a binary *numerical* system 27 would be 11011.

Non-structural linguistics has often confused what, according to the foregoing comparison, we could call the two notions of numerical system and of coding system; the abstract units of language and their substantial realizations. One can obviously say that Englishmen and Italians use the same ten figures, in spite of the fact that a 1 in ordinary Italian handwriting will look like a 7 to an Englishman, but not to an Italian who crosses the vertical stroke of his 7; attention must thus be paid to the physical shape of the figures. But one would hardly acquire an understanding of arithmetic by examining the shape of Arabic figures: all that matters is that ten different shapes are used. Similarly, one cannot understand how language works merely by studying carefully the physical aspect of the utterances. The feeling of concreteness, of keeping to the hard reality of facts, which traditional linguistics sometimes claims for itself, in opposition to the rarefied abstractions of structuralism, is thus largely an illusion. A phoneme remains the same, whether its material manifestation is a sound or a letter. A grapheme remains the same whether it is manifested by a handwritten or by a printed letter, or by dots and dashes as in the Morse code, or by gestures as in deaf and dumb sign language.

Structural linguistics has stressed that the physical realizations of an abstract unit have features which are predictable on the basis of environment; for instance phonemes are realized as speech sounds, but often one talks of conditioned or distributional variants, the nature of which depends on the sounds which are adjacent in the spoken chain. The relationship is thus twofold: the abstract unit is related on the one hand to its concrete manifestation, on the other to a particular 'distributional' variant of this manifestation.

The distinction between abstract and concrete is traditional in philosophy. From the point of view of the theory of signs Peirce elaborated his distinction between type and token, and Carnap his distinction between sign-design and sign-event. Logicians have also discussed at length the notion of *class*, which is here obviously relevant. It is possible to think of linguistic *types*, such as phonemes, as *classes*, as long as one keeps in mind that they are on a higher level of abstraction than tokens (the concrete speech sounds), and are neither a group of speech sounds (which is as concrete as a single speech sound), nor a sign belonging to metalanguage and denoting speech sounds used in the object language. It has been said that the phoneme /p/ is the name used to denote all the [p] speech sounds, and is thus a metalinguistic morpheme and not at all a (linguistic or metalinguistic) phoneme; but this statement will appear ill-conceived to linguists for whom the phoneme is obviously a phonological and not a morphological unit. A third notion is probably needed here: that of 'occurrence', which applies both at the level of concreteness of the tokens and at the level of abstraction of the types. To take an example from the written language, in the word 'that' we find four tokens ('t', 'h', 'a', 't') and three types ('t', 'h', 'a'); there are two tokens of the same type 't'. Each token is necessarily an occurrence. But we can think of the written word 'that' as a type; in it we would still find the three letter types 't', 'h', 'a', and four occurrences ('t', 'h', 'a', 't'), but no token. In other words a type can be thought of as occurring, on its own level of abstraction, without becoming, by its occurrence, a token.

This is important as it allows us to distinguish more sharply than is traditionally done between the two notions, mentioned above, of concrete manifestations and of distributional variants. The distributional variant will have certain predictable features which will depend on the substance of the manifestation. In speech the dorsal plosive of *keel* will be palatalized and the one of *coal* will not. In print there are type faces in which the dot over an 'i' will not appear if the letter immediately preceding is an 'f', and so on. Here we are at a different level of abstraction from one where we consider units which can be manifested in speech, or in writing, or in any other substance. However, one may want to consider these distributional variants as more abstract than any particular token or event: one can conceive an occurrence of *keel*, with its palatalized dorsal, and of *coal*, with its non-palatalized dorsal, not pronounced by any one particular voice, with any one particular speed or loudness etc. There is, in other words, an intermediate level of abstraction between a token occurring as one particular manifestation and a type which can be manifested by any substance whatsoever. This intermediate level of abstraction is interesting for the linguist as it allows him to discuss how distributional variation is introduced by syntagmatic relationships, without engulfing him in the description of particular speech events. To put it another way: some non-relevant features are more relevant than others. The palatalization of a dorsal stop in front of a palatal vowel is more relevant than, say, the kind of voice which pronounces that stop. The change of a male voice for a female one does not distort the message, but the change of the dorsal of *keel* for the dorsal of *coal* does. In other words, syntagmatic relations are *not* identical with relations within Saussure's

31

parole ('speech' or 'speaking'), and distributional variants can be considered as belonging to Saussure's *langue* ('language').

The criterion of relevance applies within particular languages. In English, in Italian and in Chinese we find the two sounds [n] (an alveolar nasal) and [ŋ] (a velar nasal). In English and in Chinese they belong to different phonemes: *to sing* in English is not *to sin*, and *xìng* ('sex') in Chinese is not *xìn* ('truth'). In Italian the two sounds are in complementary distribution in internal position (*manto* 'cloak' with a dental in front of a dental, *manco* 'lack' with a velar in front of a velar); in final position (*man* 'hand') there is normally a velar which can be freely substituted with an alveolar without any change in meaning.

[p] sounds appearing in English, Italian and Chinese utterances may be physically indistinguishable. But different features can be relevant in different languages. The voicelessness of [p] is relevant in English where *pin* is different from *bin*, and in Italian where *pastone* 'mash' is different from *bastone* 'stick'. The initial of English *pin* is aspirated; this is not relevant, but a matter of distributional variation (in front of a stressed vowel a voiceless initial stop will predictably be aspirated; it will be unaspirated if preceded by *s* as in *spin*). The Italian [p] is normally unaspirated: an aspirated [pᶜ] would be not a distributional but a free, unpredictable variant which could have an expressive value, but would not make *pastone* into another word. The lack of aspiration which is not relevant in English *spin* or in Italian *pastone*, is relevant in Chinese *bà* 'to cease': the Chinese *b* is unaspirated and different from the aspirated *p* of *pà* 'to fear'. Both aspirated and unaspirated Chinese bilabials are voiceless; but this time the voicelessness is not relevant, as there is no voiced counterpart; in fact the unaspirated *b* can sometimes become voiced, as a matter of free variation. Whereas in the Wade-Giles romanization the unaspirated is noted as 'p' and the aspirated as ' p ' ', in the Chinese romanization called pīnyīn (used above), the unaspirated is noted with the letter 'b', and the aspirated with the letter 'p'; in IPA transcription the unaspirated is noted [b̥].

Phonemic units are also *discrete*. A bilabial stop can be

pronounced in English or in Italian with any degree of sonoriz-
ation between a fully voiceless [p] and a fully voiced [b]. But
any of these sounds, phonetically intermediate between voiceless and voiced, will be interpreted either as the phoneme /p/
or as the phoneme /b/, without any possibility of a compromise.
From the point of view of meaning, our language gives us the
possibility of saying anything we want to say (or almost anything, for many of our experiences defy verbalization for the
normal language user). In particular we are not semantically
bound by discreteness. If the need arises, we can talk about an
object which is halfway between a pin and a bin; but we will not
be able to do so by pronouncing the word with a half sonorized
initial bilabial stop. The units with which grammar and lexis
operate are not phonemes but morphemes and lexemes; these
are also discrete units, and signs of an 'arbitrary character'.
Not only is there nothing in a bin to suggest that it should be
called *bin* rather than *pin*, but the fact that the word *bin* is more
similar in its phonemic shape to the word *pin* than to the word
container does not suggest that a bin is more like a pin than a
container.

Attention has been focused on the presence of a set of
abstract and discrete elements which are the functioning units
in language. They are connected by a complex net of relationships; they constitute a system. It is normally possible to
identify the system by examining the structures, i.e. the strings
manifested in spoken chains within which these elements
contract syntagmatic relationships. Insistence on the notion of
structure appears in the label itself of structural linguistics. The
term *structura* was already used in Latin not only with its
architectonic meaning (from *struere*, 'to construct'), but in
metaphorical applications, such as 'the structure of a speech'.
The notion became common in the nineteenth century; one may
recall in Marxist thought the use of *Struktur* and *Basis* versus
Überbau (normally rendered as 'structure' and 'superstructure'),
and the frequent use of the notion of structure in the natural
sciences, in psychology, sociology and anthropology (and
recently, not without the influence of structural linguistics

itself, in social and cultural anthropology, especially in the work of Lévi-Strauss and other French thinkers like Barthes, Foucault, Lacan, Derrida etc.).[11]

Throughout the nineteenth century the notion of language as an organism and as a system was very widespread; when Meillet wrote about linguistic structure and linguistic system as 'a whole where everything is connected' (*un ensemble où tout se tient*)[12] he was expressing a commonplace idea rather than an original view. But the histories of linguistics do not help us much in understanding how these notions were related to what structuralists called the 'atomism' of Neo-grammarians (to whom in fact both Saussure and American structural linguists owed a great debt). It is in any case interesting, and should be stressed here, that the theorists of generative grammar are today very critical of structural linguistics and of the conception of language as an inventory of units connected by systematic interrelationships (a notion which they attribute both to nine-teenth-century comparatists and to twentieth-century struct-uralists).

It must be added that in language there are many features which, though not discrete and not relevant in the above sense, are nevertheless of interest and worthy of study. This is partic-ularly clear when one looks at language from the point of view of its substantial realization in speech. It seems obvious that many phonetic features are not only non-discrete, but also non-relevant; but they constitute a sort of reservoir of elements which can be used for a particular expressive purpose, and provide the stuff out of which linguistic change is made.

But also at the level of *la langue* one has to take into account elements like intonation, which are undoubtedly linguistic, but, according to many scholars, non-discrete. Not only is there an indefinite number of states of mind between, say, annoyance and exasperation, but a sentence can be pronounced with an indefinite number of intonations to convey them. Also, what is irrelevant from one point of view can be relevant from a different point of view; and it is obvious that if we take into account functions of language other than the one of transmitting information on the 'representational' plane, we shall have to deal with all the features previously ignored, and we shall have to question even the most basic operations of structural linguistics, like the procedures used in phonemic analysis. The commutation test, for instance, as applied by Trubeckoj, is based on the assumption that *There's a pin* and *There's a bin* are different in meaning on the 'representational' plane, whereas *There's a pin* and *There's a pin!* (with different intonations) are different in meaning on the 'emotive' plane. It is well known that interpretation of the ways in which differences of emotive meaning are phonically represented poses questions which are far from satisfactorily solved, in spite of the many interesting attempts that have been made.

This is a drawback for traditional phonemic analysis as well, because the validity of the distinction between differences of 'representational' and 'emotive' meaning has never been satisfactorily established. The attempt to do away with meaning in phonemic analysis, for instance in the 'thoroughly unsemantic' pair-test, also seems to fail: when people are asked to state whether or not two bits of tape they have heard provide two repetitions of the same utterance, there is no guarantee that they will not take into account semantic criteria; and in any case their answers will reveal their degree of intellectual sophistication and their phonetic skill, i.e. factors which interfere unpredictably with the result of the test.

1.4 Trends in Structural Linguistics

I do not know when the label 'structural linguistics' was used for the first time. It seems to me that today it is used in at least three different senses. In the widest sense, every reflection on language has always been structural as, to obtain positive results, it necessarily had recourse (even though only implicitly) to the notions mentioned above; it had to consider the particular utterances as messages produced and interpreted according to particular rules, with reference to a particular code; it had to identify certain bits of speech as manifestations of the same language unit (and this was only possible when the differences between various repetitions of the same unit were considered non-relevant). In this sense the invention of writing was clearly based on structuralist intuition: a written mark (or rather, the written manifestation of a grapheme) was used to represent items of the spoken language which were widely different in their manifestations; and in particular alphabetic writing was based on the phonemic insight that linguistic messages are encoded using an inventory of a few dozen units. In this wider sense the term 'structural' is scarcely revealing, and it does little more than refer us to the capacity for abstraction which is characteristic of human thought.

There is a second, more restricted sense, in which 'structural linguistics' designates those trends of linguistic thought in this century which deliberately and explicitly tried to gain an insight into the systematic and structural character of language. This is, I believe, the more widely accepted sense, and the one referred to in the title of this present study.

The term has recently been used in a third sense, particularly by followers of the transformational generative school. This third sense is in certain respects narrower than the second one, as it applies mainly to Bloomfieldian American linguistics, particularly of the forties and fifties. Such linguistics is characterized by transformationalists as 'taxonomic', i.e. interested mainly in the *classification* of the items it identified through the *segmentation* of the spoken chain. In other respects this third sense is wider than the second one, because transformationalists associate what they call structural linguistics with most of nineteenth-century comparative grammar, ascribing to both the same restriction to surface structures, as opposed to the deeper aspects of linguistic activity which must be taken into account if one wants to *explain*, instead of only *classifying*, the facts of language. Transformationalists see themselves as heirs to the tradition of linguistic thought elaborated mostly in the seventeenth and eighteenth centuries; linguistic theory in the nineteenth and in the first half of the twentieth century they consider on the whole a stifling parenthesis.

36

Introductory Notions

In the present book a different and, in many respects, a more traditional view of the history of linguistics is adopted. I think I can see within seventeenth- and eighteenth-century linguistic thought things both more interesting than those which twentieth-century traditionalist accounts suggest, and differing more from each other than transformationalist accounts suggest. I think I can also see the connexions as well as the differences between eighteenth- and nineteenth-century linguistics, and between 'taxonomic' and transformational linguistics; and the differences as well as the connexions between nineteenth- and twentieth-century linguistics. Within this perspective trans-formational grammar is an heir to twentieth-century structural linguistics and constitutes in fact one of its most interesting developments.

In the following chapters some of the main trends in structural linguistics will be examined. The work of Saussure (Chapter 2) clarified and rendered common in linguistic thought some dichotomies such as synchrony versus diachrony, 'language' (*langue*) versus 'speech' (*parole*), syntagmatic versus paradigmatic relationships, and 'significans' or 'signifier' (*signifiant*) versus 'significatum' or 'signified' (*signifié*). The Prague School (Chapter 3) developed a functionalist view of language, and whilst taking into account many problems such as those of style, literary language, and historical linguistics, provided a detailed model for phonological analysis. The Copenhagen School, and in particular the glossematic trend expounded by L. Hjelmslev (Chapter 4) developed in the most rigorous way the Saussurean conceptions, insisting in particular on the opposition of form to substance, and on the formal character of language. American structural linguistics is discussed with reference to the work of the two major figures who represent 'mentalism' and 'behaviourism', E. Sapir and L. Bloomfield respectively (Chapter 5). After this, several developments and scholars are introduced, both from Europe and from the United States. Special attention is devoted to the work of linguists such as A. Martinet and R. Jakobson (Chapter 6) who have contributed greatly to bridging the gap between European and

Introductory Notions

American linguistics. The development of structural linguistics in the United States and Britain (Chapter 7) is outlined, with its insistence on the rigour and explicitness of the procedures of linguistic analysis. Its limitations–laid bare in the very work of the most consistent structuralists, such as Z. S. Harris, a scholar who pointed the way to the solution of some problems along 'transformational' lines–are also discussed. The transformational model was developed in an original way by N. Chomsky (Chapter 8), and provided means of syntactic analysis more powerful than those offered by more traditional structural linguistics; the generative transformational conception was extended from syntax to the domain of semantics and phonology, and brought about a widening of linguistic horizons through the new importance given to explanatory–instead of merely descriptive–adequacy, and to the renewal of connexions with other disciplines (psychology in particular). It brought about a rebirth of interest in traditional questions, such as those of language universals and innate ideas, and a new consideration of the history of linguistics (in particular a re-evaluation of seventeenth- and eighteenth-century rationalist linguistics). Finally (Chapter 9) questions which have been the object of recent attention–like statistical linguistics and machine translation–are discussed.

The different theoretical trends are presented as objectively as possible. The exposition of these trends does not leave much space for a discussion of theoretical problems as such. It is therefore perhaps not out of place if some of these are mentioned here.

Semantics, both in itself and in connexion with grammatical analysis, remains the most problematic field. The attempts to eliminate from phonological and grammatical description any recourse to meaning have, so far, been unsatisfactory; but, it is fair to add, so has the way in which meaning was introduced. In any attempt to discuss meaning, one is faced with three main interpretations of it. (1) Language is seen as a two-plane system, consisting either of the sum of, or of the relationship between, form and meaning or, less ambiguously, expression and content.

38

According to this view meaning can be described, either independently of or in necessary connexion with expression, but in any case as a logically autonomous entity. Most traditional views about language, and some modern ones like Saussure's and Hjelmslev's, are of this kind. Here belong the attempts to analyse meaning *componentially*, i.e. to identify simultaneous features (chosen from a presumably limited inventory), which are the components of each of an unlimited number of meanings. (2) Meaning is seen as the relationship (the correspondence, or lack of correspondence) between language and reality, between an utterance and the state of affairs it refers to. This point of view has been adopted mainly by philosophers and logicians, and usually does not satisfy linguists. (3) Meaning is the way signs are used; this view is connected with the previous one, in so far as it sees in meaning the relationship between signs and reality both linguistic (the linguistic context) and non-linguistic (the context of situation). This view has recently been widely supported, as it seems to substitute a hypostatized notion with a checkable set of facts–the ways in which signs are actually used. But to deny that use depends on meaning, and to state instead that meaning is use, or that it is the context of situation, offers little advantage to the linguist. The use of signs, or the context of situation, turns out to be as difficult to describe as their more traditionally conceived meaning. In spite of repeated attempts to describe meaning in an exact way, having recourse to formalized symbolism or to statistical computation, the problem still appears to be intractable.

Structural linguistics has paid less attention to syntax than to phonology and morphology. Only recently, with transformational generative grammar, has there been a major attempt to tackle its fundamental problems. Many discussions, however, are of an almost purely programmatic nature. A satisfactory description of the syntax of a language is still so distant a goal that we cannot even hazard a guess when it will be reached.

Transformational grammar has also questioned much that was taken for granted in the field of phonemic analysis, so much so that what was traditionally viewed as the most important achievement of structural linguistics, the 'phonemic principle', has been discarded altogether. Two different notions are used, corresponding approximately to the morphophonemic and the phonetic levels.

Not only have the attempts to produce interesting results in the field of machine translation failed, but, if further proof of the tremendous complexity of the problems involved were needed, not even a machine like the 'automatic secretary' has been produced, to write under dictation and to read aloud written texts.

In these fields – in which lack of success is in itself a challenge – traditional comparative and historical linguistics did not have much to offer to structural linguistics. A question which would deserve a book to itself, and which I can only mention here, is that of the relationships between comparative philology and structural linguistics. On the meaning side, comparative philology never got beyond approximate and intuitive notions which contrast strangely with the precision and complexity of its operations on the expression side. Even though early modern semantics (at the end of the nineteenth and beginning of the twentieth century) was mainly devoted to change of meaning, it never got as far as clearly establishing how related in meaning two items, between which a regular sound correspondence seemed to apply, had to be for their linguistic relationship to be accepted.

On the expression side, the status of the reconstructed sound units was never clarified: are they phonetic or phonemic? Few attempts have been made to specify the operations of comparative philology within the framework of structural linguistics. Hjelmslev attempted to distinguish genetic relationships (based on functions between expression elements) from typological relationships (based on functions between categories), but he did not solve the question posed by the correspondence between genetic relationships and real historical happenings (a correspondence which does not apply in the case of most typological criteria, which are arbitrarily set up). N. S. Trubeckoj took a more radical position, defining a language as Indo-European if it possessed certain features (more precisely six features: lack of vowel harmony; initial consonantism not poorer than the internal or final one; possibility of prefixation; possibility of apophony; morphological role of consonant alternation; same treatment of the subject of transitive and intransitive verbs). Trubeckoj played havoc with the conceptions held by most students of historical linguistics, by stating that any language can become, or can cease to be, Indo-European, just by acquiring all the six features in question, or by losing any one of them. This view, which is both stimulating and misleading, is again unsatisfactory in so far as it does not distinguish clearly between a typology which contains the reasons for its own validity within the classification it provides, and a typology whose validity depends on the truth of the historical description it allows. This is a predicament similar to that in which linguistics found itself earlier on, when it tried to interpret a synchronic classification of languages into isolating, agglutinating and flexive as a historical description of three chronologically successive stages.

CHAPTER II

Ferdinand de Saussure

🙖🙖🙖🙖🙖🙖

2.1 Saussure and the *Cours de linguistique générale*

In 1878 the Swiss scholar F. de Saussure (born in 1857) published his *Mémoire sur le système primitif des voyelles dans les
langues indo-européennes*. In this extremely original work
Saussure, then very young, 'discovered some fundamental principles, e.g. the so-called law of palatals which . . . revolutionized
the notion of Indo-European by attributing with certainty to the
early phonological system the vowels *e* and then also *o*, considered, up to then, as secondary (due to the misleading
conditions of Sanskrit in which *a* represented both the earlier *e*
and *o*), the existence of sonantic coefficients capable of lengthen-
ing a preceding vowel; and the hypothesis, rich in consequences,
that the fundamental vowel of Indo-European was *e*'.[1] The
reading of the *Mémoire* is still one of the most exciting intellectual adventures afforded by literature on Indo-European
(an intellectual adventure which perhaps remained unrivalled
until 1935, when É. Benveniste published his theory of the
Indo-European root in the *Origines*). Saussure's discoveries
depend on an analysis which today we would not hesitate to call
structural. Taking into account the whole system, he postulates
elements of an abstract character which are defined on the basis
of their structural function rather than their phonetic shape.

The exacting methodological requirements of his theoretical
rigour, which had produced such extraordinary results in the
Mémoire, afterwards seemed to paralyse Saussure's scientific
production. He published very few contributions though they

were all of great penetration.[2] In the second part of his scientific career it seems that the problems of method and theory became predominant. It was only after his death (1913) that his insights were made accessible to an audience larger than the circle of his own pupils. In 1916 Ch. Bally and A. Sechehaye published, under the title *Cours de linguistique générale*,[3] an elaboration of the notes taken by several members of his audience at three courses held between 1906 and 1911.[4] This text was to have tremendous importance in the development of contemporary linguistics. The *Cours* did not bear the imprimatur of the author: it was a posthumous compilation based on students' notes. As a result, the book's influence is derived from single passages—often detached from the rest of the work—which appeared to the reader to contain specially stimulating insights. For several decades after the publication of the *Cours* it seemed as if Saussure's conceptions were best summarized by a series of dichotomies, such as synchrony versus diachrony, 'language' versus 'speech' or 'speaking' (*langue* versus *parole*), paradigmatic versus syntagmatic, 'significans' or 'signifier' versus 'significatum' or 'signified' (*signifiant* versus *signifié*), and by notions such as the arbitrary character of the linguistic sign. These were often starting-points for theoretical excursions which moved far away from Saussure's thought.

In the pages which follow, Saussure's theory will be considered within the by now traditional framework of these isolated points. This is due in part to the fact that Saussure's influence on modern linguistics acted within this framework; in part to the fact that a satisfactory account of Saussure's intellectual development is still wanting. It is only since the mid-fifties that previously unpublished material has begun to appear in print.[5] In 1957 R. Godel published a very important book on the manuscript sources of the *Cours*;[6] and in 1967 R. Engler began the publication of a monumental critical edition of the *Cours*.[7] It is to be hoped that when this is completed, and when more unpublished material is made known and more analytical work produced on Saussure, a better understanding will be possible of his intellectual development

43

and of his theories. The present chapter is obviously not a step in this direction, but simply underlines some points which appear to be particularly important for modern linguistics.

2.2 Synchrony and Diachrony

A language can be analysed synchronically–i.e. by looking at it at a particular point in time–and, obviously, this point is not necessarily fixed in the present, but may be as distant from us as the existing documentation allows. We can also analyse a language diachronically–i.e. by taking into account its changes from one point in time to a later one. These two points of view were often not clearly distinguished before Saussure; that they must be distinguished is denied by few linguists today. This does not mean that the two approaches, synchronic and diachronic, cannot be usefully combined for the solution of specific linguistic problems.[8] In particular, whereas the Copenhagen School (one of those claiming a predecessor in Saussure) and many American structuralists insist on the strict separation of the two points of view, the Prague School has been favourable to a synthesis of the two.

In the three dichotomies, *langue-parole*, paradigmatic-syntagmatic, and synchrony-diachrony, the first two have correlative terms of which neither can be studied without taking the other into account. Not so the third one: synchrony can in fact be studied quite separately from diachrony. In a sense Saussure turned the traditional (implicit or explicit) view of historical linguistics upside down. After Saussure the problem was not whether purely synchronic linguistics was a proper subject for scientific inquiry, but whether diachronic linguistics itself was possible unless it were based on a previous synchronic analysis. From Saussure's *Cours* it is not at all clear that one can study structurally the changes of linguistic systems; it appears that elements of a system may change in an isolated way and thus give rise to new systems, though the change itself is non-systematic. One of the tasks of post-Saussurean linguistics has in fact been the attempt to bring language change within the structural consideration of linguistic phenomena. Diachronic structural linguistics has been advocated and practised with considerable success, especially by linguists connected with the Prague Circle tradition (as we shall see later, the work by A. Martinet in the field of diachronic phonemics is particularly interesting). Once the possibility of diachronic structural linguistics has been accepted, synchronic studies themselves appear in a different light: in particular those parts of the system which are less balanced and seem less amenable to structural treatment, appear now as potential 'breaking points', at which change is taking or will take place. As traditional linguistics used to repeat, language is in fact continuously changing, even though the speaker may not be conscious of it and may translate such changes as he experiences in terms of a stylistic choice between synchronically coexistent uses. There is one point of view, that of the language user, from which language does not appear to be (and, given the relationship between language and language user, is not) changing.

It is not the synchronic view of language that is an abstraction, compared with the supposedly more concrete reality of language change; on the contrary, the idea that language is continuously changing is in fact a scientific fiction on a higher level of abstraction than the idea of language as a synchronic system. In order to compare two systems, and to state that the earlier one has changed into the later one, we have first to consider the synchronic systems themselves. This does not mean that the consideration of time has no place in language study: an interesting feature of sentences is that they have a beginning and an end, that there is a sequence (a temporal one in speech, and a spatial one in writing). Whether this belongs only to the *parole* or whether, and exactly how, it belongs also to the *langue*, is a subject for discussion. But the temporal sequence in which the beginning and the end of a sentence are arranged is, from the point of view of linguistic study, of a different kind from the temporal sequence along which language changes. We do not need to worry at the possibility that we might begin a sentence in one language and finish it in a different one because our language is changing all the time even if we do not realize it. It is not merely that language takes more time to change than we take to utter a sentence: the language we use is an essentially synchronic system, even though it involves the use of strings of elements which may manifest themselves, in the spoken utterance, along a time sequence.

Saussure uses from various points of view a comparison between language and chess.[9] With reference to synchrony we read in the *Cours* (pp. 126–7): 'In a game of chess any given position has the peculiar characteristic of being independent from its antecedents . . . ; to describe this position it is perfectly useless to recall what has just happened.' But, overlooking that it is not made quite clear exactly how a game of chess is to be compared with language, there is a sense in which some 'diachronic' information is included in the rules of chess: one may need to know whether the king or the rook have moved, if one wants to castle; one may need to know whether a pawn has just been moved if one wants to take it *en passant*; and to decide whether a game ends in a draw one needs to know whether the same position occurs for the third time; or in the end game one may need to know how many moves have been made from a certain moment onwards. Nothing like this applies to language; although in any conversation it may indeed be useful to know what has just been said.

One must be careful not to identify 'diachronic' with 'historical', in spite of the fact that traditionally 'historical linguistics' does mean 'diachronic linguistics'. Indeed, from the point of view of historical studies, the label 'historical linguistics' is something of a misnomer. The study of historical linguistics has been pursued according to methods which are quite distinct from normal methods of studying history;[10] and nothing prevents a synchronic study from being conducted according to the methods normally used in historical research.

Different again is the question of what the status of synchronic linguistics would be within a general 'historicist' view. Here it may be remembered that modern theories of scientific explanation do not necessarily imply that to explain something is to explain how it came to be what it is. As to Saussure's dichotomy, it can also be studied from two points of view: with regard to its value for linguistic theory and with regard to its origin and the intellectual development of Saussure himself. Linguists have worked mostly on the first point. The second problem is perhaps a minor one, but it is certainly very difficult to tackle in the present state of our information about Saussure.

2.3 Langue and Parole

The two terms correspond roughly to language and speech. In Saussure's dichotomy two separate distinctions are conflated: one between social (*langue*) and individual (*parole*), the other between abstract (*langue*) and concrete (*parole*). The two are connected: *parole* is the individual aspect of language, as it is manifested in the concrete psycho-physiological and social reality of particular speech acts. *Langue* is the social part of language, outside the individual speaker, who cannot create it or modify it. Although to us *langue* appears to be at a more abstract level than *parole*, Saussure goes out of his way to stress that *langue* is an object of a concrete nature; the *signs*, which, as a system, constitute *langue*, are not abstractions, but real things which have their place in the brain and can be represented (in writing or otherwise) in an exhaustive way. Particular speech acts cannot be so represented because accuracy is necessarily limited (pp. 31–2). It is difficult to assess exactly the value of the distinction of *langue* and *parole* in Saussure;[11] an attempt has been made to show that the dichotomy goes back to the discussion between É. Durkheim and G. Tarde: *langue* could correspond to Durkheim's 'social fact' (*fait social*) (as it is a psycho-social phenomenon, which exists in the collective conscience of the social group, outside the individual, on whom it exerts a constraint), while *parole* would correspond to the individual element, as presented by Tarde. From this it has been concluded that Saussure's distinction was based on a philosophical conception, external, in substance, to linguistics.[12] Without necessarily subscribing to this, it may be pointed out that this distinction appears to be of a general methodological (rather than specifically linguistic) value, in so far as it represents the process of abstraction which is necessary to any scientific procedure. Among post-Saussurean linguistic trends, the Copenhagen Circle has insisted on the abstract character of *langue*, and the Prague Circle has used the dichtomy to consolidate its own distinction between phonemes and speech-sounds, placing the first on the level of *langue* and the second on the level of *parole*. Both have tried to eliminate the patently psychological character of Saussure's *langue* by confining psychology to the realm of *parole*; the psychological character of *langue*, on the other hand, would probably not be denied by transformationalists who have recently interpreted the dichotomy *langue* versus *parole* in terms of competence versus performance. More debatable seems to me the interpretation which has also been suggested, in terms of the statistical notions of population and sample.

2.4 Signifiant and Signifié

Langue is thought of by Saussure as a sign system (p. 33). The *sign* for Saussure is not something which stands for something else (i.e. is its sign), but a relationship between two things: 'the linguistic sign unites . . . a concept and an acoustic image' (p. 98), i.e. a *signifié* (signified) and a *signifiant* (signifier) (p. 99). The sign has two main characteristics: it is arbitrary (pp. 100–2), and its *signifiant* is linear (p. 103). It may be noted here that the importance of Saussure's conception of the arbitrary nature of the sign has been over-estimated, and that the cryptic and inconsistent remarks which appear in the *Cours* have stimulated far too much comment. The problem of the arbitrary character of the linguistic sign is as old as reflection on language. What is new in Saussure is his (not altogether fortunate) decision to define the sign as a *relationship* between two entities. More important than his defining the sign as arbitrary is his conception of language items as two-faced entities consisting of the relationship between a *signifiant* and a *signifié*. (The traditional

48

distinction of form and meaning is later split into four strata when glossematics compounds the dichotomy *langue-parole* and the dichotomy *signifiant-signifié*. The latter may be interpreted as a typically linguistic dichotomy between expression and content; and both within expression and within content one has to distinguish, as in any scientific analysis, a form and a substance.) When one talks about the sign being arbitrary, one has to separate an extralinguistic from an intralinguistic relationship. The extralinguistic one is the relationship between language units and things meant, the intralinguistic is the relationship between the two planes of expression and content. In what sense the former (as in the traditional view about the (lack of) correspondence between name and thing), or the latter (as in the transformationalist view of the difference between deep and surface structures), or both, can be said to be arbitrary, has been abundantly discussed.[13]

More interesting is Saussure's second principle, the linear character of the *signifiant*. In the *Cours* this point is stressed as very important, but there is not much in the way of an explanation of its importance. This is all the more regrettable as the conditions of *linearity* in language have not yet been discussed in a sufficiently clear way. Two points which are involved in the notion of linearity should be distinguished. One question concerns the relationships of the elements of a sentence, their sequential order in a string. Another question is whether the string, or its elements, must be one-dimensional, or whether they can be analysed into simultaneous components. As regards the second question, R. Jakobson[14] has criticized Saussure's idea of linearity because it does not accommodate a conception of the phoneme as composed of simultaneously occurring distinctive features. But perhaps it is possible to distinguish items which occur simultaneously and items which occur in sequence, and to ask whether the *signifiant* has not got a sequential character (in spite of the possibility of analysing each of its units into simultaneous components). One then returns to the former question, with all the problems it involves (such as the ordering of content units, or, in transformational theory, the arrangement of the abstract units appearing in the deep structures).

Language signs are, in the sense which we have mentioned, not abstract, but 'real objects'. They are the 'concrete entities' studied by linguistics (p. 144). The signs must be 'delimited' (pp. 145 ff.); they have 'values' which are 'relative', and cannot be isolated from the system to which they belong (p. 157). Not only the combination of *signifiant* and *signifié* 'produces a form and not a substance' (p. 157) (and '*langue* is a form and not a substance' p. 169), but 'what distinguishes a sign is all that constitutes it' (p. 168): 'in *langue* there are only differences, without positive terms' (p. 166; signs however can be considered, in their order, as positive entities, *ib.*). It is thus clear that for Saussure the relationship signs have with each other is essential for their own definition. Such relationships are of two kinds: syntagmatic and associative (pp. 170–84).

2.5 Syntagmatics and Paradigmatics

A sign is in contrast with other signs which come before and after it in a sentence. It has with the preceding and following signs a syntagmatic relationship. This is a relationship *in praesentia*, i.e. between elements (the sign in question, and the preceding and following ones) which are all present in the message. But a sign is also opposed to other signs not because they are in the message but because they belong to the language; it is *associated* (through similarity or difference) with these other signs, it has with them an *associative* relationship. This is a relationship *in absentia*, i.e. between the element in question, which is there, and other elements, which are not there in that particular message. Together with them, it constitutes a 'virtual mnemonic series' placed 'in the brain' (p. 171). The term in question is 'like the centre of a constellation, the point where other co-ordinated terms converge' (p. 174), in a number which may be indefinite, and without a definite order. This is clearly a psychological point of view. But in the drive against psychological notions which characterizes many trends of structural linguistics, the term 'associative' was abandoned, and replaced by the term 'paradigmatic', which did not convey psychological associations.[15] The term quickly gained wide acceptance. The dichotomy is now generally referred to as between paradigmatic and syntagmatic relationships, or, to use substantives, between paradigmatics and syntagmatics. Paradigmatics and syntagmatics (the correlational, 'either-or', and the relational, 'both-and', hierarchies, in Hjelmslev's terms, or 'choice' and 'chain', in Halliday's terms) are most often interpreted as code and message, i.e. as the distinction between an inventory of items and the strings of items constituting the message. They may also be interpreted in terms of *langue* and *parole* (particularly as Saussure is not very clear about the relationships between *syntagms* and facts of *parole*, pp. 172–3). Some structuralists have insisted on the secondary and more abstract character of paradigmatics (*langue* or system) which is conceived as a scientific construction built on the basis of the primary and concrete reality of syntagmatics (*parole* or structure). It is obviously true that a linguist describing a language he does not know will have to start from the acts of speech and try to reach the underlying system. But it may very well be that the system is no less real than the messages; it is, in fact, both logically and psychologically prior to them, even when the researcher does not know the language and the examination of the messages may have to be his starting-point. The idea that *langue* is the proper object of linguistic description is certainly consistent with Saussure's position; it is also accepted by recent developments in linguistic theory which interpret *langue* as the competence underlying the performance of the language user. What appears certain today is that it is convenient to separate the two dichotomies *langue-parole* and paradigmatics-syntagmatics more clearly than was done by Saussure; and in particular to give syntagmatic relationships the place they deserve in the *langue*. It may also be useful to stress the fact that *langue* and paradigmatics do not belong to a metalanguage. *Langue* and paradigmatics, as well as *parole* and syntagmatics, belong to the (object) language. To talk about them we use a metalanguage.

And of course within our metalinguistic expressions the *names* (of the things belonging to the language which we are talking about) will have syntagmatic relationships with each other. One can say that the consonants 'p' and 'b' have a paradigmatic relationship in the English consonant system, and a syntagmatic relationship in the word 'pub'. In stating that 'p' and 'b' have a paradigmatic relationship, we have not changed this relationship into a syntagmatic one. In our statement it is not 'p' and 'b' which have a syntagmatic relationship, but their names, "p" and "b".[16]

2.6 After Saussure

Saussure's influence was instrumental in a number of later developments of linguistic theory. But, as was to be expected from the character of this theory, such developments are far from uniform, as they include the French 'sociological' school on the one hand, and the 'logicist' Copenhagen school on the other. In Geneva, Saussure's successors were Ch. Bally (1913–1939), A. Sechehaye (1939–45), and H. Frei. They all followed original lines: one can quote Bally's theory of style and his work on the 'emotive' aspects of language; Sechehaye's theory of grammar and his work on the relationships between logic and linguistics; and Frei's acute reflections on points of Saussurean theory and his penetrating criticism of many aspects of contemporary linguistic thought.[17]

In 1940 the Geneva Society of Linguistics was constituted (known today as the 'Cercle F. de Saussure'); and from 1941 dates the publication of the interesting periodical *Cahiers F. de Saussure*, which has printed important material of relevance to Saussure's thought. It is from the same milieu that the fundamental contributions by R. Godel, and more recently by R. Engler, have originated.

CHAPTER III

The Prague School

🈂🈂🈂🈂🈂

3.1 Introduction

A connexion is sometimes made between the Prague School[1] and Saussure. This connexion is mostly made *a posteriori*, in order to stress the elements which are common to two major trends in structural linguistics. In fact Saussure's thought was only one of the sources, and perhaps not the main one, of inspiration for the Prague group; the factual question of the points which Prague linguists elaborated independently from Saussure (because they drew inspiration from Russian linguistics, or because their theories were original developments) is still not clear.

The Linguistic Circle of Prague was established in October 1926 on the initiative of V. Mathesius, and among the linguists who took part in its activities were B. Havránek, J. Mukařovský, B. Trnka, J. Vachek, M. Weingart; among the foreigners who published in the Circle's *Travaux* were the Dutch A. W. de Groot, the German philosopher and psychologist K. Bühler, the Yugoslav A. Belić, the Englishman D. Jones and the French scholars L. Tesnière, É. Benveniste, A. Martinet. Particularly significant was the participation of three Russian linguists in the Circle's activities: S. Karcevskij, R. Jakobson, N. S. Trubeckoj. These presented to the first international congress of linguists at The Hague in 1928,[2] a proposition which aroused considerable interest particularly among the members of the recently founded Linguistic Circle of Prague. The following year the Circle presented to the first conference of Slavic

53

philologists the first volume of the *Travaux du Cercle Linguisti-que de Prague*, which included nine theses[3]–the collective work of the Circle–devoted to a programmatic exposition of the Circle's interests (the first three theses), and to an indication of desired lines of research in Slavic linguistics (the following six theses). In the meantime R. Jakobson's *Remarques* appeared,[4] the first work to discuss explicitly the problems of diachronic phonology within the newly elaborated conceptual framework. In 1930 an international phonological meeting was held in Prague,[5] and an International Association for phonological studies was founded; its constitution was approved at the second international congress of linguists (Geneva 1931) and its first meeting coincided with the international congress of phonetic sciences held in Amsterdam in 1932. In the opening speech of the congress[6] J. van Ginneken recognized that phonology, in spite of its autonomous origin, is 'the crowning of the whole work', it synthesizes the results of all phonetic sciences. The phonological movement had quickly established itself and had taken its official place in linguistic studies. Recently, severe and often justified criticism has been levelled against the principles followed in particular by the American 'phonemic' trends; and there are of course many for whom phonology is but a belated and unduly domineering member among the more traditional and better established studies such as articulatory phonetics, instrumental phonetics, etc. Phonology remains, however, one of the fields in which twentieth-century linguistics has proved particularly fruitful; and this is in part due to the work of the Prague Circle.

The theories of the Prague School in this 'Classic' period–as it may be called – are documented by the scientific production of its members, and in particular by the official publications of the Circle, among which the *Travaux*,[7] published between 1929 and 1938, occupy the place of honour.

3.2 The Circle's Theses

The first three of the theses we have mentioned[8] present

programmes of research derived from certain methodological positions.

In the first thesis several points are examined. (a) There is a discussion of 'problems of method which derive from the conception of language as a system', or better, a 'functional system'. Language is a product of human *activity* which has a character of *finalism*; it is a system of means of expression appropriate to an end; this end is the realization of the subject's intention to *express* and *communicate*. (b) Synchronic analysis of contemporary facts (which alone offer complete information, and of which one can have a 'direct feeling') is the best way to know the 'essence and character' of a language. But no insuperable barrier is erected (as in the Geneva School) in order to separate the synchronic and diachronic methods. On the one hand, in order to judge language changes one has to consider the system in which they take place; on the other, synchronic description itself cannot eliminate the notion of evolution, in the shape of stylistic elements felt as archaistic, of productive and non-productive forms, etc. (c) A comparative method must be used not only for diachronic purposes, reconstruction and genealogical problems, but also for synchronic purposes, to discover the structural laws of linguistic systems; the systems which are compared need not be genetically related. (d) The laws mentioned above help in substituting for the notion of isolated and chance changes, a theory of their connexion (*enchaînement*) according to the laws of evolutionary facts (nomogenesis); the hypothesis of convergent evolution is preferred to that of mechanical and fortuitous expansion.

The second thesis concerns the tasks of a study of linguistic systems: (a) with regard to the phonic aspect it is necessary to distinguish the speech sound as a physical objective fact, the (acoustic) representation, and the element of the functional system. The 'structural principle of the functional system' attributes to objective physical facts a merely indirect relationship with linguistics, and to (acoustic-motor) images a role which depends on their 'function in differentiating meaning': their reciprocal relationships within the system are more important than their 'sensory content'. The main tasks of synchronic phonology are thus: (1) to characterize the phonological systems (using the *inventory* of the phonemes and the specification of their *relationships*); (2) to determine the *realized* phoneme clusters, in relation to the *possible* ones; (3) to determine the degree of utilization and the density of realization of phonemes and phoneme clusters, their *functional yield*; (4) to describe the morphological utilization of phonological differences (morphophonology or morphonology).[9] (b) With regard to words and word groups we find (1) the theory of naming, according to which the *word* is the result of a naming activity which decomposes reality into linguistically graspable elements;[10] (2) the theory of syntagmatic processes (essentially the act of predication); (3) the theory of 'systems of word-forms or group-forms', or morphology, which does not run parallel to the previous two, but cuts across them both.

The third thesis examines different linguistic functions in so far as they modify the phonic or grammatical structure. One must distinguish the intellectual from the emotive element, and (from a social rather than an individual point of view) the communicative from the poetic function. In the communicative function one can distinguish a gravitation towards practical language ('situational'), which takes into account extra-linguistic elements, and a gravitation towards theoretical language ('formulational') which aims at constituting a self-contained whole, introducing 'term-words' and 'statement-sentences'. It would be wrong to confuse intellectual language with *langue* and emotive language with *parole*. In the communicative function language is 'directed towards meaning'; in the poetic function language is 'directed towards the sign itself'. In describing poetic language we must remember that synchronically it appears as *parole*, it is an individual creative act which acquires its value against the background of contemporary poetic tradition (poetic *langue*) and communicative language. Poetic language has, synchronically and diachronically, a very complicated and varied network of relationships with these two systems. A poetic work must be studied as a functional structure, the elements of which cannot be understood outside their relationships with the whole.

Although Trubeckoj and many members of the Circle had extremely wide literary and cultural interests, the subject on which their influence was most widely felt was phonology, so much so that sometimes by 'Prague School theories' people mean simply its phonological theories. This is unfortunate, because the School of Prague, as we have seen, made important contributions[11] to other questions: for instance, that of literary and poetic language, mostly along lines inspired by Russian formalism.[12]

3.3 N. S. Trubeckoj

Trubeckoj, who belonged to an important Russian family, pursued historical and ethnological studies in his youth in Moscow; shortly after having taken a degree in linguistics, he emigrated to escape the Revolution, and ended up in Vienna, where he taught Slavic philology from 1922 until his death in 1938. During an active scientific career[13] he elaborated the theories which, in the field of phonology, were to find a systematic (although not definitive, due to his premature death) formulation in volume VII of the *Travaux*, published shortly after his death. It may be useful to mention some of the points discussed there, having quoted the Circle's theses, not only because Trubeckoj was the most impressive personality in the Prague movement, but also to illustrate the developments which took place during the productive decade from the late twenties to the late thirties.[14]

In the *Grundzüge*[15] Trubeckoj accepts K. Bühler's distinction of three functions of language: *expression* (*Kundgabe* or *Ausdruck*) from the speaker, *appeal* (*Appell*) to the hearer, and *reference* to, or *representation* (*Darstellung*) of a state of affairs.[16] He also accepts Saussure's distinction of *langue* and *parole* (which he calls in German *Sprachgebilde* and *Sprechakt*), and of *signifiant* and *signifié* (*das Bezeichnende* and *das Bezeichnete*). Phonetics (*Phonetik*) studies the *signifiants* of *la parole*.

Phonology (*Phonologie*) is for Trubeckoj the study of the *signifiants* of *la langue* on the representational (or referential) plane. The study of the *signifiants* on the expressive and appellative (or conative) planes is the field of phonostylistics (*Lautstilistik*), which can be divided into phonetic stylistics, that studies *parole*, and phonological stylistics, that studies *langue*. There is thus no need to subdivide phonology into three branches (for expression, appeal and reference); the term can be reserved for the study of the reference function.

On the reference plane, sound features can be grouped according to three functions: culminative (*gipfelbildende* or *kulminative*)–to show how many units there are in a sentence; delimitative (*abgrenzende* or *delimitative*)–to mark the limit between units; and distinctive (*bedeutungsunterscheidende* or *distinktive*)–to differentiate units provided with meaning (or rather, as we are on the representational plane, provided with intellectual meaning: *intellektuelle Bedeutung*, p. 29).

In order to have distinctive function, speech sounds must be opposed to each other (distinction presupposes opposition). An opposition can be either *distinctive* (or *phonological*), or non-distinctive. Only sounds which may occur in the same context (i.e. that are permutable) can be in opposition. A minimum distinctive phonological unit is a *phoneme*, which is realized by *variants*. The variants may be either facultative (individual or general) or combinatory, determined by the context. Oppositions can be classified from different points of view. If we consider their relationship with the whole system of oppositions, they may be *bilateral* (when what is common to the two terms of the opposition does not appear elsewhere: for instance in English *p* : *b* are the only bilabial stops), or they may be *multilateral* (e.g., *d* : *b*, since what they have in common appears also in *g*); they may be *proportional*, when the relationship of the two terms is identical with the relationship between the terms of other oppositions (e.g., *p* : *b* since their relationship is the same as in *f* : *v*, *t* : *d*, etc.), or they may be *isolated* (e.g., *p* : *h*, for no other pair of phonemes has the same relationship). If we consider the relationship between the two terms of the opposition itself, an opposition can be *privative* if there is a mark present in one term and absent in the other (for instance *b* : *p*, voiced : voiceless), *gradual* if the terms have the same quality in different degrees (for instance, the different degrees of opening in the vowels *o* : *u*, *e* : *i* etc.), *equipollent*, if the two terms are logically equivalent, and there is neither presence nor absence, nor different degrees of a quality (as in *p* : *t*). If we consider the extent of their distinctive power in the system, oppositions can be *neutralizable* if there are circumstances in which they cease to be oppositions (for instance *t* : *d* in German, which are not opposed in word final position), or *constant*. A *correlation* is the set of all oppositions characterized by the same mark (i.e., of all pairs of phonemes which are in bilateral, proportional, and privative opposition: for instance, *p*:*b*, *f*:*v*, *t*:*d* etc.). This classification has a purely logical basis and is valid for any kind of opposition. But phonological oppositions are constituted by distinctive *sound* differences, for which phonetic (acoustic and articulatory) notions must be used. The distinctive sound features used in different languages can be grouped into three classes: (1) vocalic qualities, which can be classified according to degree of opening, localization and resonance; (2) consonantal qualities, which can be classified according to localization, nature of the obstruction, and resonance; (3) prosodic qualities which can be differentiation qualities (*Differenzierungsarteigenschaften*) (concerned with the oppositions of rhythmic-melodic units) and contact qualities (*Anschlussarteigenschaften*) (phenomena of contiguity in the spoken chain).

3.4 Early Phonologists

Trubeckoj mentions a number of linguists who preceded him in formulating the notion of system in language, and in particular of sound system, and in distinguishing between sound and phoneme, and thus between phonetics and phonology.

J. Winteler,[17] in his study of a Swiss dialect (1876), felt the need to distinguish two kinds of sound oppositions, those which involve semantic and grammatical differences, and those which do not. Similar ideas were independently expressed by the great British phonetician H. Sweet,[18] by O. Jespersen,[19] and by A. Noreen.[20] F. de Saussure[21] distinguished the sound which is material from the *signifiant* which is not, but did not state that there should be two different methods, one for studying the sounds of *parole*, the other for studying the elements which differentiate *signifiants* in *langue*. This distinction was clearly formulated by J. Baudouin de Courtenay,[22] who gave the term 'phoneme' the value it commonly has today[23] and distinguished the physiological study of speech sounds from the psychological study of phonic images which have certain functions in language. It seems that the distinction goes back to a suggestion of Kruszewski,[24] a pupil of Baudouin's. The latter conceived the phoneme as 'that sum of phonetic features which constitutes, in comparisons both·within one language and between several related languages, an indivisible unit'.[25] Later he defined the phoneme as 'a unitary image, belonging to the phonetic world, which originates in the soul by means of the psychic fusion of impressions preserved through the pronunciation of the same sound = psychic equivalent of the sound. To the unitary image of the phoneme is bound (associated) a certain sum of single anthropophonic [i.e. articulatory and acoustic] images.'[26] Phonetics includes all phonetic facts, and is divided into anthropophonetics (which studies articulatory and acoustic facts) and psychophonetics (which studies the psychic facts which are reflexes of the anthropophonic). A key role in Baudouin's theory is played by the notion of *alternation*. This term is used in Saussure's *Mémoire* with the value relevant here: 'Italic languages have made verbal flexion too uniform for one to expect to find in them the alternation (*alternance*) between weak and strong forms.'[27] Leskien too broached the same question in 1884;[28] Baudouin in 1894–5 stated that he had already reached the concept of *alternation* eighteen years earlier, in his university lectures,[29] because he was dissatisfied with the current notions of 'passing' from one sound to another and of sounds 'giving' other sounds (also on the axis of synchrony, as we would say today). This did not explain, Baudouin states, 'the coexistence of phonetically different but etymologically connected speech sounds', or the cause of this state of affairs. In his Russian lectures he used the term *čeredovanie*, and in German *Abwechslung*. Here is the definition he offers: 'Phonetic alternants, or alternant phonemes are those phonemes or sounds which, although they are phonetically distinct from each other, refer to a common historical origin, or are etymologically related', for instance in the Polish forms *mog-ę*, *mож-esz* : *mog/mож*. There is *alternation* within one language, and *correspondence* between the sounds of different languages.[30]

Trubeckoj discusses in the *Grundzüge* several definitions of the phoneme. He criticizes, among others, Baudouin's definition because it is couched in psychological terms (whereas it is not the phoneme, but each particular variant which has a psychic equivalent), and also because it presupposes a notion of *speech sound* which is in fact definable only with reference to the phoneme. In the spoken chain there is a continuum within which we can isolate particular sounds only in so far as they 'correspond' to certain phonemes.

In the early stages of the theory phonologists tended to underline their originality rather than their dependence on previous scholars (an attitude which did not fail to provoke polemical discussions).[31] But Trubeckoj was certainly justified when he claimed that he had been the first to realize the full methodological importance of certain ideas (already adopted by Saussure and Baudouin), and to give them a currency in international thought which made them seminal in scientific research. Saussure had limited himself to statements of principle (that phonemes exist only as units of a system, that what matters in the working of language is not the *sound*, but the *opposition* of sounds, etc.); he had not attempted the actual description of phonological systems. Baudouin, although he insisted less on general theoretical points and on the notion of system, had more precise ideas on the difference between sound and phoneme; but he did not realize fully the importance of the distinction, and did not succeed in attracting to it the attention it deserved. Not one of the three Russians who had submitted the proposition mentioned above to the linguists' conference at The Hague, was a pupil of Baudouin, although he had taught mostly in Russia, at Kazan' and St. Petersburg. Baudouin's theories for a long time went almost unnoticed in Europe (where he was known mainly as a Slavist). The German version of his work on phonemes and alternation was published in 1895, but did not attract much attention. His influence is noticeable among some of his pupils: for instance, in the work of the Orientalist E. D. Polivanov (who contributed to making his ideas known in Japan),[32] and in the phonological theories of L. V. Ščerba.[33] But the phoneme appears to have been rediscovered independently by American scholars[34] as well as by several linguists who engaged in 'practical' questions of transcription.[35]

Trubeckoj polemicizes against N. van Wijk, who had stated that the notion of phonological system existed already in the work of nineteenth-century linguists, e.g. of the Neo-grammarians (particularly Brugmann), Schuchardt and others. 'It is a regrettable misunderstanding,' Trubeckoj comments; adding that it is obvious that one would need to be dumb and blind not to realize that Greek stops form three parallel series, and Sanskrit stops four. But the fragments of systems that earlier linguists constructed were only collections of isolated elements, and the regular correspondence which connected them was fortuitous, unexpected and inexplicable: it was even 'something of an embarrassment'. To start from the system in order to arrive at the phoneme would have been an unmethodical procedure for a Neogrammarian 'who had an almost superstitious distrust of any suggestion of teleology'.[36]

3.5 The Phoneme

A definition of phoneme similar to the one adopted by Trubeckoj is found in L. V. Ščerba (1912): 'The shortest general sound image of a given language, which can be associated with meaning images, and can differentiate words.' This definition remains within the field of associationist psychology, but underlines clearly the function of the phoneme to differentiate meaning. The notion of image is eliminated in N. F. Jakovlev's definition: 'any sound feature that can be extracted from the spoken chain as its shortest element used to differentiate meaning units'.[37] The definition adopted by Trubeckoj in his *Grundzüge* goes back essentially to R. Jakobson (1929)[38] and appears, in a different version, in the *Projet de terminologie phonologique standardisée* (1930).[39]

If '(distinctive) phonological opposition' is any sound opposition which in a language can differentiate intellectual meanings, and '(distinctive) phonological unit' is a term of a phonological opposition, phonemes are defined by Trubeckoj as 'phonological units which . . . cannot be analyzed into shorter successive phonological units' (p. 34). A phoneme is thus 'the smallest phonological unit in the language under consideration' (p. 34). This definition is different from the ones given by Trubeckoj in his earlier works, where he had used the term *Lautvorstellung* (phonic idea or image).[40] But that term, he states (p. 37), 'had never been intended as a precise scientific definition', and the use made of the notion of phoneme was in the earlier works 'exactly the same as today'.

A 'phonic idea', corresponds, according to Trubeckoj (p. 37), to each particular variant, and it is not possible to consider some ideas as 'conscious', and others as 'unconscious'. The degree of consciousness of an articulatory process depends on practice; but variations in the phoneme inventory do not correspond to variations in consciousness. The term *Lautabsicht* (phonic intention)[41] transposes the phonic idea into the field of will; but intention too is different for each different phonic variant. 'All these psychological expressions are not appropriate to the nature of the phoneme, and must therefore be refused . . . Recourse to psychology in the definition of the phoneme must be avoided, for the phoneme is a linguistic and not a psychological concept. Any reference to "linguistic consciousness" must be eliminated from the definition of phoneme' (pp. 37-8); 'linguistic consciousness' is either a metaphoric designation of

63

langue, or a vague, indefinite, and perhaps indefinable expression.[42]

We see here the conclusion, at least in the field of statements of principle, of the progressive flight from psychology which characterized many aspects of linguistics in this period. Trubeckoj has moved away from his initial position (on p. 39 he also considers favourably Bloomfield's definition), and strives towards a rigorously functional notion; 'the phoneme is first of all a functional concept, which must be defined according to its function' (p. 38). On the other hand any word appears as a whole, a configuration (*Gestalt*), and is distinguished from all other words by means of the phonemes which are the distinctive marks of such configurations (p. 34).

One and the same phoneme may be a member of both a phonological (distinctive) opposition, and of a non-phonological opposition (p. 35–Trubeckoj quotes the phonological opposition of *stechen* versus *stecken* in German, and the non-phonological opposition of *ich* versus *ach*; apparently he does not consider cases like *Kuchen* (cake) versus *Kuhchen* (little cow), *tauchen* (to dive) versus *Tauchen* (little rope) etc., which could be dealt with morphophonologically, as *-chen* is a diminutive suffix). This is due to the fact that a phoneme is composed of several features, and is distinguished from other phonemes not by all its features, but only by some of them. A phoneme thus coincides not with a 'concrete sound form' ('mit einem konkreten Lautgebilde') but only with the phonologically relevant features of that form; a phoneme 'is the sum of the phonologically relevant features of a sound form' ('die Gesamtheit der phonologisch relevanten Eigenschaften eines Lautgebildes') (p. 35). Concrete sounds are a kind of 'material symbol' of phonemes; a speech sound is the sum of all the (relevant and non-relevant) features which occur at the particular point of the spoken chain where a phoneme is realized.

CHAPTER IV

The Copenhagen School

꧅꧅꧅꧅꧅꧅

4.1 Introduction

In Scandinavian linguistic thought, with J. N. Madvig, A. Noreen, H. G. Wiwel, O. Jespersen (and, long before, with the great Rasmus Rask),[1] there is a rich tradition of scholars who contributed to general linguistics. Within this tradition we find the main representatives of what is often called the Copenhagen School. This also owes much to F. de Saussure, and has developed with great rigour some aspects of his *Cours*.[2] Linguistic theory, with Brøndal and Hjelmslev, becomes more formal and abstract than with their predecessors; both have strong philosophical, and particularly logical interests. The connexion between the linguistic theories of the Copenhagen School and Danish logical research in our century is a subject which cannot be dealt with here, but which certainly deserves careful study.

4.2 Viggo Brøndal

Brøndal's work[3] is informed by a constant guiding principle: it aims at finding in language the concepts of logic. 'Philosophy of language has as its object the search for the number of linguistic categories and their definitions. If it can be shown that these categories are everywhere the same, in spite of all variations, an important contribution will have been made towards a characterization of human spirit.'[4]

Brøndal's ideas on structural linguistics are summarized in

65

the article which opens the journal *Acta Linguistica*.[5] He considers comparative grammar a typical product of the nineteenth century: it is 'historical' (inspired by 'the romantic taste for remote antiquity'), 'positivist' (inspired by an interest 'for small factual truths, for exact and minute observation'), and 'legalistic' (inspired by contemporary natural sciences which aimed at setting up laws representing constant relationships between events). In the twentieth century, together with many new scientific conceptions, we also find a new linguistics. The need was felt 'to isolate, to cut out from the flux of time the object of a science, that is to separate on the one hand states, considered unchanging, and on the other hand sudden leaps from one state to another' (one is reminded of quantum physics and of mutations in biology). Analogously, in linguistics we have the distinction made by Saussure between synchrony and diachrony. Synchrony allows us to consider certain elements as simultaneous, and thus to observe their stability, unity and consistency.

As in science, the need was stated for 'general concepts, which alone give unity to particular cases, to all individual manifestations of the same object'; as in biology we find the genotype, 'sum of the factors of inheritance of which widely differing phenotypes are the manifestations' (W. Johannsen); as in sociology we find the social fact (Durkheim), which is independent of its particular manifestations, outside each individual consciousness—so in linguistics we find Saussure's separation between *parole* and *langue*; and the latter is at the same time *species* as in biology and *institution* as in sociology.

As in science, from atomic physics to Gestalt psychology, the notion of internal cohesion, structure and rational relationships within the object examined has taken root, so in linguistics Saussure uses the notion of system, and Sapir the notion of pattern.

The three main points in structural linguistics are, according to Brøndal, the notions of synchrony, *langue*, and structure.[6]

4.3 Louis Hjelmslev

Whereas Brøndal's theories do not seem to have exerted any marked influence, around Hjelmslev's theories a real school developed, centred on the Linguistic Circle of Copenhagen, and they became widely known and were discussed in international linguistics. In the United States, for instance, the European linguistic theories most often discussed are, together with those of the School of Prague and of British linguistics, those of Danish *glossematics*.

In Hjelmslev's first book, the *Principes de grammaire générale*, published in 1928,[7] there are already many of the insights that he was afterwards to develop. But glossematics was born later, and acquired its name towards the end of 1935. In 1931 two working committees were set up among the linguists active in Copenhagen,[8] one for phonological and the other for grammatical studies. Three members of the phonological group, L. Hjelmslev, P. Lier, and H. J. Uldall, established a new phonological theory which was presented to the second international congress of phonetic sciences in London in 1935.[9] In the meantime Hjelmslev and Uldall had also taken up the work of the group for grammatical studies. Discussing the relationships between phonological and grammatical systems, they elaborated a new theory, and to underline its complete originality with regard to all previous work in linguistics decided to give it a new name: 'glossematics'. The new theory was presented by Hjelmslev and Uldall on 18th December 1935 at Aarhus. In the first volume of *Humanistisk Samfunds Skrifter* of Aarhus the two authors published a *Synopsis of an Outline of Glossematics* in which reference was made to an *Outline* which the authors hoped to have ready for the international congress of linguists held in Copenhagen in 1936. In fact the work was not ready, and Hjelmslev presented a paper (*Essai d'une théorie des morphèmes*)[10] which is still one of the best summary expositions of glossematic analysis. Uldall, in the following years, developed his own formalism, which he intended to be used not only by linguistics, but by the humanities in general: his work, which constituted the first part of the promised *Outline*, was published in 1957 as volume X : 1 of the *Travaux du Cercle Linguistique de Copenhague*. When Hjelmslev, after much hesitation, decided to revert to the originally conceived algebra for the part of the *Outline* he should have written, it was too late: seriously ill, Hjelmslev was unable to complete the work, and it was still unpublished when he died, on May 30th 1965.

But during his most creative period, in the years around 1940, Hjelmslev had produced, instead of the handbook of glossematic analysis which the *Outline* was meant to be, two other books. One was a popularizing discussion of the main problems of general and comparative linguistics in glossematic terms; this was published only in 1963, under the title *Sproget*.[11] The other was an exposition of the theoretical principles of glossematics, published in Danish in 1943, and in English in 1953, with the title *Prolegomena to a Theory of Language* (in a second revised edition in 1961).[12] Hjelmslev in later years modified, although not substantially, his theories and his terminology; particularly important in this respect is the 1954 article on *La stratification du langage*.[13] But the main exposition of his theories remains the text of the *Prolegomena*.

Linguistic theory according to Hjelmslev must be *immanent*: i.e. it must interpret language in its own terms, not as 'a conglomerate of non-linguistic (*e.g.*, physical, physiological, psychological, logical, sociological) phenomena, but as a self-sufficient totality, a structure *sui generis*' (p. 7). The theory must be *arbitrary*, i.e. it must be 'a purely deductive system, in the sense that it may be used alone to compute the possibilities that follow from its premisses'. 'A theory, in our sense, is in itself independent of any experience' (p. 14). But the theory must also be *appropriate*, i.e. it must introduce premisses which 'fulfil the conditions for application to certain empirical data' (p. 14), that is 'those objects that people agree to call languages' (p. 17). The theory aims at providing a procedural method by means of which certain objects can be described. The *description* must be *empirical*, i.e. self-consistent, exhaustive, and as simple as possible (p. 12).

Hjelmslev is against the view that 'humanistic, as opposed to natural, phenomena are non-recurrent and for that very reason cannot, like natural phenomena, be subjected to exact and generalizing treatment' (p. 9); he states that '*a priori* it would seem to be a generally valid thesis that for every *process* there is a corresponding *system*, by which the process can be analysed and described by means of a limited number of premisses. It must be assumed that any process can be analysed into a limited number of elements recurring in various combinations. Then, on the basis of this analysis, it should be possible to order these elements into classes according to their possibilities of combination. And it should be further possible to set up a general and exhaustive calculus of the possible combinations. A history so established should rise above the level of mere primitive description to that of a systematic, exact, and generalizing science, in the theory of which all events (possible combinations of elements) are foreseen and the conditions for their realization established' (p. 10). Hjelmslev suggests that the humanities should test 'this thesis as a working hypothesis' (*ib.*), without realizing, apparently, the utterly unrealistic, unworkable character of the hypothesis—the impossibility of foreseeing 'all events'.

One of the main features of glossematics, compared with other trends of structural linguistics, is the rigour with which it combines the two dichotomies of form versus substance, and of expression (*signifiant*) versus content (*signifié*), obtaining four strata: content form and expression form, content substance and expression substance.

Whereas the distinction between form and substance is apparently valid for whatever object is studied scientifically, the distinction between expression and content is specific to language, or rather, to all *semiotic* objects, i.e. to all objects which are *biplanar*. The question is not whether an object is *interpretable*, but whether one has to set up—as is the case with language—two planes which do not have the same structure; which are, in other words, non-conformal (pp. 99–100).

The real objects of scientific analysis are not things, but

relationships, i.e. dependences, or *functions*; the things themselves are nothing but intersections of dependences, terminals of functions, i.e. *functives*. There are three kinds of functions: *interdependence* (A presupposes B and B presupposes A), *determination* (A presupposes B, but B does not presuppose A), *constellation* (A does not presuppose B, and B does not presuppose A). A function may be a *both-and* function, or conjunction, or *relation* (when there is coexistence between the functives), or an *either-or* function, or disjunction, or *correlation* (when there is alternation between the functives). This is what underlies the distinction between *process* (in our case a *text*) and *system* (in our case a *language*). The three kinds of functions have different designations according to whether they enter into a process or into a system.[14]

Saussure had pointed out that *langue* is form and not substance, and that the linguistic sign is a relationship between *signifiant* and *signifié*. Hjelmslev translates this into his own terminology: there is a sign-function, between expression-form and content-form. It is thus misleading to think that the sign is an expression and that it has a content. On the contrary, a sign is a function contracted by two forms; and if it 'stands for' anything we have to say that it stands for the expression-substance as well as for the content-substance: if a linguistic sign is 'the sign of' the thing meant, then it is 'a sign of' the speech sounds which manifest it as well.

In fact there is a distinction between *substance* and *purport* (in Danish *substans* and *mening*). The purport becomes substance when it is formed: 'by virtue of the content-form and the expression-form, and only by virtue of them, exist respectively the content-substance and the expression-substance, which appear by the form's being projected on to the purport, just as an open net casts its shadow down on an undivided surface' (p. 52). For example, on the content plane the same events or things (purport) are organized in different *substances* by different *forms*, in different languages: for instance English distinguishes *green*, *blue*, *grey* and *brown*, where Welsh distinguishes *gwyrdd*, *glas*, *llwyd*; Danish distinguishes *tree* and *skov* where German has *Baum, Holz, Wald*. On the expression plane the same phonic continuum (purport) is organized in different speech sounds (substance) by the different formal units introduced by different languages: for example Italian distinguishes seven vowels (*i e ɛ a ɔ o u*), where Spanish distinguishes only five (*i e a o u*), and Eskimo three (*i a u*); in the area where English has one *k* Eskimo has two (a velar and a uvular); where English has one *t* several languages in India have two (a dental and a retroflex).

A language, in order to be adequate, must be capable of forming new signs. But, in order to be practical and easy to use, it must be able to construct its unlimited number of signs out of a restricted number of non-signs called *figurae*. Thus a language is a sign system only in as far as its external functions, its relations to non-linguistic factors, are concerned. But as for internal structure, a language is a system of figurae.

The analysis into figurae is a well-known procedure on the expression plane: if at a certain stage the following syllables are registered: *sla, sli, slai, sa, si, sai, la, li, lai*, at the next stage the inventory will be reduced to *a, i, s, l*. The same kind of analysis must be carried out also on the content plane. 'Till now, such an analysis into content-figurae has never been made or even attempted in linguistics ... confronted by an unrestricted number of signs, the analysis of the content has appeared to be an insoluble problem, a labor of Sisyphus, an impassable mountain' (p. 61). The method is the same as for the expression plane. If one registers the following entities of content at one stage: 'ram', 'ewe', 'man', 'woman', 'boy', 'girl', 'stallion', 'mare', 'sheep', 'human being', 'child', 'horse', 'he', 'she', at the next stage one will reduce the inventory to: 'he', 'she', 'sheep', 'human being', 'child', 'horse', on account of the fact that 'ram' = 'he-sheep', 'ewe' = 'she-sheep', etc. And 'ram' = 'he-sheep' differs from 'ewe' = 'she-sheep' as, on the expression plane, *sl* differs from *fl*; 'ram' = 'he-sheep' differs from 'stallion' = 'he-horse' as, on the expression plane, *sl* differs from *sn* (cf. pp. 63–4).

By the *commutation test* we can check whether an exchange of elements on one plane entails a corresponding exchange on the other plane: if so we have two different elements; otherwise we have two variants of the same element. Whereas in the case of signs the same difference in one plane will entail the same difference in the other, in the case of figurae the same difference in one plane may entail different changes in the other: for instance, the same exchange of *e* for *a* in *pat, lad, tan*, entails three completely unrelated exchanges in the content, of 'pet' for 'pat', of 'led' for 'lad', of 'ten' for 'tan'; and the same exchange in the content, of 'he' for 'she' in 'she-sheep' and 'she-horse' entails two completely unrelated exchanges in the expression, of *ram* for *ewe* and of *stallion* for *mare*.

Traditional grammar imposed Latin categories on the analysis of modern European languages; in particular, content was analysed without reference to expression (for example the Latin cases were introduced even though nothing in the expression plane corresponded to their content). As a reaction, modern linguistics started from expression, trying to go from there to the content (so did Hjelmslev himself in his *Principes de grammaire générale*, 1928). Only the full realization of the importance of the commutation test gives the fundamental insight that one has to start from the interplay between the two planes, from the relation between expression and content.

Hjelmslev calls a language whose content plane is a semiotic a *metasemiotic* (the usual term is *metalanguage*; linguistics itself is a metasemiotic), and a language whose expression plane is a semiotic a *connotative semiotic*. A language, none of whose planes is a semiotic, is a *denotative semiotic*.

Having defined *operation* as a description that is in agreement with the empirical principle (p. 29), Hjelmslev calls *scientific* a semiotic that is an operation. A connotative semiotic is non-scientific, and a metasemiotic is scientific. *Semiology* is a metasemiotic with a non-scientific semiotic as an object semiotic, and *metasemiology* is a meta-(scientific) semiotic, the object semiotics of which are semiologies (p. 106).

This framework can accommodate a theory of style, based on the study of connotative semiotics; and metasemiology 'is in practice identical with the so-called description of substance' (p. 109). 'Just as the metasemiology of denotative semiotics will in practice treat the objects of phonetics and semantics in a reinterpreted form, so in the metasemiotic of connotative semiotics the largest parts of specifically sociological linguistics and Saussurean external linguistics will find their place in reinterpreted form' (p. 110).

One thus reaches 'a totality-concept that can scarcely be imagined more absolute' (p. 110). One finds 'in the final instance, no object that is not illuminated from the key position of linguistic theory' (p. 111). But a 'temporary restriction of the field of vision was the price that had to be paid to elicit from language itself its secret' (p. 112); linguistics had to be established 'on an internal and functional basis', as a discipline 'whose science of the expression is not a phonetics and whose science of the content is not a semantics', an 'algebra of language, operating with unnamed entities, *i.e.*, arbitrarily named entities without natural designation' (p. 71).[15]

It would no doubt be interesting to compare Hjelmslev's theories on the one hand with Uldall's *General Theory*, and with some of the existing applications to particular languages; on the other hand with the tenets of other structural schools. Here I shall limit myself to noting that the use made by glossematics of formal logic does not appear to be satisfactory and that the necessity for it is not convincingly shown. The net is cast wide with the intention of catching much more than natural language: but in the process the facts of natural language (not to speak of all the rest) often seem to slip through. But it must also be recognized that on several points of theory, e.g. greater precision given to some of Saussure's dichotomies, the contribution of a general semiotic framework, the specification of the idea of content form and of the analysis of content into figurae, glossematics has provided interesting insights, some of which are still proving fruitful at the present time.

CHAPTER V

The Beginning of American Structuralism

꽈꽈꽈꽈꽈

5.1 Introduction

Linguistics in the United States[1] did not differ to any great extent from European linguistics until after the first world war. We may recall the interesting popular books on language by D. W. Whitney[2] that appeared towards the end of the nineteenth century; a comparison of Whitney and Max Müller (natural not only because of the discussion in which they opposed each other) is to the full advantage of the former.

At the beginning of the twentieth century we find the work of Franz Boas which exerted an important influence on future developments in linguistics in the United States. Boas's thought had been inspired by European Neo-grammatical trends;[3] he became a specialist in American Indian languages, started the *Handbook of American Indian Languages,*[4] and founded in 1917 the *International Journal of American Linguistics*, printed in Germany until 1939, and interrupted during the second world war. When publication began again in 1944 after Boas's death, under the editorship of C. F. Voegelin of the University of Indiana, it also published many important contributions of a general linguistic and theoretical character. Boas's introduction to the first volume of the *Handbook* mentioned above is considered a milestone in the field of descriptive linguistics and made its effect felt far beyond the limits of the study of Indian languages.

The Beginning of American Structuralism

It is after 1920 that American linguistics really develops particular trends that differentiate it from European linguistics. We find the vigorous spread of structural linguistics, in the two aspects represented by Sapir and Bloomfield, and within such linguistics the prevalence of synchronic over diachronic interests. The strength of descriptive synchronic interests is partly explained by the necessity (which had also, however, been felt in the past)[5] of describing native American languages which had no written tradition which would immediately pose (as with many Indo-European languages) the problem of the history of particular languages. In the field of diachronic studies there was an energetic restatement of Neo-grammatical positions (some of which were revalidated by Sapir and Bloomfield in their work on the comparative grammar of American languages).

There was also a considerable increase of discussions on general linguistics, and particularly on structuralist methods. As native American languages had offered a challenge to descriptive linguistics, so 'practical' needs (ranging from the teaching and learning of foreign languages–particularly 'exotic' ones, to be learnt quickly in their colloquial form, during the war–to the requirements of communication engineering)[6] stimulated the development of research in certain directions (synchronic description) instead of others (diachronic studies, stylistics, lexicology, semantics, for instance).

From the point of view of 'external' history we may recall in 1924 the foundation of the Linguistic Society of America, and the publication of its organ, *Language*, 1925 ff., which was an important forum for the discussion of structuralist methods; we should also remember the activity of the Linguistic Institute, with its summer sessions (1928 ff.), and of the Summer Institute of Linguistics (1934 ff.) with Pike and Nida (where research is devoted in particular to 'exotic' languages and civilizations, with a view to Bible translation and the training of missionaries). Besides *Language* and the *International Journal of American Linguistics* that have been mentioned, there is the lively Journal of the Linguistic Circle of New York, *Word* (1945 ff.); and, also interesting from our point of view, are *Studies in Linguistics* edited by G. L. Trager (1942 ff.), and *Anthropological Linguistics* (1959 ff.).

5.2 E. Sapir

Edward Sapir, of German Jewish origin,[7] was five years old when his family moved to the United States, in 1889. He studied at Columbia University, with German philology as his main subject. But it was Boas's influence which determined his interest in general linguistics and anthropology; Swadesh relates[8] how a conversation with Boas was for Sapir a decisive experience: each of the general and universal statements about language that Sapir had absorbed from traditional linguistics was contradicted by counter-examples which Boas picked from native American languages.

In 1905 Sapir studied the language and customs of the Wishram of Washington, in 1906 the Takelma of Oregon, in 1907–8 the Yana, while he worked in the new department of anthropology of the University of California, where Kroeber taught. In 1908–10 he worked at the University of Pennsylvania (at Philadelphia he worked on Paiute); in 1910 he moved to Canada, as director of the anthropological section of the Geological Survey of the National Museum at Ottawa. Here he worked in detail on Nootka and the whole Athabaskan group. In 1925 he went to the University of Chicago, and from 1931 until his death in 1939 he was professor of anthropology and linguistics at Yale.

The breadth of his interests was exceptional. In linguistics he worked not only on theoretical questions and on Indo-European and American Indian languages (a field in which he was a specialist), but also in the African, Semitic and Sino-Tibetan domains (in particular he studied the Uto-Aztecan and Na-Dene groupings, the influence of Tibetan on Tocharian, and the possible relàtionships between Sinitic and American Indian languages). Besides his professional interests in anthropology and linguistics, he was active in the fields of music and literature, not only as a critic but as an able pianist and a sensitive poet.

These different lines do not make his work lack unity: they in fact converge and are unified by his all-pervading interest in human culture, and in the variously interrelated symbolic systems in which it is manifested. Among American linguists he was one of the most 'humanistic'; he had a sharp feeling for the complexity of linguistic and social facts, for their nuances, and for the qualities of taste, sensibility and intuition which are needed in their study. He discussed language from the social point of view of communication, and from the technical aspect of the language of science (including the question of an international auxiliary language); but he also took into account the aesthetic aspects of individual creation, the literary aspect of written or oral tradition, the ontological and psychological aspects of the relationships between language and reality, and language and thought. It is relevant in this context to recall that Sapir is one of the very few American linguists who quote B. Croce; in the penetrating little volume which Sapir published in 1921 with the title *Language*, he writes: 'Among contemporary writers of influence on liberal thought Croce is one of the very few who have gained an understanding of the fundamental significance of language. He has pointed out its close relation to the problem of art. I am deeply indebted to him for this insight' (p. v). Sapir exerted a deep influence not only through his published work, but also through his teaching; according to friends and students of his, a powerful fascination was exerted by his personality.

M. Joos wrote that Sapir's 'contribution was not the developing of any method, but rather the establishing of a charter for the free intellectual play of personalities more or less akin to his own. If their wits happen to be dimmer (and here he had few equals), their blunders may betray the essential irresponsibility of what has been called Sapir's "method".'[9]

But the intellectual liveliness of Sapir and of his school has contributed in maintaining among American linguists a healthy dissatisfaction with the stifling limitations imposed on research by a mistaken sense of scientific 'responsibility' on the part of some of Bloomfield's followers.

I shall not discuss here Sapir's work on American Indian languages, in which he made brilliant use of the methods of comparative philology in a field which was apparently best suited for synchronic descriptive studies; his insight into historical linguistic evolution, using the notion of a 'drift' (connected with the internal form of language) which can be compared with some Prague School intuitions about the same subject, and which never loses sight of language as a 'historical product'; his discussion of typological problems, and many other points.[10]

In his *Language* Sapir discusses among other things the relationships between languages (the question of borrowing) (Chapter IX); the relationships between language, race and culture (Chapter X), notions which are not necessarily correlated; the relationships between language and literature (Chapter XI). The notions of 'drift' and of phonetic law are dealt with in Chapter VII.[11] The remarkably prudent and balanced way in which he talks of linguistic structure, avoiding the scientistic attitude towards that notion which was to become all too frequent, is worth recalling. From the start he insists on 'the unconscious and unrationalized nature of linguistic structure' (p. vi), and underlines the 'purely human and non-instinctive method of communicating ideas, emotions, and desires by means of a system of voluntarily produced symbols' that is language (p. 8). Speech is 'a non-instinctive, acquired, "cultural" function' (p. 4); language cannot be definitely localized, for 'it consists of a peculiar symbolic relation—physiologically an arbitrary one—between all possible elements of consciousness on the one hand and certain selected elements localized in the auditory, motor, and other cerebral and nervous tracts on the other' (p. 10). There are, therefore, 'properly speaking, no organs of speech; there are only organs that are incidentally useful in the production of speech sounds' (pp. 8–9). And, correspondingly, 'the mere sounds of speech are not the essential fact of language, which lies rather in the classification, in the formal patterning, and in the relating of concepts' (p. 22), in the 'function and form of the arbitrary systems of symbolism that we term languages' (p. 11).

After discussing the elements of speech (particularly the notion of word) (Chapter II), and the sounds of language (Chapter III), he examines (Chapters IV–VI) the problems of form in language, and gives us what is perhaps still today the most penetrating insight into the question of a morphological classification of languages.[12] There is a 'relative independence of form and function' (pp. 58–9). Linguistic form 'should be studied as types of patterning, apart from the associated functions' (p. 60). Concerning the form (Chapter IV) we have to distinguish 'the formal methods employed by a language', its 'grammatical processes', its 'formal patterns', or 'the distribution of concepts with reference to formal expression', that is 'what types of concepts make up the content of these formal patterns' (p. 57).

The grammatical processes may be grouped into six main types: word order (p. 62), composition (p. 64), affixation (p. 67), internal vocalic or consonantal modification (p. 73), reduplication (p. 76), accentual variations (p. 79).

In the field of concepts (Chapter V), in so far as it is 'reflected and systematized in linguistic structure' (p. 82), four classes can be distinguished: (1) '*Basic (Concrete) Concepts* (such as objects, actions, qualities): normally expressed by independent words or radical elements'; they 'involve no relation as such' (for example *man*, *white*, *kill*). (2) '*Derivational Concepts* . . . normally expressed by affixing non-radical elements to radical elements or by inner modification of these' (for example *farm*ER, *duck*LING, or the German *töten* 'to kill', with the basic concept 'dead', *tot*, and the derivational one 'causing to do (or be) so and so', expressed by the vocalic change, *töt-*). They 'give a radical element a particular increment of significance and . . . are thus inherently related in a specific way to concepts of type (1)'. (3) '*Concrete Relational Concepts*', normally expressed by affixation or internal modification; they imply relations that transcend the particular word to which they are attached, thus leading over to (4) *'Pure Relational Concepts'*, normally expressed by affixation, inner modification, independent words, or position; they 'relate the concrete elements of the proposition to each other, thus giving it definite syntactic form' (p. 101). Examples of relational concepts are the singularity of *farmer*, *kills*; or the subjectivity of *farmer* and the objectivity of *duckling*, expressed by their position before and after *kills* respectively, in *the farmer kills the duckling*. The first two classes express a *material content*, the second two a *relation*. Concepts of classes 1 and 4 are essential, and appear in all languages; concepts of classes 2 and 3, although common, are not essential, and particularly class 3, which represents a psychological and formal confusion of types 1–2 and 4, is avoidable. I shall not discuss here the different types of linguistic structures (Chapter VI), which are classified according to three criteria: the four conceptual types just mentioned; the techniques of isolation, agglutination, fusion and symbolism; and the degree of synthesis or elaboration of the word (analytic, synthetic, polysynthetic).[13]

We have seen that Sapir discusses only summarily 'the sounds of language' in Chapter III. He states that 'the single sound of articulated speech is not, as such, a linguistic element at all' (p. 42), and lingers over the 'psychological "values"' of phonetic elements (p. 54). A phonetic difference which is 'objective' but 'irrelevant' to the 'consciousness' of the speaker, has no 'value'. 'Back of the purely objective system of sounds that is peculiar to a language' there is 'a more restricted "inner" or "ideal" system', which can be brought to the consciousness of the speaker 'as a finished pattern, a psychological mechanism'. This 'inner sound-system' is 'a real and an immensely important principle in the life of a language' (p. 55). Sapir relates, from his experience in teaching Indians to write, how phonetic differences (however striking) were systematically ignored when they did not correspond to 'points in the pattern', and systematically expressed (however subtle) when they hit the 'points in the pattern' of the language (p. 56). This chapter is stimulating, but poses more questions than it is able to answer. Sapir faces the

80

problem: 'If speech, in its acoustic and articulatory aspect, is indeed a rigid system, how comes it . . . that no two people speak alike? The answer is simple. All that part of speech which falls out of the rigid articulatory framework is not speech in idea, but is merely a superadded, more or less instinctively determined vocal complication inseparable from speech in practice . . . Speech, like all elements of culture, demands conceptual selection, inhibition of the randomness of instinctive behavior. That its "idea" is never realised as such in practice, its carriers being instinctively animated organisms, is of course true of each and every aspect of culture' (p. 46). This passage is interesting among other things from the point of view of the contemporary Chomskyan notion of the 'idealized language user'. Also, the phonological notions used in transformational grammar are sometimes connected to Sapir's ideas on the phonological and the phonetic systems (but some scholars interpret these ideas differently from Chomsky).[14]

In *Language* the notion of phoneme is not fully worked out; Sapir speaks here of 'points in the pattern' (p. 56), and of the feeling, which the average speaker has, that his language is 'built up, acoustically speaking, of a comparatively small number of distinct sounds' (p. 42).

The notion of phoneme emerges very clearly in an article of 1925.[15] Here too it is stated that any attempt to define speech sounds, in their function as linguistic units, from a purely physical point of view, is bound to fail. An initial *wh-*, as in English *when*, is different from a similar sound produced, say, to blow out a candle, because it is 'one of a definitely limited number of sounds' which 'belong together in a definite system of symbolically utilizable counters'. Each member of the system is characterized not only 'by a distinctive and slightly variable articulation and a corresponding acoustic image, but also—*and this is crucial*—by a psychological aloofness from all the other members of the system'. The 'relational gaps' between the sounds are as necessary to their psychological definition as the articulations and acoustic images. The patterning of speech sounds has two phases: the first concerns the fact that speech sounds 'form a self-contained system'; the second 'the inner configuration of the sound system of a language, the intuitive "placing" of the sounds with reference to one another'. Sapir distinguishes the 'point in the pattern' (a 'typical form', a 'fundamental sound') from its variations (which can be individual or conditional) (*SW* pp. 35–7).

Sapir does not give, and does not aim at giving, a procedure for identifying and placing the phonemes in a system; to the question 'How can a sound be assigned a "place" in a phonetic pattern. . . ?' the answer is that 'a "place" is intuitively found for a sound (which is here thought of as a true "point in the pattern", not a mere conditional variant) in such a system because of a general feeling of its phonetic relationship resulting from all the specific phonetic relationships (such as parallelism, contrast, combination, imperviousness to combination, and so on) to all other sounds' (*SW* p. 42). In the 1925 article the term *phoneme* was used in such expressions as 'the crossing in a single objective phoneme of a true element of the phonetic pattern with a secondary form of another such element' (*SW* p. 40). But in the 1933 article on 'The psychological reality of phonemes',[16] the phoneme is defined as 'a functionally significant unit in the rigidly defined pattern or configuration of sounds peculiar to a language', and as such opposed to the 'sound' or 'phonetic element' that is 'an objectively definable entity in the articulated and perceived totality of speech'. The term 'phonemic' is used ('phonetic (one should say "phonemic") intuitions'), and opposed to the term 'phonetic': 'the phonemic attitude is more basic, psychologically speaking, than the more strictly phonetic one' (*SW* pp. 46–7).

In the same year, 1933, L. Bloomfield published his book, *Language*, which – within structural linguistics – represented a trend in some respects opposite to that of Sapir. Sapir and Bloomfield are often considered, not without some artificiality, the two leaders, in American structural linguistics, of opposite trends called – with labels used for psychological schools – mentalist and behaviourist. Not only does Sapir consider that it is unnecessary to provide rigorous procedures which can be applied mechanically in order to analyse the data, or to test any particular analysis, but he often uses sharp polemical expressions about those researchers who were under the delusion that abstract statements of their faith in the use of rigorously naturalistic methods in all sciences, would help in any way to solve scientific problems. Sapir insists on the basically symbolic character of language in this 1921 volume, and reformulates even more clearly this position in an article published in 1933 in the *Encyclopedia of the Social Sciences*.[17] He states that 'speech as behavior is a wonderfully complex blend of two pattern systems, the symbolic and the expressive, neither of which could have developed to its present perfection without the interference of the other'; rather than stating that communication is 'the primary function' of language, 'it is best to admit that language is primarily a vocal actualization of the tendency to see realities symbolically', and that 'it is precisely this quality which renders it a fit instrument for communication' (*SW* pp. 14–15).

In his *Language* Sapir has frequent recourse to the notion of linguistic 'feeling', as something of which language may be not only an object (for instance when he talks of an inner 'feel' of the structure of a sentence, p. 102), but also a subject (for instance when he says that 'both the phonetic and conceptual structures show the instinctive feeling of language for form' p. 56). He talks of 'the phonetic genius of a language' (p. 54), and of the 'structural "genius" of the language' (p. 120). He underlines (as if to forestall the lack of interest in historical linguistics which was to contribute, with some American linguists, to widening the gap between structural methods and diachronic study) that 'languages, after all, are exceedingly complex historical structures' (p. 140).

His view of linguistic methodology is also expressed in a vigorous and ironic essay of 1924[18] in which he taunts psychologists for whom language is 'a series of laryngeal habits'. 'We may go even further', adds Sapir, 'if we select the right kind of psychologist to help us, and have thought itself put in its place as a merely "subvocal laryngeating".' The help which Bloomfield found in the psychology of J. B. Watson and A. P. Weiss springs to mind. 'To say in so many words', Sapir continues, 'that the noblest task of linguistics is to understand language as form rather than as function or as historical process is not to say that it can be understood as form alone. The formal configuration of speech at any particular time and place is the result of a long and complex historical development, which, in turn, is unintelligible without constant reference to functional factors.' (*SW* p. 152, but I have followed the 1924 text, p. 150.)

5.3 L. Bloomfield

Leonard Bloomfield is the linguist who contributed most to spreading among linguists in the United States the principles and methods which are normally associated with the label 'American structuralism'. His influence was exerted more through his writings than through his oral teaching (which apparently did not have the same fascination as Sapir's). After a handbook in 1914,[19] he produced many contributions both on general linguistics and on particular languages (his work on American Indian languages was especially influential). His ideals inspired in particular *Language*, the journal of the Linguistic Society of America; and in the numerous reviews which he published there he took the opportunity of elaborating and clarifying his positions on different points of method; he did not hesitate to criticize with the utmost severity when he thought that the traditional statement of certain linguistic facts did not meet the requirements of a strictly 'scientific' method such as the one which he aimed at following.[20]

His most influential work was a handbook, *Language*,[21] published in 1933, which has the same title as the short introduction by Sapir of twelve years before. This compact book of almost 600 pages compressed what Bloomfield at the time considered to be valid in the science of language in a synthesis which for rigour, and for both completeness and concision has remained unparalleled. But Bloomfield's own treatment of the subject made this book not so much an account and a result of what had been discovered in the past, as the beginning of a new period which was to be called 'post-Bloomfieldian'.

The twenty-eight chapters of *Language* can be grouped as follows: I–IV are devoted to general questions, V–VIII to phonology, IX–XVI to grammar and lexis, XVII–XXVIII to other points (such as linguistic geography, the comparative method, borrowing, language change etc.) which I shall disregard here.[22]

In Chapter II, on 'the use of language', Bloomfield states his behaviourist view of linguistic facts (inspired by a materialism which is mechanistic rather than dialectic, and which has accordingly been qualified by some followers of dialectic materialism as idealistic). In terms of stimulus and response this view is summarized by the formula $S \rightarrow r \ldots s \rightarrow R$. A practical stimulus (S) prompts somebody to speak instead of reacting practically: this is a linguistic substitute reaction (r). It is for the hearer a linguistic substitute stimulus (s) which prompts him to perform a practical reaction (R). S and R are '*practical* events' and remain, in a sense, outside language; r and s are speech events. Bloomfield illustrates this with a little story: Jill is hungry (or rather, 'some of her muscles were contracting, and some fluids were being secreted, especially in her stomach') and sees an apple (or rather, 'the light-waves reflected from the red apple struck her eyes') (S); instead of getting it directly (R), she 'makes a noise with her larynx, tongue, and lips' (r) (we do not actually know what she says: a little further on Bloomfield insists that 'she made a few small movements in her throat and mouth, which produced a little noise');[23] Jack hears (s), and gets her the apple (R). '*Language enables one person to make a reaction (R) when another person has the stimulus (S).*' More generally, '*the division of labor, and, with it, the whole working of human society, is due to language*'. In this way, 'the possibilities of reaction are enormously increased. . . . *The gap between the bodies of the speaker and the hearer – the discontinuity of the two nervous systems – is bridged by the sound-waves.*' And in this sense the expression 'social organism' is not a metaphor: as the single cells in a many-celled organism co-operate by means of such devices as the nervous system, so the individuals in human society co-operate by means of sound-waves.

It is clear that 'the mechanism which governs speech must be very complex and delicate'; in fact, so complex that we cannot have any actual description of a speech act in behaviourist terms. We have already seen that Bloomfield does not tell us what Jill says, because we are clearly not in a position to specify, starting from the fact that Jill is hungry, what she will say. Bloomfield obviously understood this difficulty and stated it in so many words. 'Even if we know a great deal about a speaker or about the immediate stimuli which are acting upon him, we usually cannot predict whether he will speak or what he will say.' 'A great deal', says Bloomfield; but *how much* should we actually know in order to be able to make such a prediction? 'The occurrence of a speech (and, as we shall see, the wording of it) and the whole course of practical events before and after it, depend upon the entire life-history of the speaker and of the hearer.' And, if we accept this, we must probably conclude that these life-histories depend on the whole history of the universe (but it would have been interesting to see a discussion of whether it is possible to isolate, in the history of the universe, something which is *relevant* to a particular speech-event).

The situation is obviously hopeless. Faced with the 'enormous variability' of the reactions ('the possibilities are almost infinite'), Bloomfield refuses the *mentalistic* theory which ascribes the variability of human conduct to 'the interference of some non-physical factor, a *spirit* or *will* or *mind*' which 'does not follow the patterns of succession (cause-and-effect sequences) of the material world'. He prefers the *materialistic* or *mechanistic* theory which 'supposes that the variability of human conduct, including speech, is due only to the fact that the human body is a very complex system'. In particular the nervous system acts as a trigger-mechanism: 'only so can we explain the fact that large-scale movements like Jack's fetching the apple, are set off by very slight changes, such as the minute thrumming of air-waves on his ear-drum'.

This is evidently for Bloomfield the only 'explanation' which

86

is consistent with scientific method. The problem is, of course, that, in the case of language, this is no explanation at all. There is, for the time being, nothing revealing that we can say about language in terms of stimulus and reaction, apart from stating the principle that language, as everything else, must have a mechanistic explanation.

I cannot undertake here a discussion of the differences between the two texts of 1914 and 1933. Bloomfield denies that there has been an evolution from Wundtian to behaviouristic psychology. In the preface to *Language* he states that in 1914 he had based on the psychologic system of W. Wundt the 'phase of the exposition' which consisted in discussing 'in simple terms' 'the deep-rooted things about language, which mean most to all of us'. In the meantime he has learnt that 'we can pursue the study of language without reference to any one psychological doctrine'. This seems to be begging the question: Bloomfield tries to avoid dependence on psychology; only occasionally and 'by way of elucidation' has he mentioned 'how the two main present-day trends of psychology differ in their interpretation'. This means that he has tried to avoid stating the facts of language in terms of *mind*, and by so doing he has followed a mechanistic requirement. Thus mechanism appears to be not so much one of the two present-day trends in psychology, as 'the necessary form of scientific discourse'. Bloomfield, following J. B. Watson,[24] and particularly A. P. Weiss[25] whom he admired,[26] tries to follow the methods of behaviourism. In the essay which he wrote for the *International Encyclopedia of Unified Science*[27] he states the requirements that scientific method must satisfy: these can be defined with reference to strict behaviourism ('science shall deal only with events that are accessible in their time and place to any and all observers'), mechanism ('or only with events that are placed in co-ordinates of time and space'), operationalism ('or that science shall employ only such initial statements and predictions as lead to definite handling operations'), physicalism ('or only terms such as are derivable by rigid definition from a set of everyday terms concerning physical happenings') (p. 231).

Bloomfield's theory of meaning also depends on these premises (Chapter IX of *Language*). By presenting language in terms of stimulus and reaction, he had already distinguished between the speech event (r . . . s) and the *real* or *practical* events (S, R), and he had stated that 'speech-utterance, trivial and unimportant in itself, is important because it has a *meaning*: the meaning consists of the important things with which the speech-utterance . . . is connected, namely the practical events' (p. 27). The meaning of a linguistic form is 'the situation in which the speaker utters it and the response which it calls forth in the hearer'. 'We can define the meaning of a speech-form accurately when this meaning has to do with some matter of which we possess scientific knowledge.' But 'a very important part of every situation is the state of the speaker's body' (including 'of course, the predisposition of his nervous system, which results from all his experiences, linguistic and other, up to this very moment—not to speak of hereditary and pre-natal factors'); and of all this we can hardly say that we possess scientific knowledge. 'The statement of meanings is therefore the weak point in language-study, and will remain so until human knowledge advances very far beyond its present state.' In such conditions we cannot define meanings and demonstrate their constancy: we have to take 'the specific and stable character of language as a presupposition of linguistic study', and state it as 'the *fundamental assumption of linguistics*:' '*In certain communities (speech-communities) some speech-utterances are alike as to form and meaning*' (pp. 139–44, and cf. pp. 78 and 158).[28]

The main importance of Bloomfield's theories did not in fact consist in these abstract and somewhat unproductive statements of principle, but rather in his attempt to elaborate explicitly rigorous methods for the description of linguistic forms. He distinguishes (Chapter X) the *bound* forms, which are never spoken alone, from the *free* forms. A *constituent* is *contained* in a *complex* form, i.e. a form which bears a partial phonetic-semantic resemblance to some other linguistic form. A form which is not complex is a *simple* form or *morpheme*. A complex form cannot be analysed directly into its *ultimate* constituents or morphemes: its structure is composed of *immediate* constituents. The meaning of a morpheme is a *sememe*; the stock of the morphemes of a language is its *lexicon*.

An utterance contains some significant features which are not accounted for by the lexicon: the meaning depends in part on the arrangement of the forms. 'The meaningful arrangements of forms in a language constitute its *grammar*.' There seem to be four ways of arranging linguistic forms: *order*, or succession (as in *John hit Bill* versus *Bill hit John*); *modulation* or the use of 'secondary' phonemes (as in *John!* versus *John?*); *phonetic modification* (as in *do not* versus *don't*); and *selection*, which 'contributes a factor of meaning because different forms in what is otherwise the same grammatical arrangement, will result in different meanings'. Forms accordingly belong to different form classes and sub-classes (like verbs, substantives, adjectives etc.).

'A simple feature of grammatical arrangement is a *grammatical feature* or *taxeme*. A taxeme is in grammar what a phoneme is in the lexicon—namely, the smallest unit of form.' Taxemes occur in conventional grammatical arrangements or *tactic forms*; a tactic form with its meaning is a *grammatical form*; the smallest units of grammatical form are *tagmemes*, and their meanings are *episememes*. Grammatical forms can be grouped into three classes: *sentence-types* (like statements or questions) (Chapter XI), *construction*, in which we can distinguish *syntax* (Chapter XII), when none of the immediate constituents is a bound form (as in *John ran*), and *morphology* (Chapters XIII–XIV), when bound forms appear among the constituents (like *-ess* in *duke* plus *ess* : *duchess*); and *substitution* (Chapter XV), when a form is a conventional substitute for any one of a class of other linguistic forms (as with the 'pronouns' of traditional grammar). Chapter XVI discusses the relationships between form-classes and lexicon.[29]

In Chapters V–VIII phonology is discussed. Phonemes (Chapter V) can be identified by a process of *comparison* (to establish which forms are 'the same' and which are 'different') and of *alteration* (to find forms which *partially resemble* each other). Thus if we start from *pin* we can find partially resembling forms by altering three parts of the word: the beginning (*fin, sin, tin, in*), the end (*pig, pill, pit*), the middle (*pen, pan, pun*)–or the beginning and the middle (*man, sun, hen*), the middle and the end (*pat, push, peg*), the beginning and the end (*dig, fish, mill*). (If we alter all three (as in *sag, cot, fall*) we have obviously no partial resemblance.) When we find that there are no other parts that we can replace in *pin*, we 'conclude that the distinctive features of this word are three indivisible units'. Each can occur in other combinations but 'cannot be further analysed by partial resemblances'. Each is '*a minimum unit of distinctive sound-feature, a phoneme*'. The expression 'indivisible units' must however be qualified: 'The phonemes of a language are not sounds, but merely features of sound,' and not only are the distinctive features always accompanied by non-distinctive ones; they also 'occur in lumps or bundles, each one of which we call a phoneme'.

Phonemes can be classified into 'types' (Chapter VI) in terms of practical phonetics, and can undergo 'modifications' (Chapter VII). But practical phonetic observation is necessarily haphazard, and has little scientific value, states Bloomfield discussing 'phonetic structure' (Chapter VIII). 'The important thing about language . . . is not the way it sounds', but 'its service in connecting the speaker's stimulus . . . with the hearer's response.' This connexion depends on the difference between one phoneme and another: 'for the working of language, all that is necessary is that each phoneme be unmistakably different from all the others'. 'The importance of a phoneme, then, lies not in the actual configuration of its sound-waves, but merely in the difference between this configuration and the configurations of all the other phonemes of the same language.' Phonemes must be grouped not according to their physiological character but according to the parts which they 'play in the working of the language'. To state which combinations of phonemes occur, the simplest way is to find out which phonemes can occur as 'syllabics', and which phonemes, or phoneme-clusters, can be *initial* (before the first syllabic of an utterance), *final* (after the last syllabic of an utterance), and *medial* (between syllabics).[30]

The Beginning of American Structuralism

Language proved, and still proves, very fruitful; but if for a period of over two decades after its publication it was for American linguists mainly a source of inspiration, a model of scientific method which had to be followed and put into practice, more recently its fruitfulness has been of a different kind; the text has been considered more critically, and it has been noted that on many points there were ambiguities and obscurities, or that researchers who followed it consistently would find themselves down blind alleys. Bloomfield's method has also been radically criticized in the context of the growth of a new and powerful 'mentalist' trend in American linguistics. R. A. Hall had written that 'in America, Bloomfield's *Language* is generally considered the greatest single book on linguistics published in our century, on either side of the Atlantic'. But D. Hymes has written recently that Bloomfield's influence 'although crucial for a generation to certain scholars and institutions within the United States, has proven, on a larger scale of time and space, largely transient and local'.[31] One of the most intelligent of the Bloomfieldians has tried to put the blame for many of the limitations of the School on the post-Bloomfieldians, rather than on Bloomfield himself.[32]

On the whole it seems to me quite clear that recent developments, even in aspects where they openly contradict Bloomfield's positions, are not a return to the past, so to speak after a parenthesis, but depend heavily on Bloomfield and would have scarcely been possible without his work.

CHAPTER VI
Functional Linguistics

🔃🔃🔃🔃🔃

6.1 R. Jakobson

Roman Jakobson and André Martinet can be considered the two most important heirs in international linguistic thought to the theories of the Prague School. Martinet explicitly insists on the label 'functional' to define his own positions. But the consideration of linguistic functions, which is a typical feature of the School of Prague, also occupies a central place in the work of Jakobson. He takes into account not only the functions of particular elements in the working of language, but the functions of linguistic activity itself. On the latter point, the School of Prague had distinguished, with Karl Bühler, three functions: expression, appeal, and representation or reference. More recently Jakobson has distinguished six points of view from which a linguistic act can be considered: in relation to the *speaker*, the *listener*, the *context* (to which one refers) (these three correspond to the functions just mentioned), the *contact* (the physical channel and the psychological connexion through which communication takes place), the *code* and the *message*. And accordingly there are six functions: respectively the *expressive* (typically represented by interjections), the *conative* (typically represented by vocatives and imperatives), the *denotative* (or referential, or representational, typically represented by factual statements, in the 3rd person in the indicative mood), the *phatic* (of which Malinowski had spoken, represented for instance by the *yes*'s and *hem*'s said on the telephone simply to make it clear that one is still there listening, or that the

92

line has not been cut), the *metalinguistic*, centred on the code, and the *poetic* centred on the message. The study of poetry will use a 'formal', 'stylistic', 'linguistic' approach, based on the analysis of the structure of the poetic message itself. I shall not discuss here the works of Jakobson as a philologist and literary critic, such as his admirable essays on problems of metre, textual criticism, stylistics and literary history, but shall limit myself to some observations on his linguistic activity proper.[1]

Born in Moscow in 1896, Jakobson studied in Moscow and Prague, and has taught in Moscow, Brno, Copenhagen, Oslo, Uppsala, New York (at the École Libre des Hautes Études and at Columbia University), at Harvard and at the Massachusetts Institute of Technology. This breadth of contacts was accompanied by a corresponding variety in his activity and in the influences he has exerted.

A colleague rather than an heir of Trubeckoj, Jakobson was, together with Trubeckoj and Karcevskij, one of the three signatories of the memorable proposition presented to the first congress of linguists at The Hague (which makes 1928 one of the possible dates of birth of structural linguistics in Europe; another suggestion could be 1916, the date of publication of Saussure's *Cours*).

Jakobson's work is characterized by breadth of interests and depth of insights, which allowed him to point the way to several fields where research was to prove particularly fruitful. He has even been reproached for possessing these qualities to an excessive degree, for being too intelligent, determining in advance the development of certain ideas at the very moment they were formed and anticipating conclusions which, lacking adequately detailed research, could not be completely satisfactory.[2]

Jakobson was the first to state definitely the importance of diachronic phonology. While Trubeckoj elaborated the methods of phonological description, Jakobson, as early as 1929, published his observations on the phonological evolution of Russian. These were introduced by some general notes on historical phonology.[3] Schleicher, who had identified an inner functional sense in the linguistic system, saw in language change the action of blind chance. Saussure thought it necessary to separate clearly synchrony and diachrony just because of the fortuitous and non-systematic character of language change.

The *Theses* approved at The Hague had, however, already clearly stated that Saussure's dichotomy had to be overcome, and that the history of a language must not 'be confined within the study of isolated changes, but must try to consider them in terms of the system which undergoes them'.[4] Now Jakobson declared even more firmly that—contrary to what might have appeared obvious after Saussure; namely that a diachronic study presupposes a synchronic one, whereas the reverse does not apply—there can be no synchronic study without there being a diachronic one as well. Language change belongs to the linguistic system, in the shape of stylistic tendencies (characteristic of young or old people—or of modernists and traditionalists), as well as modification, in time, of the speech of particular individuals. These ideas keep reappearing in the thought of Jakobson, revised and adapted as his theories developed. Synchrony must not be conceived statically, but dynamically; the synchronic aspect of a film, for instance, is not a frame, or the series of frames each considered individually, but the synchronic consideration of the film itself, which is dynamic, in motion by definition. The picture advertising the film, printed on a poster is, on the contrary, static; and if the poster remains for a long time in front of the cinema, and undergoes certain modifications (it may become faded, stained, etc.), there is nothing to prevent us from studying it in a work of static diachrony.

The interpretation of change must be teleological, in terms of ends and not in terms of causes: the 'final causes' of linguistic changes must be sought. A systematic synthesis of these theories is found in the 1931 essay *Prinzipien der historischen Phonologie* (which also appeared in French, in a version revised by the author himself, as an appendix to the French edition of Trubeckoj's *Grundzüge*).[5]

Sound change may be non-phonological, that is, it may bring about a change in the number and in the relationships of the variants. A phonological sound change is sudden, not gradual, and alters the relationship between two elements, from A : B to $A_1 : B_1$. The two elements can be in phonological opposition, either (a) in one relationship only, or (b) in both; accordingly we may have (a)1: dephonologization, or elimination of a phonological difference; (a)2: phonologization, or formation of a phonological difference; (b) rephonologization, in which the change may be (b)1: from correlation to disjunction, (b)2: from disjunction to correlation; or (b)3: from one correlation to another.

Jakobson devoted important studies to aphasia and to child language.[6] The use of a linguistic sign implies two aspects: *combination* and *selection* (which can be compared to the syntagmatics and paradigmatics of Saussurean linguistics. But Saussure, with his insistence on the linear character of the *signifiant*, had considered only *concatenation*, and had neglected the other variety of combination, *concurrence*).[7] Style can also be interpreted according to two different poles: the *metaphoric* (one item leads to another through their similarity), typical of poetry, particularly lyric, and of 'romantic' literary products; and the *metonymic* (one item leads to another through their contiguity), typical of prose, epic, and in general of 'realistic' literary products. Aphasic disturbances can likewise be grouped into two main kinds: *similarity disorders*, which affect the selection and substitution of items, with relative stability of combination and contexture; and *contiguity disorders*, in which selection and substitution are relatively normal, while combination is impaired with the result that one finds agrammatism, chaotic word order, elimination of inflection and of prepositions, conjunctions etc. Jakobson sees in all this a dichotomy which is typical of any symbolic process.

The predilection for dichotomies, for the interpretation of linguistic facts in binary terms, is clearly apparent in many aspects of Jakobson's work. We have seen that he disagrees with Saussure on the linear character of the *signifiant*. For Jakobson there can be simultaneous elements in language; in fact the distinctive features, which occur simultaneously with each other, correspond to Saussure's definition of 'oppositive' and 'differential' elements. What is typical of Jakobson's position, though, is not the analysis of phonemes into distinctive features, but the *binary* character of the latter. Saussure's phoneme is not an 'oppositive' element, it is not related to its 'opposite'; but the distinctive feature is. It is characterized by the presence or absence of a given quality. In examining the development of Jakobson's theory one must certainly take into account the influence of information theory, with its measurement of information in terms of binary choices.[8] But the importance of dichotomies for Jakobson precedes the development of information theory, and is in fact an original feature. Already at the first congress of linguists in 1928 Jakobson had stressed the importance of phonological correlations: 'It is useful above all to consider phonological *correlations* as a separate class of meaningful differences. A phonological correlation is made up of a series of binary oppositions defined by a common principle which can be conceived independently of each pair of opposed terms.'[9] An important step towards extending the binary hypothesis to the whole of phonology was made with the 1938 contribution to the third congress of phonetics, on the phonological classification of consonants.[10]

Traditionally consonants are classified into a variety of types, but their oppositions can be interpreted in terms of a small number of binary features. For instance the opposition, in different languages, of velars and uvulars, of explosives and affricates, of stops and fricatives, of apico-dental constrictives and sibilant constrictives, of bilabials and labiodentals etc., is due to the presence in the second term of each pair of a strong turbulence (*frottement énergique*) of the air which causes a 'Schneidenton' (C. Stumpf's term): in each pair the first term is mellow and the second strident.

Here the point is made that 'the gap formerly created by handbooks between consonant structure and vowel structure is rightly questioned by modern acoustics and appears to be bridged in phonological studies'. For instance 'the differences between four types of consonants (velars, palatals, dentals,

labials) are in fact reduced to the two oppositions of phonological features' called grave versus acute, and front versus back
(later termed diffuse versus compact), as appears from the table:

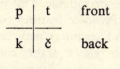

p	t	front
k	č	back

grave acute

In 1949 we find that a matrix is used in which the rows
correspond to distinctive features and the columns to different
phonemes. Two analyses are offered, for Serbocroat and for
French.[11] Each uses six distinctive features: vocality versus
consonantness, nasality versus orality, saturation versus dilute-
ness, gravity versus acuteness, continuousness versus inter-
ception and, for Serbocroat voicing versus voicelessness, which
applies only to consonants, for French tenseness versus laxness,
which applies to vowels as well.

A more complete formulation of the theory was made possible
by the technical progress of acoustics and the production of
what was called, with a term that goes back to A. M. Bell,
'visible speech'.[12] In 1952 a now famous report from the MIT
Acoustics Laboratory was produced by Jakobson, Fant and
Halle;[13] here we find a comprehensive theory of the distinctive
features (which was later modified in various ways),[14] based on
the identification, thanks to spectrographic analysis, of their
acoustic correlates. I shall follow here the version given by
Jakobson and Halle in *Fundamentals of Language*.[15] Features
may be *expressive, configurative*, or *distinctive*. Expressive
features 'put the relative emphasis on different parts of the
utterance or on different utterances and suggest the emotional
attitudes of the utterer'. Configurative features 'signal the division
of the utterance into grammatical units', by singling them out
(*culminative* features), or by delimiting them (*demarcative*
features). Distinctive features serve to differentiate linguistic
units from each other. Distinctive features occur, simultaneously,
in bundles called phonemes. The phonemes are concatenated

into sequences; the elementary pattern of such sequences is the syllable. In each syllable one part is more prominent: this is the crest; if the crest contains two or more phonemes, one of these is the peak phoneme, or syllabic. Distinctive features can be *prosodic* or *inherent*. Prosodic features (which can be of three kinds: *tone*, *force* and *quantity*) may be, according to their frame of reference, *intersyllabic*, if they contrast with features of other syllables, or *intrasyllabic*, if they contrast with features of the same syllable. Prosodic features involve polar terms: but each term is fully recognizable only when its counterpart is also present in the same message. Each of the two terms of an inherent feature, on the contrary, is recognizable by itself: there is no need for the other term to be present in the same message. For instance, a louder syllable is recognized as such only by comparison with a less loud one nearby; but a voiced consonant is recognized as such even if there is no voiceless consonant to contrast it with in the same message.

The real novelty, besides the identification of acoustic correlates of the distinctive features, is that they are reduced to a stock of twelve binary oppositions which are sufficient to analyse all the known phonological systems, and are hypothetically presented as linguistic universals. These twelve oppositions can be grouped into *sonority* features (the first nine), which are akin to the force and quantity features, and utilize the amount and concentration of energy in the spectrum; and *tonality* features (the last three), which are akin to pitch features, and involve the ends of the frequency spectrum. Here is the list of the distinctive features; after their names an indication follows of some of their acoustic or articulatory correlates, and the traditional phonetic elements to which they correspond.*

*Sound waves may be represented by oscillograms: the frequency of cycles (corresponding to sound height–perceptually pitch) is measured on the horizontal axis (time); the amplitude (corresponding to sound intensity–perceptually loudness) on the vertical axis. The shape of the wave (its 'profile') corresponds to sound quality. A complex wave can be analysed into 'fundamental' and 'harmonics'. In the production of speech sounds the cavities of the vocal tract act as 'resonators': they resonate at the frequencies of certain harmonics of the glottal tone; different positions of

I.   *Vocalic versus non-vocalic*: presence versus absence of a sharply defined formant structure; presence versus absence of a single or primary excitation at the glottis and free passage through the vocal tract. Vowels and liquids versus consonants and glides.

II.   *Consonantal versus non-consonantal*: low versus high total energy; presence versus absence of an obstruction in the vocal tract. Consonants and liquids versus vowels and glides.

III.   *Compact versus diffuse*: higher versus lower concentration of energy in a relatively narrow central region of the spectrum, and increase versus decrease of the total amount of energy; forward-flanged versus backward-flanged; the vocal tract can have a horn-shape versus a Helmholtz resonator-shape (large cavity with a small opening to which a neck may be attached). Open versus close vowels; velar and palatal versus dental and labial consonants.

IV.   *Tense versus lax*: higher versus lower amount of energy, and greater versus smaller spread of energy in the spectrum and in time; greater versus smaller deformation of the vocal tract. Tense, fortis, aspirated versus lax, lenis, unaspirated.

V.   *Voiced versus voiceless*: presence versus absence of periodic low frequency excitation; presence versus absence of periodic vibrations of the vocal cords. Voiced versus voiceless.

---

the vocal organs will produce cavities which resonate at the frequencies of different harmonics, and will thus determine the quality of the resulting speech sound.

One can also represent a complex wave placing the frequencies on one axis and the intensities on the other; the peaks of the resulting curve (i.e., the frequencies with maximum amplitude) are called 'formants'. In spectrograms time is on the horizontal axis, frequency on the vertical one; the degree of blackness at any particular point in the spectrogram represents the intensity of the frequency which corresponds to that point on the vertical axis, at the time which corresponds to the same point on the horizontal axis.

VI.   *Nasal versus oral*: wider versus narrower frequency regions over which the energy is spread, and presence versus absence of additional formants; introduction versus exclusion of the nasal resonator. Nasals versus orals.

VII.   *Discontinuous (or interrupted) versus continuant*: silence followed and/or preceded by spread of energy over a wide frequency region (as burst or as rapid transition of vowel formants) versus absence of abrupt transition between sound and such silence; presence versus absence of a rapid closure and/or opening of the vocal tract, or of one or more taps. Stops and affricates versus continuants, and flapped or trilled liquids versus continuant liquids.

VIII.   *Strident versus mellow*: higher versus lower intensity noise, rough edged (with supplementary obstruction creating edge effects) versus smooth-edged. Labiodental, sibilant, uvular versus bilabial, interdental, velar constrictives; affricates versus stops.

IX.   *Checked versus unchecked*: higher versus lower rate of discharge of energy; presence versus absence of compression of the glottis. Glottalized versus non-glottalized.

X.   *Grave versus acute*: concentration of energy in the lower versus upper frequencies of the spectrum; peripheral versus central constriction; velar, labial versus palatal, dental consonants, and back versus front vowels.

XI.   *Flat versus plain*: presence versus absence of a downward shift or weakening of some upper frequency components; narrowed versus wider slit; presence versus absence of pharyngalization, velarization, retroflection, labialization, rounding. One label is enough, because these features never function distinctively in the same phonemic context (labialization and rounding actually refer to the same articulatory process; but the latter term is restricted to vowels). In 1959 Halle called this feature 'flat versus natural', to avoid confusion with the following one.

XII.   *Sharp versus plain*: presence versus absence of an upward shift of some upper frequency components; widened versus narrower slit, and presence versus absence of an obstruction in the mouth cavity. Palatalized versus non-palatalized.

The matrices are built making each row correspond to a distinctive feature and each column to a phonological unit, and they are constructed according to different criteria in different papers. The distinctive features do not appear to be always binary: the choice is not limited to + and −, but in some matrices there are also other symbols; ±, for gradual oppositions, is still used in *Preliminaries* (1952), but is abandoned in the 1953 contribution by Jakobson, Cherry, and Halle. The 'redundant' features are put in brackets; and when a feature does not apply there is a Ø, or an empty square (it is interesting that in the 1949 article 'On the identification of phonemic entities' no distinction was made between the minuses and the zeros).[16] So in any particular square there may be a choice between seven symbols: +, −, ±, each within or without brackets, and Ø. In later contributions the ± and the brackets disappear, and the matrix is filled up with either a + or a − or a Ø for each square.

It has been stated that in these analyses 'we are concerned . . . not only with questions of logic but also with matters of fact': the binary distinctive features 'are intimately related to the physical production of speech'.[17] In fact it seems that in the specification of the distinctive features some decisions depend more on descriptive convenience than on actual consideration of the acoustic data. It is obvious that if we allow features to be ternary we need fewer features than if we want them all to be binary. In the *Preliminaries* the feature vocalic versus consonantal (with + for the vowels, − for the consonants, and ± for liquids) is split into the two features (I) vocalic versus non-vocalic and (II) consonantal versus non-consonantal. In 1957 feature (III) compact versus diffuse, which was ternary for the vowels (*a* : +; *i*, *u* : −; *e*, *ε*, *o*, *ɔ* : ±) but not for the consonants, is split into two features: (IIIa) compact versus non-compact (presence versus absence of a horn-shaped cavity) (*a* versus *i*, *e*, *ȯ*, *u*; and velars and palatals versus labials and dentals); and (IIIb) diffuse versus non-diffuse (presence versus absence of a Helmholtz resonator cavity), which applies only to the vowels (*i*, *u* versus *e*, *a*, *o*). One of the reasons for this is that it was difficult to establish an 'exchange rate' between binary and ternary features when it came to evaluation procedures for alternative phonemic solutions, or to a comparison of different phonological systems in a general typology. Halle stressed in 1957, in his apology 'in defence of the number two', that 'almost since the very beginning of modern phonology, linguists have realised that the criteria at their disposal admitted of several descriptions for the same set of facts', and referred the reader to Y. R. Chao's article on non-uniqueness.[18]

The binary distinctive feature system, like other frameworks, for example the IPA's, or Jespersen's, or Pike's, Halle noted, is basically a questionnaire, from which certain information is obtained, according to the nature of the questions. It is a hypothesis; and it appears to be preferable to others because, while it is no less satisfactory than other hypotheses in its handling of any data, it leads in many cases to a simpler description, and it allows us to formulate an evaluation procedure for alternative descriptions.

It does not seem to me that these comments succeed in dispelling the perplexities provoked by some bold statements published by Jakobson and Halle in 1956 in their *Fundamentals*. In this work too there was a reference to Y. R. Chao, but in comparison with the reference quoted above it struck rather a different note: 'The maximum elimination of redundancies and the minimum amount of distinctive alternatives is a principle that permits an affirmative answer to the focal problem raised by Chao in 1934 on whether the task of breaking down a given language into its ultimate components yields a unique solution. Not less crucial is his more recent question (1954), whether the dichotomous scale is the pivotal principle which the analyzer can profitably impose upon the linguistic code or whether this scale is inherent in the structure of language. There are several weighty arguments in favor of the latter solution.'[19]

6.2 A. Martinet

Another figure of great importance in the development of contemporary linguistics is André Martinet. He took his degree in the field of Germanic linguistics;[20] he made interesting contributions to the elaboration of the Prague School theories on such points as neutralization and segmentation;[21] he helped to spread the knowledge of phonology with clear critical expositions[22] and by his teaching as holder of the first Chair of Phonology at the École Pratique des Hautes Études in Paris. He taught at Columbia University, where he was one of the driving forces of the Linguistic Circle of New York and of its journal, *Word*, on which he impressed, in the first years of its life, an identifiable stamp which gave it an original place in the field of American linguistics. It is also worth recalling the critical exposé which he devoted to glossematics, which was a very important source for the knowledge of Hjelmslev's *Omkring Sprogteoriens Grundlæggelse* (particularly, for linguists who did not read Danish, before the publication of the English version, *Prolegomena to a Theory of Language* in 1953), and which at the same time offered a very acute criticism of those theories.[23]

Among Martinet's interests different fields can be identified which have enriched each other in their development: descriptive phonology, diachronic phonology, syntax, general linguistics. He has also applied the methods of modern linguistics to concrete questions of historical and comparative grammar.[24] His work is particularly important because it tends to bridge the gaps which have appeared in our century between different fields of linguistic study: Martinet's work has the quality, which is becoming rarer and rarer in our own time, of being interesting and comprehensible to both structuralists and traditional comparative philologists. This is due among other things to his remarkable attention to the actual reality of language, his interest in the facts and the explanations which have to fit them, rather than in explanatory theories to which the facts of language may be made to fit.

For phonological questions the title of two lectures given by

Martinet in London in 1946 is revealing: *Phonology as functional phonetics*.[25] Phonology for Martinet must interpret *phonetic* facts; these are the basic data, and not just one out of several different realizations of an abstract system. But phonology must concentrate on a particular aspect of phonetic facts: i.e. the linguistic *functions* of sound differences, the way in which they are used in the linguistic system. But it must not be assumed that, on account of this 'limitation', phonological description[26] is partial or approximate. It is, on the contrary, perfectly adequate, in as much as it reveals all that one needs to know, and only what one needs to know, from a linguistic point of view. With the label 'functional linguistics', we are saying what linguistics is or must be, we are not distinguishing one part of linguistics from another. Functional linguistics is not a sector, but the whole of linguistics.

In Martinet's phonological work an important part is devoted to the study of diachronic problems.[27] He tries here to go beyond the purely descriptive phase in which phonologizations and dephonologizations are recorded, and attempts to provide *explanations* of the changes according to general principles. A basic criterion of interpretation is offered by two contrasting elements: efficiency in communication (using as many units as possible, as different from each other as possible), and tendency to minimum effort (using as few units as possible, as similar to each other as possible). There is a tendency to reconcile these two opposing requirements. This tendency (which is not interpreted in the 'teleological' terms familiar to the School of Prague) can be conceived as a striving towards *economy*, i.e. towards attaining an improved functional load. Why then do all languages not reach an identical, economically optimum, phonological system? Optimum economy can never be reached because there are physiological disturbing factors such as the inertia and asymmetry of the speech organs.

The requirements of syntagmatic economy (to represent clusters of elements by new unique elements) and of paradigmatic economy (to represent an element by an otherwise non-existent cluster of elements already belonging to the inventory), are in opposition. The determining feature is frequency: the more frequent an element, the more likely it will be that syntagmatic economy prevails over paradigmatic.

These interpretative criteria, which had already been sketched before 1940, are discussed systematically and comprehensively in a book published in 1955 on the 'economy' of sound-change.[28] Each unit in an utterance is submitted to two contrasting pressures: a pressure in the chain, exerted by the adjacent units, and a pressure in the system exerted by the units which might have appeared in that particular place. The first is mostly an assimilating pressure, the second a dissimilating one. The phonemes which exert their dissimilating pressure on a given phoneme are not all the units of the phonological system, but in particular those which are 'near' to it, i.e., those which have 'correlative relationships' with it (they belong to those bundles of proportional oppositions which are called 'correlations', and are formed by two *series*—one with and one without the correlative feature—and a certain number of *orders*). The importance of syntagmatic pressures had been abundantly studied in the last century; the importance of paradigmatic pressures in sound change has, on the contrary, been stressed mainly by functional structuralism.

On the paradigmatic plane there is a tendency to preserve certain oppositions. On the syntagmatic plane the more marked contrasts (of the kind stop + vowel) are also preferred. It is possible to formulate a principle of *maximum differentiation*, according to which a system evolves towards a pattern in which the available phonetic space is best employed and a sort of *equidistance* of the phonemes is reached. Thus if a language has only three vowels it is likely that these will be *i, u, a*, rather than, say, *e, ε, a*, or *i, e, a*, etc. The variations—casual or conditional—in the realization of a phoneme are normally checked if they make the phoneme more easily confused with others, and are accepted if they make it more easily distinguished from others. The evolution is also influenced by the functional load of an opposition: an opposition which is little employed will disappear more easily than another which is much used.

We have seen that the analysis of phonemes into distinctive features reveals the presence of correlations; a phoneme which is *integrated* in a correlative bundle will be more stable than one which is not; an *empty hole* in a pattern is likely to be filled by a new phoneme. Complete integration would give a 'perfect' system, with a maximum number of phonemes built with a minimum number of distinctive features; this system could not be improved, and there would not be any reason to change it. But complete integration can never be reached because there are contrasting forces: on the one hand the requirement of putting next to each other in the sequence maximally different units, such as vowels and consonants, and on the other the asymmetry of the speech organs which makes certain bundles of distinctive features difficult or impossible to realize phonetically, even though they might be convenient from the abstract point of view of pattern regularity. For instance the distinction between front and back articulation, or presence versus absence of rounding, is easy for high vowels like *i* and *u*, but difficult for low vowels like *a*; and in fact the languages that distinguish *i* from *u* are much more numerous than those that distinguish a front and/or unrounded from a back and/or rounded variety of *a*.

Naturally Martinet invites us to look in the first place for the inner causes of language change, those which are within the system. But he does not forget that 'internal' explanations may not be satisfactory, in so far as they do not explain the rate of change and the specific historical occasion of particular changes. Why is a hole in the pattern, which had remained empty for centuries, filled at one particular moment? The answer will normally have to introduce an 'external' explanation of a generally historical rather than specifically linguistic character.[29]

Martinet has also studied the relationship between phonology and other levels of language, and has worked on questions of general linguistics. He has elaborated the interesting notion of '*double articulation*'.[30] A linguistic utterance undergoes a first articulation into monemes, which are the elementary grammatical units corresponding to what American linguists call morphemes. An indefinite number of utterances can be identified on the basis of a limited stock of monemes, amounting to some thousands. This is an articulation which involves both expression and content. Monemes are two-faced units: they have an expression and a content. The second articulation affects only the expression plane: the several thousands of moneme expressions can be identified on the basis of a stock limited to a few dozen phonemes. Martinet does not consider it necessary to introduce a third articulation which allows the identification of the few dozen phonemes on the basis of an even more limited stock of about a dozen distinctive features. This does not mean, obviously, that he rejects the notion of distinctive feature. On the contrary, it has an important place in his phonological analysis. For Martinet the basic concept in phonology is that of phoneme, whereas for Jakobson it is that of distinctive feature. Martinet also emphatically rejects Jakobson's theory that there is a universal inventory of distinctive features, and that these are all binary.

In recent years Martinet has also applied his *functional* views to syntax,[31] and has synthesized his theories in concise and well-balanced expositions: *Elements of General Linguistics*,[32] and *A Functional View of Language*.[33] The distinction is here clearly formulated between two kinds of elements which in traditional expositions are confused, in spite of their different, even opposite functions: on the one hand the *functional* monemes (such as prepositions, or case endings, which are connective and centrifugal: they indicate the relationship between one element and the rest of the utterance), and on the other the modifiers (such as grammatical number, or article, which are centripetal: they indicate the value–singular or plural, definite or indefinite–of the particular element to which they are attached).

Here again Martinet underlines that for syntax also *function* (as against form) is the central notion. He thus completes the functional view of language which had been suggested by the School of Prague, and which Martinet himself contributed in defining, in contrast to the formalistic and structuralist position of many American linguists. Linguistics is mainly interested in the functions of language, and in the functions of linguistic elements, rather than in language as a system of elements, or in the structures of elements. This allows one, among other things, to clarify the distinction between language and other artificial symbolic systems which may be structured in a similar way, but cannot have the same functions as language. A 'structural' view is not however irreconcilable with a functional view; on the contrary, for Martinet it is its logical complement. The choice of the label 'functional' instead of 'structural' indicates that the functional aspect is the most revealing, and not that it must be studied to the exclusion of the others.

6.3 Other Trends

The Prague School tradition has been kept alive in Czechoslovakia and has produced many works, not only in the field of phonology, but also on the problems of 'literary' language, of 'standard' language, and of syntax, with the notion of 'functional sentence perspective'.[34]

Many other positions have been elaborated which cannot be identified with those of any one particular school, but which present features which put them within the sphere of modern functional and structural linguistics. Many linguists have developed traditional views which were implicitly structuralist. In some cases there has been a fruitful convergence of different influences. I cannot do justice within the limits of this exposition to the theories, often of fundamental importance, which should be discussed at this point.[35] I shall limit myself to mentioning the French tradition, in which Saussure's teaching has been a stimulus, as is apparent from the work of the great Meillet,[36] and after him from the genial contributions of Émile Benveniste, in which a lucid conception of the system of language brings us to see (also in the most intricate problems of Indo-European grammar which he unravels with unequalled mastery) simplicity, order, norm, behind what appears complex, confused and irregular.[37] Also active in the Indo-European field is another scholar of very high distinction, the Pole Jerzy Kuryłowicz, who has taken an originally eclectic position between the Prague and the Copenhagen School conceptions, elaborating an interesting view of the parallelism between grammatical and phonological structure, and producing a large number of works which are equally fundamental for comparative grammar and for general linguistics.[38] Russian linguistics must also be mentioned, with the phonological schools going back to Fortunatov and Baudouin de Courtenay: the Leningrad School, inspired by L. V. Ščerba, with the notion of phoneme as a class of speech-sounds;[39] the Moscow School, with the notion of morphophonemic alternance;[40] and the eclectic school represented by Avanesov.[41] After the periods of 'Marrism' and 'Stalinism', there has been a revival of structural theories in the Soviet Union,[42] represented in particular by the works of S. K. Šaumjan.[43]

CHAPTER VII

Structural Linguistics

𝕾𝕾𝕾𝕾𝕾𝕾

7.1 Theoretical Questions

In the previous chapter the title 'functional linguistics' referred to some trends in European linguistics which were given currency by scholars like Jakobson and Martinet whose influence (particularly in the case of the former) was felt in the United States, but whose theories were formed in Europe. The title 'structural linguistics' in this chapter has a more restricted meaning than is usual and refers not to post-Saussurean linguistics in general, but specifically to what can be called post-Bloomfieldian linguistics.

This has been characterized by a general behaviouristic attitude and by a rather restrictive conception of scientific method, inherited from neopositivism and based on the notion of verifiability. Recourse to introspection or to the notion of mind was rejected. The sole proper object of study was thought to be a corpus of utterances; it was held that linguistics had the purpose of providing procedures for cutting up the utterances, and for grouping together the resulting segments. These two operations (segmenting and classifying) were based on the identification of partial similarities in utterances and parts of utterances; on the study of the *distribution* of the various units; on the grouping together of different units if they were in complementary distribution and were sufficiently similar (i.e. if their differences could be specified in terms of their context). The classes and categories which were set up in the process of these operations were considered to be scientific constructs,

110

conceptual fictions which were useful in the course of the description, but did not correspond to any psychological reality.

(a) *Semantics*. One of the most obvious casualties in this approach was semantic study. Semantics was traditionally the section of linguistics in which the least degree of precision had been reached, and in which recourse to 'mentalist' notions appeared to be the least dispensable. Consequently an attempt was made to achieve linguistic description without considering meaning. This gave rise to many misunderstandings which contributed to a confusion of the issue. The assumption that Bloomfield had tried to eliminate all mention of meaning from linguistics rapidly became widespread. What we actually read in *Language* is that 'the study of speech-sounds without regard to meanings is an abstraction' (p. 139); 'phonology involves the consideration of meanings' (p. 78); 'it is important to remember that practical phonetics and phonology presuppose a knowledge of meanings: without this knowledge we could not ascertain the phonemic features . . . When the phonology of a language has been established, there remains the task of telling what meanings are attached to the several phonetic forms' (pp. 137–8). And, in sum, a 'proper analysis' is defined by Bloomfield as 'one which takes account of the meanings' (p. 161).

But some linguists, on the grounds that the statement of meanings is 'the weak point in language-study' and that 'a language can convey only such meanings as are attached to some formal feature' (p. 168), armed themselves with Occam's razor and thought it convenient to eliminate this 'weak point' by excising it altogether as a useless duplication of the 'formal features' to which meaning is attached. This simplification was in fact only apparent, since it turned out to be just as difficult to account for these formal features as it was to account for meaning. The attempt to eliminate meaning was made not only in the field of phonology and morphology, but even in the field of semantics itself.[1]

In the latter a solution often adopted was the distributional one. This was based, among other things, on the suggestion that *meaning is use*.[2] If use in the context of situation was very difficult to describe, it was assumed that the use of a word within the corpus, i.e., the set of its linguistic contexts, would be easier to deal with. In order to justify the statement that two words have the same meaning, it would be necessary to prove that the two sets of their contexts coincide, and in order to state that their meanings are different, it would be necessary to point out some contexts in which the one, but not the other, can occur. But—even if we disregard the fact that this does not prove that a language-unit means something because it is used in certain contexts, rather than vice versa—the set of all the contexts of a word is impossible to define: there is an infinite number of different contexts.

In a treatment of meaning in terms of context there are other difficulties. If, for instance, we define two words *a* and *b* as synonyms only if they are interchangeable in the same context, without any change in the meaning of the sentence, we are faced by such statements as *a means b*, which are meaningful and informative (for example for somebody who knows the meaning of *b* but not of *a*), only if *a* and *b* are synonymous; but a statement like this acquires quite a different meaning if, on the grounds of the synonymity of *a* and *b*, we change it into *a means a*, or *b means b*. Besides, to check if two expressions *a* and *b* have the same meaning or not, we try to substitute one for the other in a given context $y-z$; but then to check whether $y\,a\,z$ and $y\,b\,z$ have the same meaning or not, we have to try to substitute one for the other in a wider context $w-x$; then we have to compare the meanings of $w\,y\,a\,z\,x$ and $w\,y\,b\,z\,x$ in even wider contexts, and so on ad infinitum. If we draw a line somewhere, and take into account denotation, or the context of situation, we are faced with difficulties of the kind mentioned by Bloomfield. On the one hand, a description of a meaning implies a description of the whole universe, which not only is unfeasible, but would also stultify any attempt to specify the difference between meanings. On the other hand, we are unable to state which features of a situation are relevant to particular meanings.

Useful discussions of semantic theories in modern linguistics

112

are found in the work of S. Ullmann;[3] I shall only mention here the various views according to which the meaning is either the *thing* meant, or the concept, or the content *counterpart* of expression, or the *relationship* between word and thing, or between content and expression, or the set of *contexts*, or the *rule* for the use of a linguistic expression, or simply its *use*. We are presented with conflicting theories which see linguistic signs either as two-faced entities, consisting of expression and content, or as one-faced entities, whose semantic values consist in the way in which they are used within linguistic messages, or in the way in which they are related to the non-linguistic world.

One particular trend in semantic studies, the 'Sapir-Whorf hypothesis',[4] develops suggestions earlier proposed by W. von Humboldt: that there is a *Weltanschauung* implicit in each language, and that language does not so much express our ideas, as help to condition and shape them. Some of these points were exaggerated in Korzybski's movement of 'general semantics', which finds its place in a sociological history of American culture rather than in a review of linguistic studies.[5]

Suggestions deriving from German philosophy of language were developed in the theory of 'semantic fields'.[6] Different techniques for analysing meaning have been elaborated: one may recall the 'measurement' of meaning, by Osgood and others;[7] the work on the relationship between meaning and information;[8] and the various attempts at elaborating a 'structural' semantics–from glossematics to the recent theories of Prieto and of Greimas, and to the various 'componential' analyses elaborated in the United States.[9]

(b) *Morphology*. The chapters devoted to morphology in Bloomfield's *Language* were far from explicit, and only several years after the publication of the book did the difficulties which they contained begin to be unravelled. In 1942 Harris published an article which opened the way for a series of other works in the field of morphology. He tried to specify three steps in the analytical procedures: (*a*) identify, in each phonemicized utterance, minimum parts which occur with the same meaning in other utterances: these are morphemic alternants; (*b*) group into one morpheme those alternants which (1) have the same meaning, (2) are in complementary distribution, (3) do not have a total distribution larger than other particular alternants, and (c) produce general statements applicable to all morphemes which exhibit the same differences between their alternants.[10] The discussions of this period are reflected in a manual by Nida[11] which in its different versions presents uncertainties and oscillations which are characteristic of American linguistics of that time; for instance, the 'morphological processes' of the 1946 edition become in the 1949 edition 'types of morphemes'. The author tries to eliminate all reference to processes; he does not quite succeed and has to use terms like 'assimilation' and 'dissimilation'–but these denote, he states, 'relationships' between sounds. The suggestion that the methods used in phonology could also be used in morphological analysis gained acceptance; in 1947 Hockett used the word 'morph', commenting: 'A convenient term, because it (1) eliminates the lengthy expressions "morpheme alternant" and "morpheme unit", and (2) suggests a valid analogy (*allo*)*phone: phoneme* = *morph: morpheme*.'[12] The following year Nida stated: 'Morphemic alternants can conveniently be called *allomorphs*. Accordingly, allomorphs are related to morphemes as allophones are related to phonemes.'[13] The complexity of the problem is illustrated by Hockett in 1961 with a scheme which I have adapted in this way.

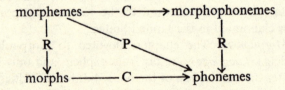

The relation of morphemes to morphophonemes and of morphs to phonemes is symbolized by 'C', which may be read: '(is) composed of (an arrangement of)'; the relation of morphemes to morphs and of morphophonemes to phonemes is symbolized by 'R', which may be read: '(is) represented by'.

114

The relation of morphemes to phonemes is symbolized by 'P', which may be read: 'is programmed into' or 'is mapped into'. We can get from morphemes to phonemes through morphs, or through morphophonemes. But it is important not to identify P with either R or C.[14]

Some of the problems connected with the treatment of the morpheme depended on the way the notion of meaning was employed. The definition of the morpheme as a minimum *meaningful* unit was in many ways misleading.[15] Besides, lacking a workable method to deal with meaning, a confusing use of 'zero' elements and of 'portmanteau' morphs was introduced. In *cats* two morphemes were identified: *cat*, meaning 'cat', and *-s*, meaning 'plural'. The way in which *cat* also meant 'singular' was not very clearly explained, and the same analysis was imposed on languages for which it was intuitively less satisfactory: for instance on Italian, in which *gatto* was analysed as one morpheme and *gatti* as two morphemes. The stem, meaning 'cat', would thus have the allomorph *gatto*, which is identical to the singular form of the substantive, and the allomorph *gatt-*, when there is the *-i* plural morpheme. Artificial solutions were suggested for cases like *foot*, *feet* or *sing*, *sang* to make them match mechanically the cases *cat*, *cats* and *love*, *loved*.

Morphological analysis also took on a rather strange aspect because it was hoped that one set of procedures would provide for the whole grammatical structure; from the utterance to the morpheme. Word-like units were almost completely obliterated from the picture, and the distinction behind the traditional separation of morphology and syntax was often blurred. The all-embracing method which was meant to provide grammatical description was a refinement and adaptation of Bloomfield's immediate constituent analysis.[16]

(c) *Phonemics*. The 'phonemic principle' is the most obvious and typical acquisition of structural linguistics. Not only has some of the earliest and most influential work in structural linguistics been devoted to phonemic analysis, but the methods of phonemic analysis have been transferred, not always for the better, to other sections of linguistics.

Particularly in the first decade after the publication of Bloomfield's *Language*, phonemic work predominated in the field of structural linguistics. Some problems and methods which were to remain for a long time of central importance for American linguistics were stated as early as 1934 by M. Swadesh.[17] Swadesh was a pupil of Sapir's, and his article on the 'phonemic principle' is worth recalling, among other things, for its eclecticism: he takes into account not only Sapir and Bloomfield, but also D. Jones and Trubeckoj. He is interested in the 'psychological' aspect of the phoneme, as we might expect from a pupil of Sapir's, and at the same time he states, in a way that would not be unsuitable for a Bloomfieldian, that 'the chief ideals' of his paper are 'theoretical comprehensiveness, consistency of treatment, and brevity'. For the identification of phonemes he proposes six criteria: (1) consistency of words: different occurrences of the same word have the same phonemic make-up; (2) partial identities: the 'significant elemental sound types' are arrived at through a comparison of all sets of words having a phonetic resemblance; (3) constant association: if a set of phonetic elements only occur together, they constitute a phonemically unitary complex; (4) complementary distribution: two similar types of sound may be sub-types of the same phoneme if only one of them occurs in certain phonetic surroundings and only the other occurs in certain other phonetic surroundings; if a type of sound is in complementary distribution with more than one other, it is to be identified with the one to which it is phonetically more similar; if it is not 'particularly similar' to either, it has to be considered as phonemically independent; (5) pattern congruity: particular formulations must be congruous with the general phonemic pattern of the given language; (6) the test of substitution which 'consists in pronouncing a word with some modification in one of the phonemes': one has 'normal deviation' if the modification cannot be perceived by a native, 'extreme deviation' or 'distortion' if it seems to trouble the native, and the substitution of one phoneme for another if the native 'definitely hears some other word or feels that one has the word wrong'.

Much of the work which followed in phonology consisted in sharpening the formulation of some of the principles which are stated here in somewhat vague terms—in particular, two cruces of phonemic theory present in the fourth and sixth criteria: the specification of phonetic similarity, and the use of the native's reaction to the commutation test. On the latter point one is faced with the question of the presence of semantic criteria in phonemic analysis.[18] In an article of 1955 Chomsky[19] tried to show that, given two utterance tokens U_1 and U_2, the statement 'U_1 is phonemically distinct from U_2 if and only if U_1 differs in meaning from U_2' is false in both directions. From right to left, examples like U_1: *I saw him by the bank* (the bank of the river) and U_2: *I saw him by the bank* (the First National Bank), prove that two utterances can be phonemically identical, and different in meaning. From left to right, examples like U_1 *ádult* and U_2 *adúlt* prove that two utterances can be phonemically distinct, and identical in meaning. When we want to know whether there is a phonemic difference between two utterances, we certainly need to know whether they differ, but the difference we are interested in is a difference in phonemic constitution, not in meaning; and the test which we use (the *pair test*, 'one of the operational cornerstones for linguistic theory') is 'a thoroughly non-semantic operational device'. The pair test consists in asking the informant to listen to U_1 and to U_2, and then to identify random repetitions of the two utterances as either U_1 or U_2. The identification will be about 50 per cent accurate if the two utterances are phonemically identical, and 100 per cent accurate if they are phonemically distinct. But, pressed by F. G. Lounsbury's question about a speaker who hears the difference between *cat* with a preglottalized and unreleased -*t*, and *cat* with a released, aspirated -*t*, Chomsky admits that if the native speaker is able to perceive a 'sub-phonemic difference between U_1 and U_2', and, repeating those utterances, consistently makes that phonetic distinction, 'then, I think, we are obliged to say that there is a phonemic distinctness there'. But this is exactly what we do not want to do. If such are the results of the non-semantic pair test, we may either have to look for a different kind of test, or show that we cannot devise a suitable test for what interests us.

Important contributions to the development of phonemic theory are offered by Y. R. Chao's 1934 article on 'the non-uniqueness of phonemic solutions of phonetic systems', by W. F. Twaddell's 1935 monograph on 'defining the phoneme', and by many discussions in the journal *Language*, in particular those by Hockett (who later produced an interesting manual of phonology) and by Bloch, who gave one of the most rigorous formulations to post-Bloomfieldian phonological procedures, and contributed, together with Trager and Smith, some extremely influential texts.[20]

This section should not be concluded without recalling the shattering effect Chomsky's theories had, not only on traditional structural linguistic tenets, but also on the view that structuralists held about the place of their own theories in the development of modern linguistics. Whereas transformationalists criticize Bloomfield and the Bloomfieldians for their 'taxonomic' linguistics, one of the most intelligent of the Bloomfieldians, C. F. Hockett, in a recent criticism of Chomsky's theories,[21] has given a reappraisal of the situation, distinguishing sharply between Bloomfield and the Bloomfieldians. Hockett states that the transformationalists have, in fact, without realizing it, on several points gone back to Bloomfield. The people who—again without realizing it—had on several points moved away from Bloomfield, were the Bloomfieldians of the 1940's and 1950's. The Bloomfieldians were right—unlike both Bloomfield and Chomsky—in their view of the status of phonology in language design. They were wrong—unlike Bloomfield and Chomsky—in defending a narrowly item-and-arrangement model. Bloomfield was right in correlating meanings and formal features, while the view taken by both the Bloomfieldians and the transformationalists that grammar and semantics should be separated was wrong. And all three—Bloomfield, Bloomfieldians and transformationalists—are wrong in the view that language is a rigid system (as Bloomfield says, commenting on Saussure's *langue*), and that grammar is a 'well-defined system' in the sense of the theory of computability and unsolvability (as presupposed by Chomsky).[22] Hockett states that no physical system is well-defined: well-defined systems are the inventions of human intelligence. Mathematical or algebraic linguistics is irrelevant in the study of natural languages, because these are ill-defined. But he does not explain why mathematical theories (scientific abstractions), which are necessary in the study of many aspects of physical reality, should not also be used by an empirical science such as linguistics in its study of the natural phenomenon that is language. Hockett's views are, as usual, very stimulating. As Chomsky's innovations were in many respects a return to the past, so Hockett's repudiation of the post-Saussurean conception of language as a 'rigid system' is also backward-looking. But the past is represented by opposite traditions: a rationalist one for Chomsky, and an empiricist one for Hockett. In fact it seems that, according to Hockett, the actual practice of linguistics has not changed very much: 'transformations are largely a corrective to certain temporary extremisms of the 1940's, a reintroduction, with improvements and under a new name, of certain useful features of the Bloomfieldian and Sapirian view of language'. As there is no algorithm for the discovery of facts about the real world, it appears that in the actual research of the transformationalists 'the trial-and-error manipulation of data is entirely the same in spirit as it was in the 1940's'.[23]

7.2 Some Trends and Personalities of Structural Linguistics

Within the context of what we have called structural linguistics many linguists have elaborated their own theories, sometimes trying to apply rigorously and consistently the methods that had already been outlined, sometimes developing new theories on distinct and original lines. This short survey cannot do justice to all the trends that should have their place in a comprehensive discussion of structural linguistics. I shall limit myself to mentioning only some linguists whose work I have found of particular interest. B. Bloch and G. L. Trager have contributed authoritatively to the elaboration and propagation of Bloomfieldian methods;[24] an analogous position is that of R. A. Hall, Jr., a specialist in Romance, and particularly Italian linguistics, who has also produced influential popularizing works,[25] and A. A. Hill, who has developed in an important handbook a systematic description of spoken English.[26] Among other scholars whose work has been significant I should like to mention Y. R. Chao, J. H. Greenberg, D. L. Bolinger, and P. L. Garvin.[27]

The work of Zellig Sabbettai Harris[28] has sometimes been considered as most typically representative of American structural linguistics because of the rigour with which he tried to develop consistently and explicitly formal descriptive techniques, based on the shape of linguistic units and their distribution. This is misleading, in so far as Harris's rigour was not typically representative of post-Bloomfieldian linguistics in general, but rather a distinctive element of his own contributions. His work, until the late 1940's, was synthesized in a compact handbook on 'methods in structural linguistics',[29] which represents a point of arrival rather than of departure. Pursuing with the most remarkable pertinacity the methods of 'taxonomic' analysis, Harris came to realize that they had limitations which could not be overcome within the traditional framework. He then worked out a transformational method which he later developed into 'string analysis'.[30] His 1951 volume came to be considered as a symbol and a turning-point for American post-Bloomfieldian linguistics. At the end of the preface, dated 1947, he acknowledged the help of Noam Chomsky in the preparation of the manuscript. And it was Chomsky who developed Harris's ideas on transformation along original lines, making them into a new theory of language, and rejecting the structuralist framework. The developments initiated by Harris caused a radical change in perspective. This appears, for instance, from the two following passages, the juxtaposition of which has a curious effect: 'With the publication of *Methods in Structural Linguistics* American structuralism clearly reached its majority, and could take its place in the world of scholarship as a mature

120

discipline uncompromisingly dedicated to the scientific study of language.'[31] 'The student who learns linguistics from [Chomsky's] *Syntactic Structures* is, in effect, learning a different subject from the student who learns linguistics from, say, Zellig Harris's *Structural Linguistics*.'[32]

Charles Francis Hockett, whose works have been repeatedly mentioned, occupies in the group of the so-called post-Bloomfieldians a position of exceptional interest. Besides two influential handbooks, he has made important contributions to the fields of phonemic and morphemic analysis, of grammatical theory, of general linguistics and methodology of science, and of the relationships of psychology, biology and mathematics with linguistics.[33] His work is always stimulating, among other reasons because it reveals a salutary restlessness, an impatience and dissatisfaction with the limitations of theoretical points that he is discussing or applying, and a readiness to abandon them and try different ones (even when the discarded theory was his own to start with). Examples of this can be found in the ambivalent attitude towards the Bloomfieldian framework within which he was working; for instance, in his article on 'two models of grammatical description', in which he discusses the item-and-process and the item-and-arrangement models (and then in his reaction to the interpretation of that article as a defence of item-and-arrangement).[34] And again it can be found more recently in his attitude towards transformational grammar, and at the same time towards Bloomfield's theories and his own.[35]

S. M. Lamb has elaborated a stratificational view of language according to which linguistic structure comprises several structural layers or strata. Language relates sounds to meanings; much of structural linguistics appears (from this point of view) to have been based on a monostratal view: between phonology and semantics only the morphemic level was recognized. A morpheme was a combination of phonemes, and a sentence was a combination of morphemes. The traditional distinction between morphology and syntax was thus eliminated. The unit called 'morpheme' turned out to be a conflation of a morpheme and a lexeme. Those on the other hand who preserved the traditional distinction between morphology and syntax made the mistake of basing syntax on words or combinations of morphemes. Syntax should be based on lexemes, and to confuse word with lexeme is a mistake analogous to confusing syllable with morpheme: the two units belong to different strata. Lamb suggests that many more strata are needed: all natural languages appear to have at least four; some languages, like English, have six strata: semology, grammar, and phonology, each comprising two stratal systems. These are called hypophonemic or phonetic, phonemic, morphemic, lexemic, sememic, and hypersememic or semantic. Each system has a structure analogous to that traditionally ascribed to language as a whole. One reason for this complexity of language organization is that sounds and meanings are patterned differently: the former are adapted to the speech organs, and take place in time, in linear succession; the latter conform to thought patterns and may be multidimensional.[36]

An original position is occupied by Kenneth Lee Pike, a pupil of Sapir who, even when the restrictions that post-Bloomfieldian linguistics imposed on itself were more acutely felt, never abandoned, for the sake of rigour of method or elegance of solution, realistic analysis of actual linguistic facts. He always insisted on the one hand on the importance of field procedures, and on the other on the necessity of having recourse to the 'culture' of the informant, of using extralinguistic factors in elaborating a description. Pike fought an important battle in defence of the interpenetration of different linguistic levels (phonemic, morphemic or syntactic), opposing the post-Bloomfieldian prohibition of mixing the levels with his own concept of *integration*.[37] A subtle phonologist,[38] and a pioneer in the study of 'suprasegmentals',[39] Pike produced in his book *Language*[40] a wide-ranging discussion of current methods in linguistics and an attempt to lay the foundation of a comprehensive interpretation of language within its cultural setting. He insists on the importance of distinguishing *emic* and *etic* elements (from the endings of the words *phonemic* and *phonetic*) not only in language, but in the analysis of human behaviour in general. The method of linguistics can offer useful suggestions for the identification, in the objective or etic data, of the relevant or emic features. To identify significant events, the notion of *purpose* can be used in the study of behaviour as the notion of meaning is used in linguistics.

Pike has more than once stated, with a metaphor drawn from physics, that language can be considered from three points of view, in terms of particles, of waves, and of field. In terms of particles (phonemes, morphemes etc.) we have a static notion, based on the distribution of the various units which are like bricks juxtaposed in a permanent structure. This view is well represented among Bloomfieldians. In terms of waves we have a dynamic notion (close to Sapir's view, or to Firth's prosodic analysis) which accounts for the fact that in language there is a continuum of movements which merge in complex and over-lapping systems. Units like phonemes and morphemes are not then successive, separated from each other like beads in a necklace, nor simply fused at their points of contact, but variously overlapping. In terms of field we have a view in depth which is functional, and takes into account at the same time both the text and the memory reservoir against which the text can be interpreted. These three views are all needed: the particle approach must be supplemented by wave and field outlooks which provide dynamic and functional components in the analysis.[41]

Concerning the actual techniques of linguistic analysis, Pike has elaborated a theory which he called *gram(m)emics*, and later *tagmemics*,[42] based on the notion that utterances can be analysed simultaneously according to three hierarchies: a lexical one (in which the minimum unit is the morpheme), a phonological one (in which the minimum unit is the phoneme, or the distinctive feature), and a grammatical one in which the minimum unit is the gram(m)eme or tagmeme. Much attention is devoted by Pike to matrix theory:[43] in phonology matrices have for a long time been used as the basis of phonetic charts; tagmemic theory is now introducing them in grammar and also in lexicon and culture: 'the most recent articles on tagmemics depart farthest from emphasis upon the perspective of a linear order of segmentation (or from attention to a linear ordering of statements of rules). Ordering of a strikingly different type is exploited – the *ordering of adjacency, or of distance, or of classes, in reference to points or vectors in a network of intersecting dimensions* ... Ordering by network leads to directness of insight into relations between many functional classes of units of various types of systems or subsystems.'[44]

In Britain we find linguistic trends which developed in contact with both European and American structuralism. Besides the phonological studies of D. Jones,[45] we find the theories of J. R. Firth[46] and of his school.[47]

Firth thought that the concept of unity could not be conveniently applied to language and hence, that it was not advisable to attempt a structural and systemic account of a language as a whole. It was preferable to consider language as multistructural and polysystemic. His work is particularly interesting in the field of semantics, where he used B. Malinowski's notion of 'context of situation', and in the field of phonology, where he developed the concept of 'prosody', a unit which can be associated with more than one phonematic unit. Prosodic analysis was used in the phonological descriptions of many languages produced within the framework of the 'London school'.

M. A. K. Halliday (who besides being an original general linguist is also a brilliant sinologist) contributed to the creation of a trend which has been called 'neo-Firthian' and which is one of the most interesting developments of contemporary structural linguistics. Halliday's framework has been called a 'scale and categories' theory, because it uses three scales of abstraction (rank, exponence and delicacy), and, at the level of grammar, four main categories (unit, structure, class, system). The *unit* corresponds to the bit of chain which carries grammatical patterns; each unit consists of one or more units immediately lower in *rank*. Along the rank scale five grammatical units (sentence, clause, phrase, word, morpheme) and four phonological units (tone group, foot, syllable, phoneme) are used in English. The *structure* concerns the organization of elements in certain *places*; a place is characterized by *order* (*sequence* is only one of the possible ways of exposing order). In English, subject and complement are elements within the clause structure. The choice of an element of structure is limited to a certain *class*. In English the class Noun consists of the items which operate as heads in a noun phrase. Each place in the structure of a certain unit is a place in which a class of members of a lower-rank unit operates; so a structure is defined in relation to the classes of the lower unit, and a class is defined in relation to the structure of the higher unit. The distinction between class and structure corresponds to the traditional distinction between form and function, and depends on the point of view: in *I met him*, *met* is a group (unit) belonging to the class Verb (which can be defined on the basis of the function of the group); *met* is also an instance of a predicator, exponent of an element of the clause structure (which can be defined on the basis of the form of the clause).

The distinction between grammar and lexis is based on the distinction (which is not clear-cut, but gradual) between closed systems and open sets of terms from which a choice is made. In grammar the syntagmatic notion of structure corresponds to the paradigmatic notion of system, and similarly, in lexis the syntagmatic notion of collocation corresponds to the paradigmatic notion of set.

We have seen that the relationship of rank is a hierarchical relationship between higher and lower units. The other two scales of abstraction are *exponence*, which relates the categories to formal items (realization) and these to the substance (manifestation), and *delicacy*, along which richness in detail can be measured (there may be secondary structures, identified with more delicate distinctions, which belong to the same unit as the primary structure, and not to a lower one).[48]

CHAPTER VIII

Transformational Grammar

꙱꙱꙱꙱꙱꙱

The most striking innovation in the field of linguistic theory during the last fifteen years has been the development of generative transformational grammar, mainly in the work of Avram Noam Chomsky, a former pupil of Z. S. Harris, and now Professor of Linguistics at the Massachusetts Institute of Technology.

Chomsky's work is animated by interests in the history of culture, psychology, philosophy, and scientific methodology. These are not conflicting interests which make his contributions any the less consistent. They are, he would claim, legitimate aspects of linguistic research; indeed, aspects which it is necessary to take into account if linguistics is to provide a meaningful and interesting insight into language. Thus the progress of Chomsky's research has corresponded to a widening of horizons for linguistics, to a re-establishment of links with other fields which had been severed in the search for 'language considered in and for itself' (*la langue envisagée en elle-même et pour elle-même*),[1] to a reintegration of linguistics as a branch of psychology after the attempt to establish it as a completely autonomous science. The rapid spread of transformational ideas among linguists not only in the United States but throughout the world, and the readiness to throw aside traditional views have brought into the open a widely-felt dissatisfaction with the narrowness of purpose and method imposed on itself by linguistics.

The work which gave transformational linguistics a wide

126

international reputation was Chomsky's *Syntactic Structures*.[2] Here three models of language are discussed.[3] The first two are a *finite state* grammar and a *phrase structure* grammar. Both are presented in a formalized way as *generative* models. The first corresponds to a communication-theory conception of language as a Markov process, employed in statistical linguistics. The second and more powerful model is not limited to the consideration of the transitions from one word to the following in a sentence, but uses symbols representing syntactic constituents like *Noun Phrase* (NP) and *Verb Phrase* (VP) (which may contain more than one word); it incorporates an analysis in terms of parsing which had been elaborated by structural linguistics as *immediate constituent analysis*. Both models start with a finite amount of apparatus and can generate an infinite number of sentences; but both are inadequate: they do not account for all, and only, the grammatical sentences of a language.

It is immediately obvious that it would be impossible to account for sentences in terms of rules of phoneme succession only; it can be shown that a left-to-right generation, unit by unit, in terms of morphemes or words also cannot account for the sentences of a language, and that one needs to consider larger units which are more directly the building blocks in sentence structure: the immediate constituents.

But there are processes, as for instance grammatical conjunction, which are not satisfactorily described in terms of phrase structure (*John and Peter* is neither *John/and Peter* nor *John and/Peter*). There are cases, like the one of the active-passive relation (which exists between *John admires sincerity* and *sincerity is admired by John*) which, in spite of being grammatical rather than semantic relations, cannot be expressed by a phrase structure grammar; in such cases there are also restrictions applying to the active (like the one on the non-sentence *sincerity admires John*) which have to be repeated, with unnecessary duplication, if the passive is included directly in the grammar (to prevent *John is admired by sincerity*). Difficulties of this kind are eliminated if the phrase structure

127

grammar is limited to the sentences constituting the *kernel* of the language: a set of 'simple, declarative, active sentences (in fact, probably a finite number of these)',[4] while all other sentences are considered *transforms* of the kernel sentences, are derived from these through the application of *transformational rules*. In fact transformations do not operate on actual sentences but on more abstract structures, or strings of symbols underlying the sentences.[5]

Grammar is composed of three parts: the first consists of a sequence of phrase structure rules, which apply to the kernel, and the third of a sequence of morphophonemic rules. The second part, which connects the first and the third, consists of a sequence of transformational rules, which may rearrange strings and add or delete units.

There are ambiguities which offer an interesting confirmation of the necessity of the transformational level. A sequence of phonemes can be ambiguously represented on the morphological level: e.g. *an aim* and *a name*; *the sun's rays meet* and *the sons raise meat*; or *Gal, amant de la Reine, alla* (*tour magnanime*),/*Gallamment, de l'arène à la Tour Magne, à Nîmes* (Gal, lover of the queen, went–lofty expedition–/Gallantly from the arena to the great tower in Nîmes). Other ambiguities, to be represented, need the level of phrase structure; there may be differences in segmentation, as in *they are flying planes*, which can be *they/are/flying planes* or *they/are flying/planes*; or in *what disturbed John was being disregarded by everyone*, which can be either *was/being disregarded* or *was being disregarded*. In cases like *flying planes can be dangerous*, or *I don't approve of John's cooking* we have ambiguities which can also be represented on the level of phrase structure, although not in differences of segmentation; in any case their origin is transformational: *flying planes* can be Adjective + Noun, or it can be a transform of a verb phrase where *planes* is the object of *fly*; *John's cooking* can be a Modifier + Noun construction, or a transform of an embedded sentence *John cooks* (the meaning is 'I disapprove of the way John cooks' in the first case, and 'I disapprove of the fact that John cooks' in the second). Other ambiguities are completely unmarked at the level of phrase structure and can only be described in terms of transformations, for instance cases like *the shooting of the hunters*. Structural linguistics lacked the means of representing this kind of ambiguity and would probably have put it together with referential ambiguities (like *son* and *sun*, or *light* in colour and *light* in weight, etc.) which are not explained by grammar. Transformational theory is able to represent the ambiguity of this phrase, because it has two different transformational origins, being a transform either of *the hunters shoot* or of *they shoot the hunters*.

During the ten years following the publication of *Syntactic Structures* transformational theory has been variously modified and extended. A new synthesis is offered in *Aspects of the Theory of Syntax*.[6] In its new form grammar has three components; the semantic and the phonological components are interpretive; the only creative one is the syntactic component. The syntactic component contains a *base* that generates a set of basic strings, each with an associated structural description or phrase-marker. The base phrase-markers are the elementary units of which deep structures are constituted. The syntactic component also contains a transformational subcomponent which generates surface structures from the deep structures, through formal operations called *transformations*. The *deep structures* are the input of the semantic component which interprets them, the *surface structures* are the input of the phonological component which assigns to them a phonetic representation. 'Thus the syntactic component consists of a base that generates deep structures and a transformational part that maps them into surface structures. The deep structure of a sentence is submitted to the semantic component for semantic interpretation, and its surface structure enters the phonological component and undergoes phonetic interpretation. The final effect of a grammar, then, is to relate a semantic interpretation to a phonetic representation–that is, to state how a sentence is interpreted. This relation is mediated by the syntactic component of the grammar, which constitutes its sole 'creative' part ... Notice that in this view one major function of the transformational rules is to convert an abstract deep structure that expresses the content of a sentence into a fairly concrete surface structure that indicates its form.'[7] So 'the grammar assigns semantic interpretations to signals, this association being mediated by the recursive rules of the syntactic component'.[8]

The base has a categorial subcomponent and a lexicon. The categorial subcomponent consists of rules which serve 'to define a certain system of grammatical relations that determine semantic interpretation, and to specify an abstract underlying order of elements that make possible the functioning of the transformational rules'.[9] The lexicon consists of lexical entries, each of which is a set of features, some phonological and some semantic, both drawn from a universal inventory.

In the first phase of transformational grammar the stress was on the connexion between apparently different sentences (like an active and a passive one) through transformations. In the second phase the insistence was rather on the difference (which appears in the deep structures) between sentences which are, in their surface structures, apparently similar: for example, sentences which appear to have the same construction, like *John is eager to please* and *John is easy to please*, are interpreted with reference to differently constructed deep structures like *John is eager; John pleases somebody*, and *it is easy; someone pleases John* respectively. Or, if we analyse sentences like *I expected the doctor to examine John, I expected John to be examined by the doctor*, and *I persuaded the doctor to examine John, I persuaded John to be examined by the doctor*, we find that *persuade* and *expect* behave similarly on the surface, but are fundamentally different in some features of deep structure which determine the semantic content: the first two sentences are in a relation of paraphrase, but the second two are not.

One of the interesting points in the evolution of transformational theories concerns the semantic value of transformations. In the first stages of transformational theory Chomsky noted that 'the transformations are, by and large, meaning-preserving, so that we can view the kernel sentences underlying a given sentence as being, in some sense, the elementary "content elements" in terms of which the actual transform is "understood"'.[10]

In spite of some uncertainties on this point,[11] there has been a trend to eliminate the qualifications from this kind of statement, and to consider the transformations as operations which do not affect the semantic interpretations of a sentence at all. Syntactic research has tended to eliminate *generalized* transformations, which operated on more than one string and involved the presence of particularly complicated rules in the semantic component; the negative, passive, interrogative and other sentences are now also interpreted not as transforms from strings underlying the corresponding positive, active, declarative sentences, but as derived from an underlying phrase-marker within which a particular manner-adverbial (negative, passive, interrogative etc.) has been generated.[12] We now have 'quasi-transformational rules in the base component.'[13] But in this way one of the intuitively compelling arguments originally proposed in favour of the introduction of transformations has been eliminated. With the importance given to the distinction between *deep* and *surface* structures, and the necessity 'to specify an abstract underlying order of elements' in the deep structures,[14] 'the primary motivation and empirical justification for the theory of transformational grammar' is now provided by examples like *John was persuaded by Bill to leave*, in which '*John* is simultaneously Object–of *persuade* (*to leave*) and Subject–of *leave*', and '*Bill* is the ("logical") Subject–of the Sentence, rather than *John*, which is the so-called "grammatical" Subject–of the Sentence, that is, the Subject with respect to the surface structure'.[15] This, it is alleged, illustrates the necessity for distinguishing grammatical *categories* (like NP, VP, etc.) from grammatical *functions* (like Subject, Predicate, Object, etc.). Functions are *relational*, and thus already represented in the phrase-markers, where categories occur in a certain relation: 'Object-of' is the relation between the NP of a VP of the form V + NP and the whole VP, etc.

131

Besides, there is 'the need for an even more abstract notion of grammatical function and grammatical relation than any that has been developed so far, in any systematic way' for cases like *John strikes me as pompous* and *I regard John as pompous*, in which 'in some sense the relation of "John" to "strike" is the same as that of "John" to "regard", and the relation of "strike" to "me" is the same as that of "regard" to "I" ',[16] although it 'is not at all obvious' that *John* is the subject of *strike* in the deep structure.[17] Thus it seems that besides the notions of surface structure ('grammatical subject'), and of deep structure ('logical subject') there is an even more abstract, and still unexplained, notion of 'semantic function'.[18]

It seems to me that what has been gained in depth, in the progress from *Syntactic Structures* to *Aspects*, has been lost in precision, that the two notions of *function* and *relation* have not been sufficiently developed, and that the distinction between relations within deep structures and relations within surface structures has not been sufficiently illustrated.[19]

The phonological component is a system of rules which assign to the surface structures a phonetic representation in the shape of a matrix, with columns corresponding to the successive segments, and rows associated with features of a universal phonetic alphabet (like Jakobson and Halle's distinctive features); the surface structures to be represented phonetically are phonological representations in the shape of a matrix of the same kind. The two representations, phonological and phonetic, have also been called systematic phonemic and systematic phonetic. The traditional phonemic approach (with its *invariance* and *linearity* conditions, which require that a phoneme be defined by a set of physical features always present in its allophones alone, and that all phonemes correspond to particular stretches of sound arranged in the same way in which phonemes are arranged) is definitely rejected. According to this traditional phonemic approach, with its often implicit assumption of the necessity for a biunique correspondence between an utterance and its phonemic representation, it should be possible to provide a unique phonemic representation for a phonetic signal, without taking into account any information about the grammatical structure of the sentence. The phonological representation, in a transformational grammar, includes, on the contrary, information about morphological and syntactic structure (and aims at accounting for, among other things, cases like *divine–divinity*, *various–variety*, *electric–electricity* etc.).[20]

The semantic component is the least satisfactory part of this theory. It consists of projection rules which assign a semantic interpretation to the deep structures, combining the meanings of the lexical items as indicated by the syntactic description, and thus providing a full analysis of the 'cognitive meaning' of the whole string and of each of its components. The dictionary entries break down the meaning of the lexical item into its most elementary components, into atomic concepts, and state the relations between them. An entry (an example which keeps being repeated is *bachelor*) consists of *syntactic markers* (like *Noun*); *semantic markers* (like *Human, Animal, Male*, etc.) expressing general semantic properties; *distinguishers* (like *serving under the standard of another*, *having the academic degree . . .* , etc.) expressing what is idiosyncratic in the meaning of the lexical item (the same semantic markers appear in many lexical items, but each distinguisher appears only once in the dictionary). Finally there are selection restrictions. The analysis can be represented by a tree diagram in which each complete path represents a different 'reading' of the lexical item, corresponds to a 'distinct sense'. If there are n readings, the lexical item is n-ways semantically ambiguous. The example of *bachelor* (with semantic markers in ( ), distinguishers in [ ], and selection restrictions in < >), appears as shown on p. 134.[21]

This does not seem to escape the usual difficulties of any componential analysis of meaning; in particular it is not clear how *cognitive* meaning is to be distinguished from other kinds of meaning; how one is to decide whether a particular *reading* (or *sense*) qualifies for an independent path, and so for representation in the diagram, or not; how one can differentiate between semantic *markers* and *distinguishers* (i.e. how one can decide whether a property is general or particular); *how many*

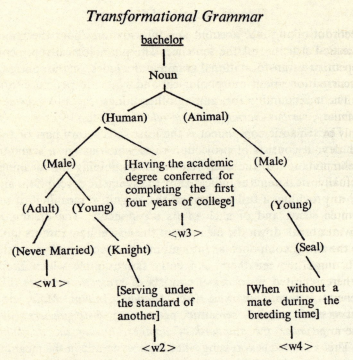

markers and *how many* distinguishers are going to appear in a complete dictionary. That *seal* or *knight* are taken to express general semantic properties appears strange; and as the single item *bachelor* exhibits as many as three distinguishers, and each distinguisher should appear only once in the dictionary, I wonder about the appropriateness of calling these components *atomic concepts*.

I shall not be able to discuss within the limits of this chapter other aspects of transformational theory which have been mentioned above. Chomsky has repeatedly stressed the creative aspect of language use. He states that any sentence we produce has (if we leave out marginal cases: utterances like *good morning* and similar expressions which are not representative of our linguistic abilities) a very low (in fact, for all practical purposes, a zero) probability of having already been heard or said by the same speaker, or even of having been uttered at all. Not only does the normal use of language rarely involve repetition, but, according to Chomsky (and this is a point which would be questioned by most structural linguists) it rarely involves 'even repetition of items of the "same pattern" as those that have occurred before'.[22]

The number of grammatical sentences of any language is infinite. Our linguistic performance is necessarily limited – if only by the limited duration of a lifetime (however much it may be devoted to speaking). But our competence is obviously unlimited, in the sense that the number of sentences we *could* actually use, should the need arise, is infinite. Hence the vanity of any corpus-oriented description; the classification of any limited corpus is, in a sense, from a linguistic point of view, a trivial operation, unless it provides generalizations which apply to the language as well as to the corpus. If it comes to the worst, a listing of the units appearing in the corpus is always possible. Whereas, if we want to analyse linguistic competence, the generative device which is built into our linguistic ability, no listing could possibly be adequate. Language is competence of the mind, not a system of behavioural habits.

This view has some important consequences. Our linguistic competence is an aspect of our general psychological capabilities; and there is no possible interpretation of language learning in terms of conditioning, of repetition of a stimulus, reinforcement, analogy etc., which could explain how, from casual exposure to scattered fragments of speech during the first few years of his life, a child can develop the formidably complex and precise system of rules that is his linguistic competence. What is involved in the understanding of a sentence is not a technique of association, of recognition of partial similarities between the presented utterance and others previously heard, but the whole of our linguistic competence. Such competence cannot possibly be learnt, on the basis of any existing learning theory, and must then be an innate, species-specific feature of human beings. As such it is universal: i.e., it applies to the whole of the linguistic activities of mankind, without limitations of space or time. Within transformational theory considerable attention is devoted to universals: not only to the fact that the form of grammatical descriptions contains certain universal features, such as deep and surface structures, or transformational rules, but also to actual inventories of semantic and phonetic universal items.

This 'rationalist' view is, according to transformationalists, the only one compatible with scientific method; it is a view which should be shared by empiricists, if they followed an *authentically* empiricist approach. In front of a black box (the language user) the output of which (the infinitely varying linguistic performance) cannot be derived from the input (the not only finite, but very limited set of actually heard utterances), a scientist would promptly suggest that built in the box there is a complex device with its own structure (in our case: linguistic competence), rather than cling to the *a priori* statement that the box is there only to store some of the input strings, cut them up, match the various bits, and throw them out in different combinations. A scientist should not be perturbed by the notions of *innateness* and *universality*. They do not mean anything more than that there are abilities which we do not learn (just as we do not *learn* to walk), and that some of these abilities are specific to our species and to the *whole* of our species (just as the ability of a cat to turn over and fall on its feet if it is thrown into the air is not learnt, but innate, and specific to its species and to the whole of its species). In fact a biological interpretation of these notions has been offered, in which one calls 'the internal structure *innate mechanisms* and the modes of operation that are determined by these mechanisms *innate behavior*'.[23] It is refreshing, in view of the wide acceptance of an empty identification of thought and language, to find Chomsky stating boldly: 'I think, in fact I am quite convinced, that thinking can proceed perfectly well without language . . . I am quite convinced that thinking is not dependent on language.'[24]

On these grounds it is not surprising that Chomsky has revalued a chapter of the history of linguistics (which he calls Cartesian) from Descartes to Humboldt, in which many of the notions now rediscovered by transformational theory (such as innatism, universals, creativity and even, he states, deep and surface structures and grammatical transformations) had already been formulated, only to be forgotten by modern taxonomic linguistics. The latter (including most of the work produced in the field of linguistic theory in the nineteenth century and in the first half of the twentieth century) limited its attention to surface structures and its aims to the discovery of segmentation and classification procedures.[25]

It can be briefly observed that, although the usefulness of Chomsky's work on the history of linguistics is undoubted, this work–as Chomsky himself notes–may be misleading, not only from the point of view of a historical understanding of seventeenth- and eighteenth-century linguistics, but also from the point of view of the relationship of transformational grammar to modern linguistics. The criticism of structural linguistics made by transformationalists could lead to a wrong idea being formed of the dependence of transformational theory on American Bloomfieldian tradition. Chomsky is a pupil of Harris, not just in the sense that he has developed transformational ideas put forward by Harris: phrase structure grammar is unthinkable without American structural linguistics; and if structuralists have sometimes questioned the equivalence of their theories to phrase structure grammars, and transformationalists have insisted on the limitations of phrase structure grammar, it must not be forgotten that such grammar plays an essential part in transformational theory.

A general point which to my mind has been insufficiently clarified in transformational theory concerns what the language user *knows* about his language. Transformationalists sometimes state that grammar should account for and satisfy the intuitions of the native users of a language. The rather confusing expression *tacit knowledge* is often used. In opposition to the behaviourist approach adopted in Bloomfieldian linguistics, transformationalists adopt a mentalist approach. A fundamental question with which a synchronic description must deal is: 'what is known by a speaker who is fluent in a natural language? That is, what facts about his language underlie his ability to communicate with others in that language?'[26] But here we have not one but two quite different questions, and connecting them with 'that is' is misleading. The further statement that this kind of knowledge is *tacit* (i.e. it refers to 'thoughts and ideas' which 'need not be present in conscious experience and so need not be available to introspective observation'–it is obvious that 'they are not publicly observable either'),[27] is far from reassuring, especially as it is apparently on this knowledge that we have to rely in deciding about the *grammaticalness* (or rather the *degree* of grammaticalness) of a sentence.

There is no doubt, however, that transformational grammar is one of the most interesting and important developments in linguistic theory, both for its widening of the scope of linguistic research and for the new impulse it has given to the much neglected field of syntax.[28]

CHAPTER IX

Mathematical Linguistics and Machine Translation

🕉🕉🕉🕉🕉🕉

9.1 Introduction

In this last chapter I shall discuss briefly a trend sometimes called 'mathematical' or 'computational' linguistics, which has been (wrongly, I think) separated from the mainstream of linguistic research.

One of the reasons for the separation is that this study is often pursued not in the traditional centres of academic linguistic research, but in circles where mathematicians and engineers, rather than philologists, work with their electronic computers; besides, this study, unlike more traditional linguistics, often aims at direct practical applications: economizing in the field of electric communications and building machines which can read out a written text, or write a spoken message (one will need some sort of identification of the phonemes), or translating machines (which will have, in some sense, to *understand* the sentence they have to translate). These are obviously inadequate reasons for separating this branch of linguistic studies from others; as is also the conventional linguists' distrust of methods to which they are unaccustomed, and the mathematicians' and engineers' ignorance of even the most elementary traditional linguistic notions.

In fact some of the studies which we shall mention in this chapter are of an obviously linguistic nature–more so than certain aspects of sociological and historical linguistics–as they deal with linguistic facts as such, and not in terms of cultural or social history, of aesthetics or literary tradition etc. These

139

studies sometimes have a 'practical' application: the 'pure' linguist may very well be indifferent to this; but he is hardly entitled to ask for an apology for possible practical applications; he should, on the contrary, be grateful that–even if he is not interested in 'practical' results–the requirements, say, of computer programming may be a healthy incentive for explicit and rigorous formulation.

'Mathematical linguistics' is a label which has at least two clearly different values. One refers to 'quantitative' linguistics, which takes into account numerical magnitudes, and is also called 'statistical linguistics'. The other refers to the use of symbols, and to operations performed on symbols; here 'mathematical' has the same value as in 'mathematical logic', and this kind of linguistics is also called 'algorithmic', or 'algebraic'.

9.2 Statistical Linguistics

Traditionally the 'counting' of linguistic elements has a marginal place in linguistics proper. This is not contradicted by the interest of philologists in *hapax legomena* (for which the counting is quite simple, as it is limited to checking that they appear only once in a corpus). Nor is it contradicted by various computations on the frequency of words or letters in such texts as the Bible or certain classics; or by the 'word lists' compiled for research in psychology or language teaching; or by the letter counting produced by inventors of shorthand systems, or of typewriter keyboards. Interesting results have been obtained also in works produced for purely mathematical reasons, which is not surprising, given the amount of knowledge of statistical methods often needed in these computations.

I shall not touch here on the problems involved in the use of statistical methods in the social sciences, and in particular the question of the relevance of the frequency of a phenomenon for its characterization, or the fact that a population of events may conform to certain statistical laws, even though each particular event may be considered not probabilistic, but either mechanistically 'determined' or 'free' and unforeseeable. What is certain is that language events have been considered particularly amenable to statistical treatment.[1] When we speak we choose our words and sentences according to what we want to say. But a sufficiently large corpus of utterances appears to conform to certain statistical regularities.

These studies[2] are obviously difficult, among other things because they require of researchers a double qualification–linguistic and mathematical. Many basic problems concerning the relevance of statistical methods in linguistics are still far from being solved: one can recall Chomsky's denial of the interest of statistics in this field, and Herdan's attempt at interpreting in statistical terms some of Saussure's dichotomies.[3]

A pioneering work in this field has been produced by a linguist whose influence has only belatedly been felt, G. K. Zipf.[4] In the thirties the Prague School had underlined the importance of statistical considerations of linguistic facts (the notion of functional yield can be mentioned, which was meant to be statistically based).[5] In fact it was Zipf who identified many laws and tendencies which appear to be particularly interesting (and which were later modified by other scholars). Some can be mentioned here.[6]

If we order the words of a text according to decreasing frequency (f), and we number them progressively according to their rank (r) in the list, the relation between frequency and rank is obviously *inverse* (this depends on the way we have prepared our list); what is interesting, and does not depend on the way we have prepared our list, is that this relation turns out to be inversely *proportional*, i.e. to be such that the product of frequency by rank is approximately constant. From Joyce's *Ulysses* the following data can be extracted:

rank (r)	frequency (f)	f . r = C
the 10th word is used	2653 times	26530
100th	265	26500
1000th	26	26000
10000th	2	20000
29000th	1	29000

From V. A. C. Henmon's *French Word Book* (based on a corpus of 400,000 words) one finds that

the 100th word is used	314 times	31400
200th	158	31600
1000th	31	31000

There is another interesting statistical relation (connected to the one just mentioned) between the words of a text. If we compare the frequency (f) of any given word, and the number (n) of words which have the same frequency as the given word, we find that $n.f^2$ is approximately constant. Also from *Ulysses* we see that

n	f	$n.f^2 = C$
16432	1	16432
4776	2	19000
2194	3	19600
1400	4	20239
900	5	22400
770	6	22700
480	7	23500
370	8	23600
300	9	24300
220	10	22000

These two laws should be modified as they are not exact for certain groups of words (those with the highest and those with the lowest frequency).[7] It is certainly important for them to be statistically correct.[8] The linguist, however, will be interested mainly in their interpretation.

Zipf had suggested a simple and attractive explanation based on the law of minimum effort. The statistical regularities mentioned, he maintained, represent a compromise between a striving towards rest (always using the same word in a message, with minimum effort, but also with minimum information), and a striving towards effectiveness (using in a message the most specific words, with maximum effort, but also maximum information). This explanation has been reformulated in a more complex way by Mandelbrot, who corrects Zipf's formulae and shows that they are 'explained' by their being (from a 'limited but not negligible' pragmatic point of view) the 'best' properties which a text can have, with regard to the requirements of communication. Martinet has arrived at similar results, on purely linguistic grounds, without having recourse to mathematical apparatus.

Zipf also shows, on a statistical basis, that there is an inverse relation between the length of a word and its frequency (consequently a tendency to shorten words when their frequency of use rises); [9] between the degree of 'complexity' of the phonemes and their frequency (consequently phonemes which are 'complex' usually become 'simpler' if their frequency rises: and here may lie one of the causes of sound change, as again Martinet maintains without having recourse to mathematical data).

There are other interesting features which have emerged from the work done in this field. It is possible, for instance, starting from a normal one-volume dictionary of a language (containing, say, 50,000 words), to prepare a list of words, in order of decreasing frequency, such that the first 15 words account for 25 per cent of any text (or corpus of texts) which uses only words included in the dictionary; the first 100 account for 60 per cent, the first 1,000 for 85 per cent, the first 4,000 for 97·5 per cent of any text. But if we want to account for the remaining 2·5 per cent of any text, we need all the remaining 46,000 words in the dictionary.

An attempt has also been made to establish certain relations between frequency and some semantic aspects of lexis; distinctions such as that between 'empty' words (which have a 'grammatical' meaning) and 'full' words have a statistical relevance; and statistics comes into the definition of the 'theme-words' (which are the most used, in absolute terms, by an author), and 'key-words' (the frequency of which, in an author, is different from the average). Also, using the number of meanings given in each entry of a dictionary, it has been found that the number (n) of words which have a particular number of meanings (m) is inversely proportional to the square of the number of meanings: $n \cdot m^2 = C$.

On the basis of the study of frequency lists, the conclusion has been reached that the most frequent words are (1) the shortest, (2) the oldest, (3) the simplest morphologically, (4) those with the greatest semantic coverage.[10] The value of this information depends obviously on the linguist's ability to interpret it and to use it for a better understanding of language.

There are other aspects of linguistic research in which quantitative considerations have been used: for instance, the so-called stylo-statistics which looks for certain statistical constants typical of a text or of an author (or of an author in a certain period of his life, or when writing in a certain style). These studies have been used in the discussion of problems of authorship and of dating, and have a long history which we shall not relate here. Nor shall we discuss the use of statistical criteria in historical linguistics which is known as 'glottochronology'.[11]

From a linguistic point of view it may not be out of place to mention some elementary points which have occasionally been disregarded in statistical work: (1) distinction (to use the terms also employed by Guiraud) between *vocabulary*, i.e. the list of the words used in a text, and *lexis*, i.e. the inventory of the words of a language, from which any text draws its particular vocabulary. Statistical computations are obviously made on the vocabulary of a text (or are based on a dictionary taken as a text); then they are sometimes made more 'interesting' by attributing their result to the lexis of the language in which the text is written. But often one forgets to discuss whether the text examined can be taken as a reliable sample. The same difficulty applies to the results of corpus-oriented and of language-oriented grammars. (2) Distinction between homography and polysemy: it is useful to decide clearly how to deal with cases like *calculus* 'concretion' and *calculus* 'a branch of mathematics', which have different meanings and the same etymology, and cases like *post* 'pole' and *post*, as in 'post-office', which have different meanings and different etymologies. Even when the problem of deciding whether it is a question of different words, or of one word with different meanings, has been solved, one still has to decide, depending on the particular purpose of the statistics, whether two different words which are homographs should be treated as one or two items. (3) Defining the notion of *word*. In particular it must be clear whether the different inflected forms of a word are counted as one item only (as in Guiraud) or as one item each (as in Zipf). (4) Distinction between type, token and occurrence: one may want to know how many times the article *a* is used in a text; or how many times the indefinite article is used, counting both *a* and *an*; or how many adjectives are used in a text (including repetitions of the same adjectives); or how many different adjectives are used (not taking into account whether any particular adjective is used more than once).

9.3 Information Theory

In non-technical terms we may say that the more unexpected a linguistic element is, the greater will be the information it conveys. In a word like *universally* the final *-y*, in a sense, does not add information to *universall-*, because no other letter could take its place, and consequently one could not expect anything but a *-y* (this is already a conventional sense of the term 'information': the absence of the *-y* would in fact be surprising—and thus 'informative', just because one expects it to be there). In *sally*, the *-y* gives more information, as the word could be *salli(es)* or *sallo(w)* etc. The same sort of reasoning may apply to phonemes, morphemes, words or any other linguistic units. Some units can be eliminated without preventing the understanding of the message. It is well known that in English, as in many other languages, words written without vowels remain fairly legible—far less so if the consonants are deleted (w.rds wr.tt.n w.th..t v.w.ls r.m..n f..rl. l.g.bl.–.a. .e.. .o i. ..e .o..o.a... a.e .e.e.e.). Some elements are redundant: of course they may be useful if certain conditions make communication more difficult: for instance in a badly written manuscript the absence

145

of vowels could add just that amount of difficulty to make the text totally incomprehensible.

All this is rather obvious; and, although it appears to be based on the central notion of information theory, it is, from a technical point of view, also misleading. The connexion between the technical notions of information theory, and a non-technical interpretation of the value of such notions for natural languages poses rather delicate questions (especially when by 'information theory' one does not mean–restrictively–the theory of transmission of signals, but something much wider, according to the general use of cybernetics).[12]

The main point in the theory of Hartley and Shannon is that it is possible to measure exactly one particular aspect in the transmission of signals. This aspect is the relative frequency of a symbol i, or rather something which depends on that frequency and which–for reasons we will not discuss here–scientists define as the logarithmic function of the reciprocal of relative frequency. This quantity $\log 1/fr(i)$ is the central notion of information theory.[13] Usually one makes the frequency refer to a source which emits infinite symbols; in this case one talks of *probability p* of the symbol i; the quantity of information associated with the symbol i is then $\log 1/p(i)$. The notion of quantity of information was studied by Nyquist (1924), Hartley (1928) and Szilard (1929).[14] The founder of information theory in the modern sense is considered to be C. E. Shannon (1948) together with N. Wiener and others.[15]

There are some philosophical problems–the terms of which are sometimes insufficiently clear–involved in the relationships between *frequency* (concerning occurrences in the past) and *probability* (concerning expectation of future events, or in any case unknown events). Some misunderstandings are connected with the notions of *probability* and *information*. Shannon repeatedly insisted that his theory allowed us to measure the *quantity* of information, that is a function of the rarity of certain symbols, and not to measure *information* in the ordinary sense of the word.[16] But others have been less cautious, and the notion has been extended in the attempt to measure linguistic *meaning*, and even the *circulation of information* in society as a function of freedom, democracy and the like. Another point which is not always as clear as it should be–given the fact that the symbols used in natural languages are not equiprobable and independent–concerns the relationships between the frequency of a symbol (its quantity of information) and the number of units belonging to the inventory out of which particular choices are made at particular points in the message.

9.4 Machine Translation

I shall end with a few remarks about a recent field of research: that of machine translation.[17] I shall not touch on the problem of the 'possibility' of translation; leaving aside the question of whether two utterances in different languages are ever (or can possibly be) completely equivalent, and accepting the ordinary use of the term 'translation', one should not be surprised that an attempt has been made to use computers in the operation of translating.

If we disregard the 'precedents' offered by the work on *ars combinatoria, characteristica universalis*, etc., the first project for a translating machine goes back, it seems, to Petr Petrovič Smirnov Trojanskij who patented one in 1933.[18] But modern research, based on computers, begins with Booth and Weaver. The idea was stimulated by the desire to find the computers something to do. Booth at first wanted to make the computers perform operations comparable to those of a human translator who looks up a word in a dictionary. But soon the possibility was considered of making the computer analyse the syntactic structure of sentences. The main steps in this development are the discussions of Booth and Weaver (1946), the research by Booth and Britten at Princeton (1947), and by Booth and Richens (1948), mainly devoted to the question of an automatic dictionary. In 1949 we find the memorandum by W. Weaver,[19] and in 1950 the work by the sinologist E. Reifler,[20] based on the idea of collaboration between man and machine: even if there is a pre-editor and a post-editor, they would not need to be

147

bilingual, and the conversion of the pre-edited text from one language into a text (to be post-edited) in another language would be done entirely by machine. In 1951 we find an important contribution by Oswald and Fletcher on automatic analysis of German syntax;[21] in June 1952 there took place, at the Massachusetts Institute of Technology, the first meeting devoted to machine translation, organized by Y. Bar-Hillel.[22]

There were eighteen participants at this meeting; and the number of people in the world working on machine translation was probably not much higher. Since then it has increased enormously. On 7th January 1954 there was a public experiment with machine translation, in New York, organized by Dostert and Garvin of Georgetown University and by Sheridan of IBM, on an IBM 701. The translation was from Russian into English with a dictionary of two hundred and fifty Russian words and the use of six syntactic rules. Here is an example: *veličina ugla opredeljaetsja otnošeniem dliny dugi k radiusu*, translated as *magnitude of angle is determined by the relation of length of arc to radius*.[23] In 1955 there was a Russian experiment, with a dictionary of nine hundred and fifty-two English words, on the computer BESM by the Academician S. A. Lebedev. Here is an example: *When a practical problem in science or technology permits mathematical formulation, the chances are rather good that it leads to one or more differential equations*, translated as *Esli praktičeskaja zadača v nauke ili texnike dopuskaet matematičeskuju formulirovku, šancy dovol'no veliki čto èto privodit k odnomu ili bolee differencial'nym uravnenijam*.[24]

Machine translation had become one of the fields of competition between the USA and the USSR, and this was no doubt one of the reasons why a large amount of energy was devoted to it. In 1956 the University of Moscow organized a seminar of mathematical linguistics, and the Massachusetts Institute of Technology organized the first international conference on machine translation. In the following years the meetings devoted to the subject were fairly numerous.

In the meantime some healthy doubts began to be voiced. Bar-Hillel, who had worked with great penetration in this field from the start, came to the conclusion that a high quality completely automatic translation was in principle impossible.[25] His arguments have not been answered; and recently the attitude towards machine translation appears to have become slightly more realistic. A solution had been looked for in psychological research on human translation. But this did not lead far, because we know very little about the working of human translation.[26]

In some cases translation as such has been abandoned and research has concentrated on automatic analysis of the source language and automatic synthesis of the target language. What is meant by these notions is fairly clear; but whether it is possible to write a programme for a computer which enables it to produce any sentence in a language, and no non-sentence (or to recognize and analyse any sentence of a language) is a different matter. The models used in machine translation projects are usually based on some form of constituent structure grammar — be it 'predictive analysis', 'dependency grammar', 'projective grammar', or 'push-down store grammar', etc.[27] But these grammars have been shown to be inadequate in principle for natural languages, even leaving aside the problem of ambiguities. A computer, provided with a dictionary in which each lexical item is accompanied by an indication of its category (Verb, Noun, etc.), and with syntactic rules which specify possible syntactic patterns, may resolve certain ambiguities: for instance in *iron grips well* the computer will be able to reject the interpretation Verb + Noun + Verb, or Verb + Verb + Noun, as incompatible with the syntax of an English sentence. But within the boundaries of acceptable syntactic patterns (like Noun + Verb + Adverb, Verb + Noun + Adverb, Noun + Verb + Noun, Modifier + Noun + Verb, etc.) the computer will be unable to choose. It was fashionable in the past to talk optimistically about the possibility of sub-classifying lexical items according to their privileges of occurrence, and of programming the computer to take into account the relevant context. In fact this is beyond our present possibilities.

A human translator is normally (but not always) able to

resolve the ambiguities he meets because he knows the context of the sentence, and its meaning, and a great deal besides. What the translator brings to bear on his activity (and in general, what the language user brings to bear on his use of language) is not only his knowledge of the language, but also his knowledge of the world, his experience as a human being, and in fact that complex of qualities which we call his intelligence. All this is something which we are not only unable to programme, but also about which we know very little. A language user will be able to decide that, in a given situation, it is more likely that *iron grips well* refers to iron gripping hard, rather than to ironing grips accurately, or gripping wells with iron, or to metal grips which well up—although he will know (even if he has never thought about this before) that these other alternatives are not impossible. What one needs, if one wants a translating machine, is a thinking and knowing machine, as has been stated by an acute Italian theorist, Silvio Ceccato.[28]

'If a human being can do it, a suitably programmed computer can do it too,' Bar-Hillel used to repeat in 1952 at the MIT meeting on machine translation. In 1963 he commented soberly: 'Though this slogan is doubtless correct, "in principle", its value lies more in its being an expression of willingness to work towards a certain goal than in exhibiting a deep philosophical insight. Its practical content is close to nil.'[29]

What precedes should not suggest that computers are of no use to linguists, or that the research produced in the field of machine translation has been useless. The contrary is true. Computers, when they are employed for what they can do, are invaluable aids to linguistics; and research in the field of machine translation has been very fruitful, both as a stimulus for clear and precise formulation, and as a test revealing how little we still know about many basic facts of language: it acts therefore as a spur to remedy our ignorance.

Notes

Chapter I

1 For the history of linguistics it is sufficient to mention here H. Pedersen, *The Discovery of Language*, Bloomington 1962 (a reprint of the English translation by J. W. Spargo, 1931, of the Danish original *Sprogviden-skaben i det nittende aarhundrede*, København 1924); R. H. Robins, *Ancient and Mediaeval Grammatical Theory in Europe*, London 1951; A. Graur, L. Wald, *Scurtă istorie a lingvisticii*, București 1961, 1965²; M. Ivić, *Pravci u lingvistici*, Ljubljana 1963 (and in English trans. *Trends in Linguistics*, The Hague 1965); C. Tagliavini, *Panorama di storia della linguistica*, Bologna 1963; G. Mounin, *Histoire de la linguistique des origines au XXᵉ siècle*, Paris 1967; R. H. Robins, *A Short History of Linguistics*, London 1967. Th. A. Sebeok, ed., *Portraits of Linguists. A Biographical Source Book for the History of Western Linguistics, 1746–1963*, Bloomington 1966 is a collection of essays on linguists. A useful anthology of passages by linguists, from G. B. Vico to the present day is T. Bolelli, *Per una storia della ricerca linguistica. Testi e note intro-duttive*, Napoli 1965. Other collections of texts and commentary are offered by H. Arens, *Sprachwissenschaft*, Freiburg 1955; V. A. Zvegincev, *Istorija jazykoznanija XIX i XX vekov v očerkax i izvlečeni-jax*, Moskva 1960; W. P. Lehmann, *A Reader in Nineteenth-Century Historical Indo-European Linguistics*, Bloomington 1967.

2 K. Brugmann, B. Delbrück, *Grundriss der vergleichenden Grammatik der indogermanischen Sprachen*, Strassburg 1886 ff., 1897 ff.²

3 A. Schleicher, 'Eine fabel in indogermanischer ursprache', *Beiträge zur vergleichenden Sprachforschung*, 5, 1868, 206–8; H. Hirt, *Die Haupt-probleme der indogermanischen Sprachwissenschaft*, hgg. und bearbeitet v. H. Arntz, Halle 1939, 113–15.

4 Cf. A. Meillet, *Introduction à l'étude comparative des langues indo-européennes*, Paris 1953, 85, 100 (first ed. 1903). The examples in the text are simplified; different views of the Indo-European sound system are generally held today.

5 A. Meillet, *Introduction* cit., viii, 41, 47.

6 H. Schuchardt in his inaugural lecture at Leipzig in 1870. This was published thirty years later: *Über die Klassifikation der romanischen*

Notes

Mundarten, Graz 1900; but as early as 1873 Schuchardt had written in a footnote to a lecture of 1872: 'In the opening lecture of my 1870 course in Leipzig I tried to show that it is impossible to establish a classification of the Romance languages, and their historical relationships cannot be represented by the image of a genealogical tree,' *Romania*, 3, 1874, 9; J. Schmidt, *Die Verwantschaftsverhältnisse der indogermanischen Sprachen*, Weimar 1872.

7 J. Bédier, in *Romania*, 54, 1928, 161–96, 321–56 objected to the 'bifid trees' (*arbres bifides*) of textual criticism; on the relationship between the philological 'stemma codicum' and the linguistic 'genealogical tree' cf. chapter viii of S. Timpanaro, *La genesi del metodo del Lachmann*, Firenze 1963.

8 B. Croce, *Estetica come scienza dell'espressione e linguistica generale*, Milano 1902.

9 On structural linguistics there is an extensive bibliography. At this stage I shall only mention some expositions inspired by different principles: V. Bröndal, 'Linguistique structurale', *AL*, 1, 1939, 2–10; L. Hjelmslev, 'Structural Analysis of Language', *SL*, 1, 1947, 69–78; E. Buyssens, 'La conception fonctionelle des faits linguistiques', *JPsych*, 43, 1950, 37–53; A. Martinet, 'Structural Linguistics', in A. L. Kroeber, ed., *Anthropology Today*, Chicago 1953, 574–86; C. E. Bazell, 'The Choice of Criteria in Structural Linguistics', *Word*, 10, 1954, 126–35; J. R. Firth, 'Structural Linguistics', *TPhS*, 1955, 83–103; R. A. Hall, Jr., 'Scopi e metodi della linguistica', *AGI*, 42, 1957, 57–69 and 148–61. Some discussions in E. Haugen, 'Directions in Modern Linguistics', *Lg*, 27, 1951, 211–22; A. Sommerfelt, 'Tendances actuelles de la linguistique générale', *Diogène*, 1, 1952, 77–84; T. Bolelli, *Considerazioni su alcune correnti linguistiche attuali*, Pisa 1953; É. Benveniste, 'Tendances récentes en linguistique générale', *JPsych*, 47–51, 1954, 130–45 (reprinted in Id., *Problèmes de linguistique générale*, Paris 1966, 3–17); L. Heilmann, 'Orientamenti strutturali nell' indagine linguistica', *RALinc*, 10, 1955, 136–56; S. K. Šaumjan, 'O suščnosti strukturnoj lingvistiki', *VJa*, 5: 5, 1956, 38–54; W. Doroszewski, 'Historyczne podstawy strukturalizmu', *PJ*, 151, 1957, 241–55 (reprinted in Id., *Studia i szkice językoznawcze*, Warszawa 1962, 102–15); L. Heilmann, 'Origini, prospettive e limiti dello strutturalismo', *Convivium*, 5, 1958, 513–26; H. H. Christmann, 'Strukturelle Sprachwissenschaft', *RJb*, 9, 1958, 17–40 and 12, 1961, 23–50; B. Malmberg, *Nya vägar inom språkforskningen*, Stockholm 1959, 1966[3] (and in a revised version *New Trends in Linguistics. An Orientation*, Stockholm 1964); L. Wald, 'Structuralismul', *PLG*, 2, 1960, 143–73; Zs. Telegdi, 'Über die jüngere Entwicklung der Sprachwissenschaft', *ALH*, 11, 1961, 233–54; C. Mohrmann etc., edd., *Trends in European and American Linguistics 1930–60*, Utrecht 1961, and *Trends in Modern Linguistics*, Utrecht 1963 (these are two volumes prepared for the CIPL on the occasion of the 9th Intern. Congress of Linguists); J. Svartvik, 'Thirty Years of Linguistics', *MSpråk*, 56, 1962, 8–17; M. Leroy, *Les grands courants de la linguistique moderne*,

Notes

Bruxelles 1963 (and in English trans. *Main Trends in Modern Linguistics*, Oxford 1967); J. T. Waterman, *Perspectives in Linguistics*, Chicago 1963, devotes about 40 pages to linguistic theory after 1900; É. Benveniste, *Coup d'œil sur le développement de la linguistique*, Paris 1963 (reprinted in Id., *Problèmes* cit., 18–31); Th. A. Sebeok, ed., *Current Trends in Linguistics* (a large collective enterprise published by Mouton), 1: *Soviet and East European Linguistics*, The Hague 1963; M. M. Guxman, V. N. Jarceva, edd., *Osnovnye napravlenija strukturalizma*, Moskva 1964; N. Ruwet, 'La linguistique générale aujourd'hui', *Archives Européennes de Sociologie*, 5, 1964, 277–310; D. Hymes, 'Directions in (Ethno-)Linguistic Theory', *AmA*, 66: 3, part 2, 1964, 6–56; M. de Paiva Boléo, 'Algumas tendências e perspectivas da linguística moderna', *RPF*, 13, 1964–5, 279–346; *Problèmes du langage*, Paris 1966 (a reprint of *Diogène* 51); Th. A. Sebeok, ed., *Current Trends in Linguistics*, 3: *Theoretical Foundations*, The Hague, 1966; M. Bierwisch, 'Strukturalismus', *Kursbuch*, 5, 1966, 77–152; F. P. Dinneen, S.J., *An Introduction to General Linguistics*, New York 1967, devotes pp. 192–399 to post-Saussurean linguistics; *Lo strutturalismo linguistico*, *Il Verri*, 24, 1967; *Linguistics and Communication, ISSJ*, 19: 1, 1967.

10 Cf. I. I. Revzin, *Modeli jazyka*, Moskva 1962 (and in English trans. *Models of Language*, London 1966); N. D. Andreyev, 'Models as a Tool in the Development of Linguistic Theory', *Word*, 18, 1962, 186–97; Y. R. Chao, 'Models in Linguistics and Models in General', in E. Nagel etc., edd., *Logic, Methodology and Philosophy of Science* [1960], Stanford Calif. 1962, 558–66; R. Katičić, 'Modellbegriffe in der vergleichenden Sprachwissenschaft', *Kratylos*, 11, 1966, 49–67.

11 Particularly interesting for a linguist are the essays collected in C. Lévi-Strauss, *Anthropologie structurale*, Paris 1958; and cf. R. Barthes, *Essais critiques*, Paris 1964; M. Foucault, *Les mots et les choses*, Paris 1966; J. Lacan, *Écrits*, Paris 1966; J. Derrida, *De la grammatologie*, Paris 1967; J. Piaget, *Le structuralisme*, Paris 1968. Cf. also R. Bastide, ed., *Sens et usage du terme structure dans les sciences humaines et sociales*, 's-Gravenhage 1962 (and G. C. Lepscky, 'Osservazioni sul termine *Struttura*', *ASNP*, 31, 1962, 173–97); J. Viet, *Les méthodes structuralistes dans les sciences sociales*, Paris 1965; *La notion de structure*, *Revue internationale de philosophie*, 19: 73–4, 1965; *Structuralism*, *Yale French Studies*, 36–7, 1966; *Problèmes du structuralisme*, *Les temps modernes*, 22: 246, 1966. A. D. Momigliano has illustrated the traditional distinction between the study of 'history' and the study of 'antiquities' or 'institutions', cf. 'Ancient History and the Antiquarian', *Journal of the Warburg and Courtauld Institutes*, 13, 1950, 285–315 (reprinted in Id., *Contributo alla storia degli studi classici*, Roma 1955, 67–106 and in Id., *Studies in Historiography*, London 1966, 1–39), and his introduction to the Italian translation J. Burckhardt, *Storia della civiltà greca*, Firenze 1955, xxiii–xliii (reprinted in Id., *Secondo contributo alla storia degli studi classici*, Roma 1960, 283–98); S. Timpanaro compares this distinction with the

structuralist one between synchronic and diachronic method, in *Belfagor*, 18, 1963, 4–5.
12 A. Meillet, *Introduction* cit., vii–ix. Cf. also G. Mounin, 'La notion de système chez A. Meillet', *Linguistique*, 1966: 1, 17–29; K. H. Rensch, 'Organismus-System-Struktur in der Sprachwissenschaft', *Phonetica*, 16, 1967, 71–84.

Chapter II

1 T. Bolelli, *Per una storia della ricerca linguistica. Testi e note introduttive*, Napoli 1965, 358.
2 Saussure's works are collected in *Recueil des publications scientifiques de F. de Saussure*, Genève 1922 (also Heidelberg 1922); this includes pp. 1–268, the *Mémoire sur le système primitif des voyelles dans les langues indo-européennes*, Leipsick 1879 (but published in 1878).
3 F. de Saussure, *Cours de linguistique générale, publié par* Ch. Bally *et* A. Sechehaye, *avec la collaboration de* A. Riedlinger, Lausanne 1916. The page references in the text are to the fourth edition Paris 1949. On Saussure cf. A. Meillet, in *BSL*, 18 (61), 1913, CLXV–CLXXV (reprinted in Id., *Linguistique historique et linguistique générale*, II, Paris 1951, 174–83); Ch. Bally, *F.d.S. et l'état actuel des études linguistiques*, Genève 1913 (reprinted in Id., *Le langage et la vie*, Genève 1952³, 147–60); W. Streitberg, in *IJ*, 2, 1914, 203–13; *Ferdinand de Saussure (1857–1913)*, Genève 1915, 1962²; J. Wackernagel, in *Sonntagsbl. d. Basler Nachrichten*, 11, 1916, 165–6, 172; L. Gautier, in *Gazette de Lausanne*, Aug. 13 1916; A. Oltramare, in *La semaine littéraire* (Genève), May 27 1916, 256–9; J. Ronjat, in *Journal de Genève*, June 26 1916; K. Jaberg, in *Sonntagsbl. d. 'Bund'*, Dec. 17 and 24 1916, 790–5, 806–10 (reprinted in Id., *Sprachwissenschaftliche Forschungen und Erlebnisse*, Bern 1937, 1965², 123–36); A. Meillet, in *BSL*, 20 (64), 1916, 32–6; Id., in *Revue critique*, 83, 51, 1917, 49–51; H. Schuchardt, in *LGRP*, 38, 1917, 1–9 (also dismembered in L. Spitzer, ed., *Hugo Schuchardt-Brevier*, Halle 1922); O. Jespersen, in *NTF*, 6, 1917, 37–41 (reprinted in Id., *Linguistica*, Copenhagen 1933, 109–15); A. Sechehaye, in *Rev. Philos.* 84, 1917, 1–30; M. Grammont, in *RLaR*, 59, 1917, 402–10; B. A. Terracini, in *Bollett. Filol. Class.*, 25, 1919, 73–9; J. Vendryes, in *JPsych*, 18, 1921, 617–24 (reprinted in Id., *Choix d'études linguistiques et celtiques*, Paris 1952, 18–25); H. Lommel, in *GGA*, 183, 1921, 232–41; Id., in *Philol. Wochenschr.*, 42, 1922, 252–7; Id., in *DLZ*, 45, 1924, 2040–46; L. Bloomfield, in *MLJ*, 8, 1924, 317–19 (reprinted by É. Benveniste in *CFS*, 21, 1964, 133–5); G. Devoto, in *La cultura*, 7 1928, 241–9 (cf. also Id., *I fondamenti della storia linguistica*, Firenze 1951); L. Weisgerber, in *Teuthonista*, 8, 1932, 248–9; H. Ammann, in *IF*, 52, 1934, 261–81; N. van Wijk, in *Album Th. Baader*, Tilburg 1939, 9–14; A. Sechehaye, in *VR*, 5, 1940, 1–48; K. Rogger, in *ZRPh*, 61, 1941, 161–224; E. Buyssens, in *RLaV*, 1942, 1, 15–23 and 2, 46–55; A. Sechehaye, in *CFS*, 4, 1944, 65–9; R. Pipping, in *ÅVsLund*, 1946, 17–28; R. S. Wells, in *Word*, 3, 1947, 1–31; E. Buyssens, in *CFS*,

Notes

8, 1949, 37–60; H. Frei, in *CFS*, 9, 1950, 7–28; E. Buyssens, in *CFS*, 10, 1952, 47–50; R. A. Budagov, *Iz istorii jazykoznanija (Sossjur i sossjurianistvo)*, Moskva 1954; B. Malmberg, in *CFS*, 12, 1954, 9–28; A. J. Greimas, in *FM*, 24, 1956, 191–203; J. T. Waterman, in *MLJ*, 40, 1956, 307–9; H. Birnbaum, in *Filol. meddel. f. Ryska inst. v. Stockholms högskola*, 1957: 1, 7–10; Sh. Hattori, in *GK*, 32, 1957, 1–42; A. S. Čikobava, *Problema jazyka kak predmeta jazykoznanija*, Moskva 1959, 96–125; S. Heinimann, in *ZRPh*, 75, 1959, 132–7; E. Buyssens, in *CFS*, 18, 1961, 17–33; É. Benveniste, in *CFS*, 20, 1963, 7–21; Id., in *CFS*, 21, 1964, 131–5; Id., in École Pratique des Hautes Études IV sect., *Annuaire 1964–5*, 21–34; M. Fleury, *ib.*, 35–67; R. Godel, in *CFS*, 22, 1966, 53–68; Id., in Th. A. Sebeok, ed., *Current Trends in Linguistics*, 3, The Hague 1966, 479–93; K. H. Rensch, in *Phonetica* 15, 1966, 32–41; R. Engler, in *CFS*, 22, 1966, 35–40; I. von Niederhäusern, *Zu F. de Saussures Cours de linguistique générale*, Zürich 1966; T. Pavel, in *SCL*, 18, 1967, 571–80 and 19, 1968, 183–95; G. Mounin, *Saussure ou le structuraliste sans le savoir*, Paris 1968; R. Engler, in *Ulisse*, 9 (63), 1968, 158–64; B. Collinder, in *ASLU*, 1: 5, 1968, 181–210. For the fortune of the *Cours* it may be useful to recall its translations: into Japanese by H. Kobayashi, *Gengogaku-genron*, Tokyo 1928; into Russian by A. M. Suxotin, *Kurs obščej lingvistiki*, Moskva 1933 (and cf. N. Slusareva, 'Quelques considérations des linguistes soviétiques à propos des idées de F.d.S.', *CFS*, 20, 1963, 23–46); into German by H. Lommel, *Grundfragen der allgemeinen Sprachwissenschaft*, Berlin 1931, 1967²; into Spanish by A. Alonso, *Curso de lingüística general*, Buenos Aires 1945; into English by W. Baskin, *Course in General Linguistics*, New York 1959; into Polish by K. Kasprzyk, *Kurs językoznawstwa ogólnego*, Warszawa 1961; into Italian by T. De Mauro, *Corso di linguistica generale*, Bari 1967 (the latter takes into account Engler's work, has a large number of notes, and sketches a portrait of Saussure, his thought and his influence; cf. also T. De Mauro, 'Saussure in Italia', *Il Veltro*, 4–5, 1967, 727–30).

4 F. de Saussure, *Cours* cit., 7.

5 Cf. 'Notes inédites de F.d.S.', *CFS*, 12, 1954, 49–71; 'Cours de linguistique générale (1908–1909). Introduction', *CFS*, 15, 1957, 3–103; R. Godel, 'Nouveaux documents saussuriens. Les Cahiers É. Constantin', *CFS*, 16, 1958–9, 23–32; 'Souvenirs de F.d.S. concernant sa jeunesse et ses études', *CFS*, 17, 1960, 12–25; 'Inventaire des manuscrits de F.d.S. remis à la Bibliothèque publique et universitaire de Genève', *CFS*, 17, 1960, 5–11; É. Benveniste, 'Lettres de F.d.S. à Antoine Meillet', *CFS*, 21, 1964, 89–130. Some extracts from Saussure's notes on the 'anagrams' (or 'hypograms', or 'paragrams') have been published by J. Starobinski, in *Mercure de France*, 350, 1964, 243–62 and in *To Honor R. Jakobson*, The Hague 1967, 1906–17. Cf. also A. Rossi, in *Paragone*, 218, 1968, 113–27; G. Nava, in *CFS*, 24, 1968, 73–81. Saussure was apparently convinced that writers (particularly poets of Old German, Indian, Greek, and Latin literatures) analysed certain key words (usually names of Gods or Heroes)

into syllables or into phonemes which they sprinkled in their compositions.

6 R. Godel, *Les sources manuscrites du Cours de linguistique générale de F. de Saussure*, Genève 1957.

7 F. de Saussure, *Cours de linguistique générale, édition critique par* Rudolf Engler, Wiesbaden 1967 ff. (cf. also Id., 'CLG und SM; eine kritische Ausgabe des Cours de linguistique générale', *Kratylos*, 4, 1959, 119–32; and 'Zur Neuausgabe des Cours de linguistique générale', *Kratylos*, 12, 1967, 113–28). Another valuable aid has been provided by the same author: R. Engler, *Lexique de la terminologie saussurienne*, Utrecht 1968.

8 The combination of the two points of view has been upheld by W. v. Wartburg, 'Das Ineinandergreifen von deskriptiver und historischer Sprachwissenschaft', *SbSAW*, 83: 1, 1931; Id., 'Betrachtungen über das Verhältnis von historischer und deskriptiver Sprachwissenschaft', *Mélanges Ch. Bally*, Genève 1939, 3–18; Id., *Einführung in Problematik und Methodik der Sprachwissenschaft*, Halle 1943, 125–79 (*Problems and Methods in Linguistics*, Oxford 1969, 138–93). A. G. Haudricourt, A. G. Juilland, *Essai pour une histoire structurale du phonétisme français*, Paris 1949, 3 consider the opposition of synchronic and diachronic a paradoxical thesis which contradicts the rest of Saussure's teaching; but É. Benveniste, 'Tendances récentes en linguistique générale', *JPsych*, 47–51, 1954, 132 (= Id., *Problèmes de linguistique générale*, Paris 1966, 5) notes very appropriately that 'the novelty of Saussure's point of view ... was the realization that language in itself does not entail any historical dimension, that it is synchrony and structure, and that it only functions thanks to its symbolic nature. It is not so much historical consideration which is condemned by this as a way of "atomizing" language and mechanizing history.' On the whole question cf. also R. Jakobson, in *La cultura*, 12, 1933, 637–8; J. Vendryes, 'Sur les tâches de la linguistique statique', *JPsych*, 30, 1933, 172–84; B. Trnka, 'Synchronie a diachronie v strukturálním jazykozpytu', *ČMF*, 20, 1934, 62–4; Ch. Bally, 'Synchronie et diachronie', *VR*, 2, 1937, 345–52; A. Sommerfelt, 'Points de vue diachronique, synchronique et panchronique en linguistique générale', *NTS*, 9, 1938, 240–9 (reprinted in Id., *Diachronic and Synchronic Aspects of Language*, 's-Gravenhage 1962, 59–65); B. Malmberg, 'Système et méthode. Trois études de linguistique générale', *ÅVsLund*, 1945, 3–52 includes 'Synchronie et diachronie', 22–32; V. M. Žirmunskij, 'O sinxronii i diaxronii v jazykoznanii', *VJa*, 7: 5, 1958, 43–52; E. Coseriu, *Sincronía, diacronía e historia*, Montevideo 1958; *O sootnošenii sinxronnogo analiza i istoričeskogo izučenija jazykov*, Moskva 1960; A. Avram, 'Syntagme et paradigme, synchronie et diachronie', *PhP*, 8, 1965, 120–4; M. Cohen 'Synchronie?', *Beiträge W. Steinitz*, Berlin 1965, 74–7; H.-H. Lieb, ' "Synchronic" versus "Diachronic" Linguistics: a Historical Note', *Linguistics* 36, 1967, 18–28; G. Mihăilă, in *PLG*, 5, 1967, 49–68; E. S. Kubrjakova, in *VJa*, 17: 3, 1968, 112–23; W. P. Lehmann, 'Saussure's Dichotomy between Descriptive and

Notes

Historical Linguistics', in W. P. Lehmann, Y. Malkiel, edd., *Directions for Historical Linguistics. A Symposium*, Austin 1968, 3–20 (in the same volume cf. also U. Weinreich, W. Labov, M. I. Herzog, 'Empirical Foundations for a Theory of Language Change', 95–195).

9 Cf. on this point P. A. Verburg, 'Het schaakspel-model bij F. de Saussure en bij L. Wittgenstein', in *Wijsgerig perspectief op maatschappij en wetenschap*, Amsterdam, I, 1960–1, 227–34.

10 Cf. Y. Malkiel, 'Linguistics as a Genetic Science', *Lg*, 43, 1967, 223–45.

11 Cf. Th. Absil, 'Sprache und Rede', *Nph*, 10, 1925, 100–8, 186–93; Ch. Bally, 'Langue et parole', *JPsych*, 23, 1926, 693–701; W. Doroszewski, ' "Langue" et "parole" ', *PF*, 14, 1929, 485–97 (in Polish in Id., *Studia i szkice językoznawcze*, Warszawa 1962, 80–8); J. M. Kořínek, 'Einige Betrachtungen über Sprache und Sprechen', *TCLP*, 6, 1936, 23–9; J. von Laziczius, 'Die Scheidung langue-parole in der Lautforschung', *3rd Congr. Phon.*, 13–23 (reprinted in Th. A. Sebeok, ed., *Selected Writings of G. Laziczius*, The Hague 1966, 77–89); Z. S. Harris, in *Lg*, 17, 1941, 345ff.; L. Hjelmslev, 'Langue et parole', *CFS*, 2, 1943, 29–44 (reprinted in Id., *Essais linguistiques*, *TCLC*, 12, 1959, 69–81); B. Malmberg, *Système et méthode* cit., 5–21, K. Møller, 'Contribution to the Discussion Concerning "langue" and "parole" ', *TCLC*, 5, 1949, 87–94; H. Frei, 'Langue, parole et différenciation', *JPsych*, 45, 1952, 137–57; A. Gill, 'La distinction entre *langue* et *parole* en sémantique historique', in *Studies Presented to John Orr*, Manchester 1953, 90–101; K. Rogger, 'Langue-parole und die Aktualisierung', *ZRPh*, 70, 1954, 341–75; N. C. W. Spence, 'A Hardy Perennial: The Problem of *La Langue* and *La Parole*', *ArchL*, 9, 1957, 1–27; E. Vasiliu, ' "Langue", "parole", stratification', *RLing*, 5, 1960, 27–32; L. Geschiere, 'Plaidoyer pour la Langue', *Nph*, 45, 1961, 21–37; N. C. W. Spence, '*Langue* and *parole* yet again', *Nph*, 46, 1962, 197–201; L. Geschiere, 'La "langue": Condamnation ou sursis?', *Nph*, 46, 1962, 201–10; *Tezisy dokladov Mežvuzovskoj konferencii na temu 'jazyk i reč'*, Moskva 1962; A. G. Volkov, 'O teoretičeskix osnovanijax dixotomičeskoj gipotezy *jazyka* i *reči* F.d.S.', *VMU*, 19: 2, 1964, 40–53; Ju. A. Levickij, G. V. Petrova, 'Terminy "jazyk" i "reč'" v sovremennom jazykoznanii', *VMU*, 23: 6, 1968, 14–25. The interesting contributions by E. Coseriu, *Sistema, norma y habla*, Montevideo 1952, and *Forma y sustancia en los sonidos del lenguaje*, Montevideo 1954, are reprinted in Id., *Teoría del lenguaje y lingüística general*, Madrid 1962, 11–113 and 115–234. R. Jakobson, in *La cultura*, 12, 1933, 637–8, and A. Alonso in the preface to the Spanish translation of the *Cours* (*Curso* cit., Buenos Aires 1961[4], 10) refer Saussure's dichotomies, through V. Henry, *Antinomies linguistiques*, Paris 1896, to Hegel's dialectic.

12 W. Doroszewski on Durkheim (1930) in Id., *Studia i szkice* cit., 89–101; Id., in *2nd Congr. Ling.*, 146–7; Id., in *JPsych*, 30, 1933, 82–91; Id., in *8th Congr. Ling.*, 544 (cf. also R. Godel, *Les sources* cit., 282). Cf. É. Durkheim, *Les règles de la méthode sociologique*, Paris 1956[13]; G. Tarde, *Psychologie économique*, Paris 1902.

13 Cf. the important contribution by É. Benveniste, in *AL*, 1, 1939, 23–9,

157

Notes

and the surveys by G. C. Lepscky, in *ASNP*, 31, 1962, 65–102, R. Engler, in *CFS*, 19, 1962, 5–66 and 21, 1964, 25–32. See also G. Derossi, *Segno e struttura linguistici nel pensiero di F. de Saussure*, Udine 1965.

14 Cf. R. Jakobson, in *TCLC*, 5, 1949, 207; Id., in *4th Congr. Phon.*, 440–55 (both in Id., *Selected Writings*, I, 's-Gravenhage 1962, 419–20 and 631–58, particularly 636 and 653).

15 Cf. L. Hjelmslev, in *4th Congr. Ling.*, 140.

16 Cf. G. C. Lepschy, in *SSL*, 5, 1965, 36.

17 Cf. for instance Ch. Bally, *Le langage et la vie*, Paris 1926, 1952³; Id., *Linguistique générale et linguistique française*, Paris 1932, 1965⁴; A. Sechehaye, *Programme et méthodes de la linguistique théorique*, Paris 1908; Id., *Essai sur la structure logique de la phrase*, Paris 1926; H. Frei, 'Zéro, vide et intermittent', *ZPhon*, 4, 1950, 161–91; Id., 'Désaccords', *CFS*, 18, 1961, 35–51; Id., 'Syntaxe et méthode en linguistique synchronique', in *Methoden der Sprachwissenschaft* (*Enzyklopädie der geisteswissenschaftlichen Arbeitsmethoden*, 4), München 1968, 39–63. See also A. Sechehaye, 'L'école genevoise de linguistique générale', *IF*, 44, 1927, 217–41; H. Frei, 'La linguistique saussurienne à Genève depuis 1939', *AL*, 5, 1945–9, 54–6; R. Godel, 'L'école saussurienne de Genève', in C. Mohrmann etc., edd., *Trends in European and American linguistics 1930–60*, Utrecht 1961, 294–9.

Chapter III

1 On the Prague School cf. J. Vachek, J. Dubský, *Dictionnaire de linguistique de l'école de Prague*, Utrecht 1960; J. Vachek, *A Prague School Reader in Linguistics*, Bloomington 1964; Id., *The Linguistic School of Prague. An Introduction to its Theory and Practice*, Bloomington 1966. See also N. Trubetzkoy, in *JPsych*, 30, 1933, 227–46; R. Jakobson, in *La cultura*, 12, 1933, 633–41; Ch. Møller, 'Thesen und Theorien der Prager Schule', *Acta Jutlandica*, 8: 2, 1936; A. Martinet, in *FM*, 6, 1938, 131–46; Id., in *CILP*, 6, 1938, 41–58 (cf. Id., *La linguistique synchronique. Études et recherches*, Paris 1965, 44 ff., 59 ff.); O. Leška, in *VJa*, 2: 5, 1953, 88–103; K. Horálek, in *SS*, 15, 1954, 29–38; B. Trnka etc., in *PhP*, 1, 1958, 33–40; J. Vachek, in *PhP*, 4, 1961, 65–78; T. V. Bulygina, in M. M. Guxman, V. N. Jarceva, edd., *Osnovnye napravlenija strukturalizma*, Moskva 1964, 46–126; J. Svoboda, in *PI*, 6, 1964, 239–42; G. C. Lepschy, in *Il Verri*, 24, 1967, 19–34.

2 *1st Congr. Ling.*, 33–6. On Trubeckoj and Jakobson information will be given below; on S. Karcevskij cf. R. Jakobson, in *CFS*, 14, 1956, 9–16; N. S. Pospelov, in *VJa*, 6: 4, 1957, 46–56.

3 *TCLP*, 1, 1929, 5–29.

4 *TCLP*, 2, 1929.

5 Cf. *TCLP*, 4, 1931.

6 *1st Congr. Phon.*, 106–7.

7 Cf. on the Circle's activity *ČMF*, 1928 ff., and *SS*, 1935 ff. See

158

Notes

Trubeckoj's bibliography in *TCLP*, 8, 1939, 335–42, and Jakobson's bibliography in *For Roman Jakobson*, The Hague 1956, 1–12 and in *To Honor Roman Jakobson*, The Hague 1967, xi–xxxiii. Of other prominent members of the Circle I shall mention J. Mukařovský, *Kapitoly z české poetiky*, Praha 1948; V. Mathesius, *Čestina a obecný jazykozpyt. Soubor statí*, Praha 1947. Here follows the complete list of the *Travaux*: 1, 1929: *Mélanges linguistiques dédiés au Ier Congrès des philologues slaves*; 2, 1929: R. Jakobson, *Remarques sur l'évolution phonologique du russe comparée à celle des autres langues slaves*; 3, 1930: B. Trnka, *On the Syntax of the English Verb from Caxton to Dryden*; 4, 1931: *Réunion phonologique internationale tenue à Prague (18–21 XII 1930)*; 5: 2, 1934: *Description phonologique du russe moderne, II*: N. Trubetzkoy, *Das morphonologische System der russischen Sprache* (fascicule 5: 1 was never published); 6, 1936: *Études dédiées au quatrième congrès de linguistes*; 7, 1939: N. S. Trubetzkoy, *Grundzüge der Phonologie*; 8, 1939: *Études phonologiques dédiées a la mémoire de M. le prince N. S. Trubetzkoy.*

8 *TCLP*, 1, 1929, 5–21.

9 Cf. N. S. Trubetzkoy, 'Gedanken über Morphonologie', *TCLP*, 4, 1931, 160–3.

10 Cf. on this point E. Cassirer, 'Le langage et la construction du monde des objets', *JPsych*, 30, 1933, 18–44, and for Cassirer's views on modern linguistics, Id., 'Structuralism in Modern Linguistics', *Word*, 1, 1945, 99–120.

11 Cf. P. L. Garvin, *A Prague School Reader on Esthetics, Literary Structure, and Style*, Washington 1964[3].

12 On Russian formalism cf. B. Tomaševskij, in *RESl*, 8, 1928, 226–40; V. Erlich, *Russian Formalism. History-Doctrine*, 's-Gravenhage 1955; T. Todorov, ed., *Théorie de la littérature*, Paris 1966.

13 On various aspects of Trubeckoj's work cf. W. F. Twaddell, in *AL*, 1, 1939, 60–3; R. Jakobson, in *AL*, 1, 1939, 64–76; Z. S. Harris, in *Lg*, 17, 1941, 345–9; A. Martinet, in *BSL*, 42 (125), 1942–5, 23–33 (and 45 (131), 1949, 19–22; cf. Id., *La linguistique synchronique* cit., 83 ff.); J. Krámský, in *AO*, 16, 1948, 225–64; E. Stolte, in *ZPhon*, 3, 1949, 277–82; R. Jagoditsch, in *WSlJb*, 4, 1955, 28–50; the proceedings of two symposia devoted to his work, in a supplement to *Phonetica*, 4, 1959, and in *WSlJb*, 11, 1964, 5–166. C. Hagège publishes extracts from Trubeckoj's correspondence in *Linguistique*, 1967: 1, 109–36.

14 Of Trubeckoj's works I shall mention 'Zur allgemeinen Theorie der phonologischen Vokalsysteme', *TCLP*, 1, 1929, 39–67; 'Die phonologischen Systeme', *TCLP*, 4, 1931, 96–116; *Anleitung zu phonologischen Beschreibungen*, Brno 1935 (in English trans. *Introduction to the Principles of Phonological Descriptions*, The Hague 1968); 'Essai d'une théorie des oppositions phonologiques', *JPsych*, 33, 1936, 5–18. His statements on comparative grammar (cf. 'Gedanken über das Indogermanenproblem', *AL*, 1, 1939, 81–9) undermine many traditional conceptions, and have not been generally accepted by structurally inclined comparatists (cf. for instance H. M. Hoenigswald, *Language*

Notes

Change and Linguistic Reconstruction, Chicago 1960; O. J. L. Szemerényi, *Trends and Tasks in Comparative Philology*, London 1961).

15 N. S. Trubetzkoy, *Grundzüge der Phonologie*, TCLP, 7, 1939, reproduced unchanged in a second edition, Göttingen 1958.

16 Cf. K. Bühler, *Sprachtheorie*, Jena 1934. On Bühler cf. G. Ungeheuer, 'Die kybernetische Grundlage der Sprachtheorie von Karl Bühler', *To Honor R. Jakobson* cit., 2067–86.

17 J. Winteler, *Die Kerenzer Mundart des Kantons Glarus*, Leipzig 1876.

18 H. Sweet, *A Handbook of Phonetics*, Oxford 1877, 103–5 with the distinction between narrow and broad transcription: the latter is a kind of phonological transcription. Cf. R. Jakobson, 'H. Sweet's Path Towards Phonemics', in C. E. Bazell etc., edd., *In Memory of J. R. Firth*, London 1966, 242–54. P. Passy must also be recalled; in his *Étude sur les changements phonétiques*, Paris 1890 (1891), A. Martinet, *Économie des changements phonétiques*, Berne 1955, 42 ff. finds a clear statement of the functional theory of phonetic change.

19 Cf. O. Jespersen, *Fonetik*, København 1897–9 (in German *Lehrbuch der Phonetik*, Leipzig 1904).

20 B. Collinder, in a polemic against phonology, *4th Congr. Ling.*, 122–7 quotes a passage from A. Noreen, *Vårt Språk*, Lund 1903 ff. (on this cf. J. Lotz, in *SL*, 8, 1954, 82–91), in which the notion of phoneme is clearly present. (Collinder continues his polemic against structuralism in *ASLU*, 1: 1, 1962, 1–15. A. Dauzat, in *FM*, 7, 1939, 40 states that he has anticipated the phonologists with his *Essai de méthodologie linguistique*, Paris 1906, 254–5).

21 F. de Saussure, *Cours de linguistique générale*, Paris 1949⁴, 36–7.

22 Cf. J. Baudouin de Courtenay, *Versuch einer Theorie phonetischer Alternationen. Ein Capitel aus der Psychophonetik*, Strassburg 1895 (a German summary of 'Próba teorji alternacyj fonetycznych', *Rozprawy Akademii Umiejętności: Wydział filologiczny*, 20, 1894, 219–364). On Baudouin cf. R. Jakobson, in *Slav. Rundsch.*, 1, 1929, 809–12; L. V., Ščerba, *Izbrannye raboty po russkomu jazyku*, Moskva 1957, 85–96 (an article of 1929); M. Weingart, in *Ročenka slovanského ústavu za rok 1929*, 1930, 172–98; M. Z. Arend, in *MPhon*, Jan.–March 1934, 2–3; M. Vasmer, in *ZPhon*, 1, 1947, 71–7; W. Doroszewski, in *PJ*, 1949: 1, 1–4; E. A. Zemskaja, in *RJaŠ*, 12: 6, 1951, 61–73; K. Nitsch, in *JP*, 34, 1954, 322–4; S. Urbańczyk, in *JP*, 34, 1954, 377–9 (and cf. *ib.*, 35, 1955, 233–6); W. Doroszewski, in *Nauka Polska*, 3, 1955: 1, 47–58 (reprinted in Id., *Studia i szkice językoznawcze*, Warszawa 1962, 68–75); Z. Štiber, in *VJa*, 4: 4, 1955, 88–93; L. Wald, in *LbR*, 7: 4, 1958, 5–10; A. A. Leont'ev, in *VJa*, 8: 6, 1959, 115–24; R. Jakobson, in *BPTJ*, 19, 1960, 3–34; A. A. Leont'ev, in *VJa*, 10: 4, 1961, 116–24; S. Szlifersztejn, in *PJ*, 1964: 7, 317–24; A. A. Leont'ev, in *RJaŠ*, 29: 2, 1965, 87–93; Id., in *IzvAN*, 25, 1966, 329–32; H. G. Schogt, in *Linguistique* 1966: 2, 15–29; R. Jagoditsch, in *To Honor R. Jakobson* cit., 1009–14. See also the commemorative vol. *I. A. Boduèn de Kurtenè (k 30-letiju so dnja smerti)*, Moskva 1960; and a Russian collection of his works, *Izbrannye trudy po obščemu jazykoznaniju*, Moskva 1963.

Notes

23 Cf. N. Trubetzkoy, in *JPsych*, 30, 1933, 229; J. R. Firth, 'The Word "Phoneme"', *MPhon*, April–June 1934, 44–6; D. Jones, *The History and Meaning of the Term 'Phoneme'*, Suppl. to *MPhon*, July–Dec. 1957 (1964²; also as an appendix to Id., *The Phoneme*, Cambridge 1967³). R. Godel, *Les sources manuscrites du Cours de linguistique générale de F. de Saussure*, Genève 1957, 160 refers us to the introduction of the term 'phonème' by A. Dufriche-Desgenettes in a paper read to the Société de linguistique de Paris on May 24 1873, cf. *BSL*, 2 (8), 1873, LXIII; *Revue critique*, 1, 1873, 368; cf. the interesting papers by the same author in *BSL*, 2 (12), 1875, CLXVIII–CLXXII; 3 (13), 1875, XLIV–XLVII; 3 (14), 1875, LXXI–LXXVI.

24 Cf. J. Baudouin, *Versuch* cit., 7; N. Kruševskij, 'Novejšija otkrytija v oblasti ario-evropejskago vokalizma,' *RFV*, 4, 2, 1880 (33–45) 36. Cf. R. Jakobson 'L'importanza di Kruszewski per lo sviluppo della linguistica generale', *RSlav*, 13, 1965, 3–23.

25 J. Baudouin, *Versuch* cit., 7; cf. Id., in *RFV*, 5, 3, 1881, 325, 338–40.

26 J. Baudouin, *Versuch* cit., 9.

27 F. de. Saussure, *Mémoire sur le système primitif des voyelles dans les langues indo-européennes*, Leipsick 1879, 12 (in *Recueil des publications scientifiques de Ferdinand de Saussure*, Genève 1922, 13).

28 Cf. A. Leskien, *Der Ablaut der Wurzelsilben im Litauischen*, Leipzig 1884.

29 Cf. J. Baudouin, *Podrobnaja programma lekcij v 1876–1877 uč. godu, Kazan'*, Varšava 1878, 56–61; 62–3; 85; and *ib.* for 1877–78, Varšava 1881, 85; 86–8; 105–6; 145; cf. *RFV*, 5, 3, 1881, 338.

30 Cf. J. Baudouin, *Versuch* cit., 3–4, 11–2 and for Saussure cf. R. Godel, *Les sources* cit., 40 ff.

31 Cf. J. Schrijnen, in *1st Congr. Phon.*, 115–18.

32 Cf. E. D. Polivanov, *Lekcii po vvedeniju v jazykoznanie i obščej fonetike*, Berlin 1923; Id., *Vvedenie v jazykoznanie*, Leningrad 1928; Id., *Stat'i po obščemu jazykoznaniju*, Moskva 1968.

33 Cf. L. V. Ščerba, *Court exposé de la prononciation russe*, Suppl. to *MPhon*, Nov.–Dec. 1911; Id., *Russkie glasnye v kačestvennom i količestvennom otnošenii*, S.-Peterburg 1912 (now in part reprinted in Id., *Izbrannye raboty po jazykoznaniju i fonetike*, I, Leningrad 1958, 124 ff.)

34 Cf. E. Sapir, 'Sound Patterns in Language', *Lg*, 1, 1925, 37–51 (reprinted in Id., *Selected Writings*, Berkeley 1949, 33–45).

35 Cf. N. Trubetzkoy, in *JPsych*, 30, 1933, 227 ff.

36 Cf. N. van Wijk, in *NTg*, 26, 1932, 65; N. Trubetzkoy, in *JPsych*, 30, 1933, 234. See Ph. Munot, in *Word*, 23, 1967, 414–21.

37 Cf. both definitions in N. S. Trubetzkoy, *Grundzüge* cit., 34.

38 Cf. *TCLP*, 2, 1929, 5.

39 Cf. *TCLP*, 4, 1931, 311.

40 Cf. N. Trubetzkoy, in *TCLP*, 1, 1929, 39 and in *SbÖAW*, 211: 4, 1930, 111.

41 Cf. N. Trubetzkoy, in *2nd Congr. Ling.*, 120 ff. See also K. Bühler, in *TCLP*, 4, 1931, 22–53 and in *2nd Congr. Phon.*, 162–9.

Notes

42 On the notion of linguistic consciousness cf. A. Mirambel, in *JPsych*, 51, 1958, 266–301; H. Weinrich, in Suppl. to *Phonetica*, 4, 1959, 45–58.

Chapter IV

1 Cf. R. Rask, *Ausgewählte Abhandlungen, hgg. von* L. Hjelmslev, *mit einer Einleitung von* H. Pedersen, Kopenhagen 1932–7; *Breve fra og til Rasmus Rask, udgivet ved* L. Hjelmslev, København 1941; L. Hjelmslev, 'Commentaires sur la vie et l'œuvre de Rasmus Rask', *CILP*, 10, 1951, 143–57. See also P. Diderichsen, *Rasmus Rask og den grammatiske tradition*, København 1960.

2 N. Ege, in *TCLC*, 5, 1949, 23–24 writes: 'It is Saussure who formulated the principle that language is form, . . . but it is Hjelmslev who followed it.'

3 Cf. V. Bröndal, *Substrat et emprunt en roman et en germanique. Étude sur l'histoire des sons et des mots*, Copenhague 1948; Id., *Essais de linguistique générale*, Copenhague 1943; Id., *Les parties du discours*, Copenhague 1948; Id., *Théorie des prépositions*, Copenhague 1950. Cf. Brøndal's bibliography in *Essais* cit., 141–68.

4 V. Brøndal, *Les parties* cit., 76.

5 V. Bröndal, in *AL*, 1, 1939, 2–10 (reprinted in *Essais* cit., 90–7).

6 For a more detailed exposition cf. G. C. Lepscky, in *ASNP*, 30, 1961, 223–9.

7 L. Hjelmslev, *Principes de grammaire générale, Kgl. Danske Vidensk. Selskab, Hist. Filol. Medd.*, 16: 1, 1928, 1969².

8 Cf. E. Fischer-Jørgensen, in *Lingua*, 2, 1949, 95–109; K. Togeby, in *Symposium*, 3, 1949, 226–37; B. Siertsema, *A Study of Glossematics. Critical Survey of its Fundamental Concepts*, The Hague 1955, 1965² (cf. W. Haas, in *ArchL*, 8, 1956, 93–110); H. Spang-Hanssen, 'Glossematics', in C. Mohrmann etc., edd., *Trends in European and American Linguistics 1930–60*, Utrecht 1961, 128–64. See the applications by K. Togeby, *Structure immanente de la langue française, TCLC*, 6, 1951, and Paris 1965²; E. Alarcos Llorach, *Gramática estructural (según la Escuela de Copenhague y con especial atención a la lengua española)*, Madrid 1951. For other information see G. C. Lepscky, in *ASNP*, 30, 1961, 229–48; K. Togeby, in *SNPh*, 37, 1965, 269–78; E. Fischer-Jørgensen, in *AL*, 9: 1, 1965, iii–xxii; J. Holt, in *Kratylos*, 12, 1967, 103–7; K. Togeby, ed., *La glossématique. L'héritage de Hjelmslev au Danemark*, Paris 1967; G. C. Lepschy, 'Hjelmslev e la glossematica', introduction to L. Hjelmslev, *I fondamenti della teoria del linguaggio*, Torino 1968, ix–xxxiv. Particularly important for glossematic discussions are the two periodicals *TCLC* and *AL*.

9 Cf. L. Hjelmslev, 'On the Principles of Phonematics', *2nd Congr. Phon.*, 49–54; H. J. Uldall, 'The Phonematics of Danish', *ib.*, 54–7.

10 L. Hjelmslev, 'Essai d'une théorie des morphèmes', *4th Congr. Ling.*, 140–51 (reprinted in Id., *Essais linguistiques, TCLC*, 12, 1959, 152–64).

11 L. Hjelmslev, *Sproget. En introduktion*, København 1963 (and in French trans. with a preface by A. J. Greimas, *Le langage. Une introduction*, Paris 1966).

Notes

12 L. Hjelmslev, *Omkring sprogteoriens grundlæggelse*, København 1943; in the English translation by F. J. Whitfield, revised by the author, *Prolegomena to a Theory of Language*, Suppl. to *IJAL*, 19: 1, 1953; Madison 1961². (I quote from the second edition of the English translation, and give the page references of the Danish original: this is more convenient because the pagination of the two English editions is different, but both give the references of the pages of the Danish original). The Danish text was summarized and discussed in an important article by A. Martinet, 'Au sujet des Fondements de la théorie linguistique de Louis Hjelmslev', *BSL*, 42 (124), 1942–5, 19–42; cf. also H. Vogt, in *AL*, 4, 1944, 94–8; C. E. Bazell, in *ArchL*, 1, 1949, 89–92; and on the English translation P. L. Garvin, in *Lg*, 30, 1954, 69–96; E. Haugen, in *IJAL*, 20, 1954, 247–51. Interesting contributions were published in *Recherches structurales 1949. Interventions dans le débat glossématique, publ. à l'occasion du cinquantenaire de M. Louis Hjelmslev, TCLC*, 5, 1949; and cf. G. L. Trager, in *SIL*, 8, 1950, 99; C. E. Bazell, in *ArchL*, 2, 1950, 177–80; R. Wells, in *Lg*, 27, 1951, 554–70; P. L. Garvin, in *IJAL*, 17, 1951, 252–5; C. F. Hockett, in *IJAL*, 18, 1952, 86–99; W. Preusler, in *IF*, 60, 1952, 329–31.

13 L. Hjelmslev, 'La stratification du langage', *Word*, 10, 1954, 163–88 (reprinted in Id., *Essais* cit., 36–68).

14 Determinations, interdependences, and constellations, if they are relations, are called selections, solidarities, combinations; if they are correlations, they are called specifications, complementarities, autonomies respectively. Hjelmslev gives some examples: there is selection between *sine* and the ablative in Latin; there is solidarity between case morpheme and number morpheme in a Latin noun; there is combination between *ab* and the ablative in Latin (because not only can an ablative occur without *ab*, but *ab* can also occur without an ablative, if it is used as a preverb). Examples of complementarity are vowel and consonant, or substantive and adjective; examples of autonomy which are not trivial and examples of specifications which are convincing seem to be more difficult to find. There is a basic point which is not clear. Determination, interdependence and constellation are three *different kinds of functions*. Relation and correlation are two *different kinds of functions*. The former three on the one hand and the second two on the other are also *different kinds of functions*, but this time in another sense: in what sense exactly Hjelmslev does not explain; S. M. Lamb, in *RomPh*, 19, 1966, 561 criticizes Hjelmslev for having put the three dependences at the base of his system, instead of the two notions of relation and correlation.

15 On glossematics cf. also C. H. Borgström, in *AL*, 5, 1945–9, 1–14; V. Skalička, in *SS*, 10, 1948, 135–42; E. Fischer-Jørgensen, in *TCLC*, 5, 1949, 214–34; S. Johansen, in *AL*, 6, 1950, 17–30; E. Fischer-Jørgensen, in *JACS*, 24, 1952, 611–17; Ead., in *AL*, 7, 1952, 8–39; F. J. Whitfield, in *For Roman Jakobson*, The Hague 1956, 670–6; E. Fischer-Jørgensen, *ib.*, 140–51; B. Siertsema, *8th Congr. Ling.*, 142–4; P. Diderichsen, *ib.*, 156–82; H. Spang-Hanssen, *ib.*,

Notes

182–94; Ju. K. Lekomcev, in *VJa*, 11: 4, 1962, 90–7; V. P. Murat, in M. M. Guxman, V. N. Jarceva, edd., *Osnovnye napravlenija strukturalizma*, Moskva 1964, 127–76; A. Rosetti, in *LbR*, 13, 1964, 543–551; S. M. Lamb, in *RomPh*, 19, 1966, 531–73; E. Fischer-Jørgensen, in *AL*, 10, 1966, 1–33.

Chapter V

1 On American linguistics cf. the important book by J. B. Carroll, *The Study of Language. A Survey of Linguistics and Related Disciplines in America*, Cambridge Mass., 1955². Other surveys: R. A. Hall, Jr., in *ArchL*, 3, 1951, 101–25 and 4, 1952, 1–16; H. Müller, in *ZPhon*, 7, 1953, 1–23; K. Koch, in *ÅVsLund*, 1954, 27–52; K. L. Pike, in *RBF*, 2, 1956, 207–16; N. D. Arutjunova, G. A. Klimov, E. S. Kubrjakova, 'Amerikanskij strukturalizm', in M. M. Guxman, V. N. Jarceva, *Osnovnye napravlenija strukturalizma*, Moskva 1964, 177–306; R. A. Hall, Jr., 'American linguistics, 1950–1960', *AION–L*, 6, 1965, 241–60. Useful information also in several articles in C. Mohrmann etc., edd., *Trends in European and American Linguistics 1930–60*, Utrecht 1961. A very useful aid is offered by E. P. Hamp, *A Glossary of American Technical Linguistic Usage 1925–50*, Utrecht 1957, enlarged ed., 1963. See also M. Joos, ed., *Readings in Linguistics. The Development of Descriptive Linguistics in America since 1925*, New York 1958² (a companion volume, E. P. Hamp, F. W. Householder, R. Austerlitz, edd., *Readings in Linguistics II*, Chicago 1966 is inspired by different criteria and covers a different and wider range of theoretical positions). In the last ten years there has been a widespread change of attitude towards Bloomfieldian and neo-Bloomfieldian linguistics: cf. K. V. Teeter, in *Word*, 20, 1964, 197–206; D. Hymes, in *AmA*, 66: 3, part 2, 1964, 6–56; S. R. Levin, in *FL*, 1, 1965, 83–94; P. Valesio, in *Il Verri*, 24, 1967, 35–74.

2 Cf. W. D. Whitney, *Language and the Study of Language*, New York 1867; Id., *The Life and Growth of Language*, New York 1875.

3 Cf. R. Jakobson, in *IJAL*, 10, 1944, 188–95; W. Goldschmidt, ed., *The Anthropology of F. Boas, AmA*, 61: 5, part 2, 1959, which includes another important contribution by R. Jakobson, 139–45.

4 F. Boas, *Handbook of American Indian Languages*, I, Washington 1911; II, Washington 1922; III, New York [Glückstadt] 1933–8.

5 Cf. R. A. Hall, Jr., in *ArchL*, 3, 1951, 112 ff.

6 Cf. R. A. Hall, Jr., in *ArchL*, 4, 1952, 9–15; J. B. Carroll, *The Study* cit., 140–95; W. G. Moulton, in C. Mohrmann etc., edd., *Trends* cit., 82–109. The work by C. C. Fries must be recalled in this context.

7 He knew Hebrew from childhood, and kept up his interest in Yiddish and Talmudic philology throughout his life. He took part in the activities of the Yiddish Scientific Institute and of the Conference for Jewish Relations. M. Swadesh in his obituary of Sapir, *Lg*, 15, 1939, 132–3, wrote openly about his fight against antisemitism and racial discrimination. It may be recalled that after having been strongly criticized in the Soviet Union, cf. for instance Mirra Moiseevna

Notes

Guxman, in *VJa*, 3: 1, 1954, 110–27, Sapir was 'rehabilitated' in an editorial article in *Voprosy Jazykoznanija*: 'the great American linguist E. Sapir has been accused without any ground of propagating racism. It is well known on the contrary that E. Sapir fought bitterly against antisemitism and every manifestation of racial discrimination, in the United States and other capitalist countries.', *VJa*, 5: 4, 1956, 5.

8 Cf. M. Swadesh, in *Lg*, 15, 1939, 132–3.

9 M. Joos, *Readings* cit., 25.

10 E. Sapir, *Language. An Introduction to the Study of Speech*, New York 1921 (I quote from the Harvest Books edition, New York 1957). Many important works are collected in D. G. Mandelbaum, ed., *Selected Writings of Edward Sapir in Language, Culture, and Personality*, Berkeley 1949 (I quote from this edition with the abbreviation *SW*); there is also a reduced version, E. Sapir, *Culture, Language, and Personality. Selected Essays* ed. by D. G. Mandelbaum, Berkeley 1957. On Sapir cf. F. Boas, in *IJAL*, 10, 1939–44, 58–63; L. Hjelmslev, in *AL*, 1, 1939, 76–7; M. Swadesh, in *Lg*, 15, 1939, 132–5; Z. S. Harris, in *Lg*, 27, 1951, 288–333; S. Newman, in *IJAL*, 17, 1951, 180–6; F. Mikuš, in *CFS*, 11, 1953, 11–30; R. J. Preston, in *AmA*, 68: 5, 1966, 1105–28.

11 Cf. E. Sapir, *Language* cit., 150, 155, 181–2; see also Z. S. Harris, in *Lg*, 27, 1951, 306 ff.

12 Cf. É. Benveniste, in *CILP*, 11, 1952–3, 33–50 (reprinted in Id., *Problèmes de linguistique générale*, Paris 1966, 99–118); Z. S. Harris, in *Lg*, 27, 1951, 293–4.

13 Cf. also E. Sapir, 'Grading. A Study in Semantics', *Philosophy of Science*, 11, 1944, 93–116 (reprinted in *SW*, 122–49); Id., *Totality*, Baltimore 1930; Id., M. Swadesh, *The Expression of the Ending-Point Relation in English, French, and German*, Baltimore 1932.

14 Cf. N. Chomsky, in *9th Congr. Ling.*, 944 ff.; Id., *Current Issues in Linguistic Theory*, The Hague 1964, 65 ff., Id., M. Halle, in *JL*, 1, 1965, 120; J. D. McCawley, in *IJAL*, 33, 1967, 106–111; K. L. Pike, *Language in Relation to a Unified Theory of the Structure of Human Behavior*, The Hague 1967², 352–3; C. F. Hockett, *The State of the Art*, The Hague 1968, 26–7.

15 E. Sapir, 'Sound Patterns in Language', *Lg*, 1, 1925, 37–51 (reprinted in *SW*, 33–45); cf. Z. S. Harris, in *Lg*, 27, 1951, 291 ff.

16 E. Sapir, 'La réalité psychologique des phonèmes', *JPsych*, 30, 1933, 247–65 (the English original in *SW*, 46–60).

17 E. Sapir, 'Language', in *Encyclopedia of the Social Sciences*, 9, New York 1933, 155–69 (reprinted in *SW*, 7–32).

18 E. Sapir, 'The Grammarian and his Language', *American Mercury*, 1, 1924, 149–55 (reprinted in *SW*, 150–9); see also Id., 'The Status of Linguistics as a Science', *Lg*, 5, 1929, 207–14 (reprinted in *SW*, 160–6).

19 L. Bloomfield, *An Introduction to the Study of Language*, New York 1914. Cf. G. S. Lane, in *SPh*, 42, 1945, 465–83; G. L. Trager, *ib.*, 43, 1946, 461–4; E. H. Sturtevant, in *Year Book of the American Philosophical Society*, 1949, 302–5; G. L. Trager, in *MPhon*, July–Dec. 1949,

Notes

24–6; R. A. Hall, Jr., in *Lingua*, 2, 1950, 117–23; B. Bloch, in *Lg*, 25, 1949, 87–94; C. C. Fries, in C. Mohrmann etc., edd., *Trends* cit., 196–224; Y. Malkiel, in *RomPh*, 16, 1962–3, 83–91 (reprinted in Id., *Essays on Linguistic Themes*, Oxford 1968, 165–74); E. A. Esper, *Mentalism and Objectivism in Linguistics. The Sources of L. Bloomfield's Psychology of Language*, New York 1968. See Bloomfield's bibliography in *Lg*, 25, 1949, 94–8.

20 Cf. L. Bloomfield, in *Lg*, 1, 1925, 1–5; *Lg*, 2, 1926, 153–64; *MPh*, 25, 1927, 211–30; *SPh*, 27, 1930, 553–7; *Philosophy of Science*, 2, 1935, 499–517; *Lg*, 12, 1936, 89–95; *Lg*, 17, 1941, 59; *Lg*, 20, 1944, 45–55; *Lg*, 22, 1946, 1–3; and see his reviews of works by E. Sapir, *CW*, 15, 1922, 142–3; O. Jespersen, *AJPh*, 43, 1922, 370–3; F. de Saussure, *MLJ*, 8, 1924, 317–19; O. Jespersen, *JEGP*, 26, 1927, 444–6; G. G. Kloeke, *Lg*, 4, 1928, 284–8; J. Ries, *Lg*, 7, 1931, 204–9; E. Hermann, *Lg*, 8, 1932, 220–33; W. Havers, *Lg*, 10, 1934, 32–40; A. F. Bentley, *Lg*, 12, 1936, 137–41; L. H. Gray, *MLF*, 24, 1939, 198–9; M. Swadesh, *Lg*, 19, 1943, 168–70; F. Bodmer, *AS*, 19, 1944, 211–13.

21 L. Bloomfield, *Language*, New York 1933 (I quote from the London 1957 edition).

22 For the importance of Bloomfield's work in the comparative field see his contributions on Central Algonquian, in *Lg*, 1, 1925, 130–56; *Lg*, 4, 1928, 99–100; *Language* cit., 359–60; and cf. E. Sapir, 'The Concept of Phonetic Law as Tested in Primitive Languages by L. Bloomfield', in S. A. Rice, ed., *Methods in Social Science: A Case Book*, Chicago 1931, 297–306 (reprinted in *SW*, 73–82); C. F. Hockett, 'Implications of Bloomfield's Algonquian Studies', *Lg*, 24, 1948, 117–31; É. Benveniste, in *CILP*, 11, 1954, 35 (reprinted in Id., *Problèmes* cit., 101); C. F. Voegelin, in *Lg*, 35, 1959, 109–25.

23 Cf. also L. Bloomfield, in *Lg*, 12, 1936, 93.

24 Cf. J. B. Watson, *Behaviorism*, Chicago 1924.

25 Cf. A. P. Weiss, *A Theoretical Basis of Human Behavior*, Columbus Ohio 1925, 1929²; Id., in *Lg*, 1, 1925, 52–7; see also in *Lg*, 4, 1928, 33–8.

26 Cf. L. Bloomfield, in *Lg*, 7, 1931, 219–21; 12, 1936, 89–95. See also M. Schlauch, in *Word*, 2, 1946, 25–36; P. K. Alkon, in *L&S*, 2, 1959, 37–51.

27 Cf. L. Bloomfield, 'Linguistic Aspects of Science', in O. Neurath etc., edd., *International Encyclopedia of Unified Science*, I, Chicago 1955, 215–77 (originally publ. as part 1:4 of the *Encyclopedia*, Chicago 1939).

28 Cf. also L. Bloomfield, 'Meaning', *Monatshefte*, 35, 1943, 101–6. See C. C. Fries, in *Lg*, 30, 1954, 59; Id., in C. Mohrmann etc., edd., *Trends* cit., 215.

29 L. Bloomfield, *Language* cit., 264: 'The meaningful features of linguistic signaling are of two kinds: lexical forms, which consist of phonemes, and grammatical forms, which consist of taxemes.' The parallelism of lexical and grammatical features can be exhibited as follows:

Notes

		lexical	grammatical
smallest meaningless unit	phememe	phoneme	taxeme
smallest meaningful unit (its meaning)	glosseme (noeme)	morpheme (sememe)	tagmeme (episememe)

30 Cf. The analysis of English phonemes in L. Bloomfield, *Language* cit., 129–38.
31 Cf. R. A. Hall, Jr., in *ArchL*, 3, 1951, 110; D. Hymes, in *AmA*, 66: 3, part 2, 1964, 45.
32 Cf. C. F. Hockett, *The State* cit., 24 ff.

Chapter VI

1 For these functions cf. R. Jakobson, 'Linguistics and Poetics', in Th. A. Sebeok, ed., *Style in Language*, New York 1960, 350–77. A bibliography 1916–67 of R. Jakobson appeared in *To Honor Roman Jakobson*, The Hague 1967, xi–xxxiii. A large collection of *Selected Writings* (which I quote with the abbreviation *SW*) is being published by Mouton, The Hague 1962 ff. A one volume collection has been ed. by N. Ruwet in French, *Essais de linguistique générale*, Paris 1963 (and in Italian, with preface by L. Heilmann, *Saggi di linguistica generale*, Milano 1966). Even though I shall not discuss Jakobson's stylistic and philological studies (from the volume *O češskom stixe, preimuščestvenno v sopostavlenii s russkim*, Moskva 1923, to the contributions on Russian epic, to the dissection, with C. Lévi-Strauss, of '"Les Chats" de Charles Baudelaire', *Homme*, 2, 1962, 5–21), I shall recall the programme for a structural treatment of linguistics and poetics which he published with Ju. Tynjanov, 'Problemy izučenija literatury i jazyka', *Novyj lef*, 1928:12, 36–7 (cf. L. Matejka, ed., *Readings in Russian Poetics*, Ann Arbor 1962, 99–102), and the mention he made, as early as 1919, of the distinction between sound and phoneme, in *Novejšaja russkaja poèzija. Nabrosok pervyj*, Praga 1921, 48 (the text is dated May 1919). (Cf. P. Ivić, in *Linguistics*, 18, 1965, 38).
2 Cf. the criticisms of some aspects of Jakobson's work in A. Martinet, *Économie des changements phonétiques. Traité de phonologie diachronique*, Berne 1955, 45–6, 73–7, 150; Id., *La linguistique synchronique. Études et recherches*, Paris 1965, 79–83, 97–105, 128, 133–8.
3 R. Jakobson, in *TCLP*, 2, 1929 (*SW*, 1, 7–116).
4 *1st Congr. Ling.*, 86.
5 R. Jakobson, in *TCLP*, 4, 1931, 247–67 (*SW*, 1, 202–20).
6 R. Jakobson, 'Les lois phoniques du langage enfantin et leur place dans la phonologie générale' (1939), in N. S. Troubetzkoy, *Principes de phonologie*, Paris (1949) 1957, 367–79 (*SW*, 1, 317–27); Id., *Kindersprache, Aphasie und allgemeine Lautgesetze*, Uppsala 1941 (*SW*, 1, 328–401)

Notes

and in English trans. *Child Language, Aphasia and Phonological Universals*, The Hague 1968; Id., 'Two Aspects of Language and Two Types of Aphasic Disturbances', in Id., M. Halle, *Fundamentals of Language*, 's-Gravenhage 1956, 53–82.

7 Cf. R. Jakobson, in *6th Congr. Ling.*, 5–18; in *TCLC*, 5, 1949, 205–13 (*SW*, 1, 418–25); in *Fundamentals* cit., 58 ff.

8 Cf. R. Jakobson, in *IJAL*, 19: 2, Suppl. (Memoir 8) 1953, 15; in *PSAM*, 12, 1961, 245–52.

9 R. Jakobson, in *1st Congr. Ling.*, 33 (*SW*, 1, 3).

10 R. Jakobson, 'Observations sur le classement phonologique des consonnes', *3rd Congr. Phon.*, 34–41 (*SW*, 1, 272–9).

11 R. Jakobson, 'On the Identification of Phonemic Entities', *TCLC*, 5, 1949, 205–13 (*SW*, 1, 418–25); Id., J. Lotz, 'Notes on the French Phonemic Pattern', *Word*, 5, 1949, 151–8 (*SW*, 1, 426–34).

12 Cf. A. M. Bell, *Visible Speech*, London 1867 (cf. J. R. Firth, in *TPhS*, 1946, 92–132; D. Jones, in *ZPhon*, 2, 1948, 127–35; E. Dieth, *Vademekum der Phonetik*, Bern 1950, 5–18; R. W. Albright, *The International Phonetic Alphabet. Its Background and Development*, *IJAL*, 24: 1, part 3, 1958, 30–4). See R. K. Potter, G. A. Kopp, H. C. Green, *Visible Speech*, New York 1947; a lucid presentation is offered by E. Pulgram, *Introduction to the Spectrography of Speech*, 's-Gravenhage 1959.

13 R. Jakobson, C. G. M. Fant, M. Halle, *Preliminaries to Speech Analysis. The Distinctive Features and their Correlates*, Cambridge Mass. 1967 (MIT Acoustics Lab. Techn. Rep. No. 13, 1st edition 1952).

14 Cf. E. C. Cherry, M. Halle, R. Jakobson, in *Lg*, 29, 1953, 34–46 (*SW*, 1, 449–63); M. Halle, in *Word*, 10, 1954, 197–209; R. Jakobson, M. Halle, 'Phonology and Phonetics', in *Fundamentals* cit., 1–51 (*SW*, 1, 464–504) (a slightly different version in L. Kaiser, ed., *Manual of Phonetics*, Amsterdam 1957, 215–51. There is now a 2nd revised edition of this *Manual*, ed. B. Malmberg, Amsterdam 1968). Cf. also E. C. Cherry, in *For Roman Jakobson*, The Hague 1956, 60–4; M. Halle, 'In Defense of the Number Two', *Studies J. Whatmough*, 's-Gravenhage 1957, 65–72; Y. Bar-Hillel, in *Word*, 13, 1957, 323-35; G. Ungeheuer, in SL, 13, 1959, 69–97. A comprehensive survey is given by P. Ivić, 'Roman Jakobson and the Growth of Phonology', *Linguistics*, 18, 1965, 35–78.

15 R. Jakobson, M. Halle, *Phonology and Phonetics* cit.

16 This is lost in *SW*, 1, 418–425, where minuses are inscribed in some of the empty squares of the matrix printed in *TCLC*, 5, 1949, 205–13, as noted by P. Ivić, in *Linguistics*, 18, 1965, 36.

17 E. C. Cherry, M. Halle, R. Jakobson, in *Lg*, 29, 1953, 37–8 (*SW*, 1, 453–4).

18 M. Halle, *In Defense* cit., 71.

19 R. Jakobson, M. Halle, *Phonology and Phonetics* cit., 47 (*SW*, 1, 499). The two articles by Y. R. Chao are 'The Non-Uniqueness of Phonemic Solutions of Phonetic Systems', *BIHP*, 4: 4, 1934, 363–97, and the review of *Preliminaries* cit., in *RomPh*, 8, 1954–5, 40–6.

Notes

20 Cf. his dissertations, A. Martinet, *La gémination consonantique d'origine expressive dans les langues germaniques*, Copenhague 1937; *La phonologie du mot en danois*, Paris 1937 (and in *BSL*, 38 (113), 1937, 169–266). See also his *Initiation pratique à l'anglais*, Lyon 1947, and the part devoted to pronunciation in I. de Stemann, *Manuel de langue danoise*, Paris 1949². A bibliography of his writings in *Linguistic Studies Presented to A. Martinet*, I, *Word*, 23, 1967, 1–11. See also the collective works edited by A. Martinet, *Le Langage* (*Encyclopédie de la Pléiade*), Paris 1968 (with important theoretical chapters by F. François, B. Malmberg, E. Buyssens, L. J. Prieto and others), and, on a more elementary level, *La Linguistique. Guide alphabétique*, Paris 1969.

21 Cf. A. Martinet, 'Neutralisation et archiphonème', *TCLP*, 6, 1936, 46–57; Id., 'Un ou deux phonèmes?', *AL*, 1, 1939, 94–103 (reprinted in Id., *La linguistique synchronique* cit., 109–23).

22 Cf. A. Martinet, 'La phonologie', *FM*, 6, 1938, 131–46; Id., 'Où en est la phonologie?', *Lingua*, 1, 1948, 34–58 (partly reprinted in Id., *La linguistique synchronique* cit., 59–76).

23 A. Martinet, 'Au sujet des Fondements de la théorie linguistique de Louis Hjelmslev', *BSL*, 42 (124), 1942–5, 19–42.

24 Cf. A. Martinet, 'Linguistique structurale et grammaire comparée', *TIL*, 1, 1956, 7–21; Id., 'Les "laryngales" indo-européennes', *8th Congr. Ling.*, 36–53, and several contributions in *Économie* cit.

25 A. Martinet, *Phonology as Functional Phonetics*, Oxford 1949.

26 See for example A. Martinet, *La prononciation du français contemporain. Témoignages recueillis en 1941 dans un camp d'officiers prisonniers*, Paris 1945; Id., *La description phonologique, avec application au parler franco-provençal d'Hauteville (Savoie)*, Genève 1956.

27 Cf. his contributions in *3rd Congr. Phon.*, 30–4; *CILP*, 6, 1938, 41–58; *TCLP*, 8, 1939, 273–88; *Lingua*, 1, 1948, 34–58; *Word*, 8, 1952, 1–32; *Word*, 9, 1953, 1–11; L. Kaiser, ed., *Manual* cit., 252–73; *5th Congr. Phon.*, 82–102. General bibliographical information in A. G. Juilland, 'A Bibliography of Diachronic Phonemics', *Word*, 9, 1953, 198–208. See also the *Miscelánea homenaje a André Martinet*, ed. D. Catalán, Tenerife Canarias 1957, with the revealing title *Estructuralismo e historia*.

28 A. Martinet, *Économie* cit.

29 Cf. on these questions the observations by O. Szemerényi, 'Structuralism and Substratum. Indo-Europeans and Aryans in the Ancient Near East', *Lingua* 13, 1964, 1–29 (also W. S. Allen, in *Lingua*, 13, 1965, 111–24; O. Szemerényi, in *Phonetica*, 17, 1967, 65–99); Id., 'Methodology of Genetic Linguistics', in *Methoden der Sprachwissenschaft* (*Enzyklopädie der geisteswissenschaftlichen Arbeitsmethoden*, *4*), München 1968, 3–38.

30 A. Martinet, 'La double articulation linguistique', *TCLC*, 5, 1949, 30–7; Id., 'Arbitraire linguistique et double articulation', *CFS*, 15, 1957, 105–16 (both articles are reprinted with some modifications in Id., *La linguistique synchronique* cit., 11–35).

31 A. Martinet, 'Quelques traits généraux de la syntaxe', *Free University Quarterly*, 1959: 2, 115–129; Id., 'Elements of a Functional Syntax',

Notes

Word, 16, 1960, 1–10; Id., 'Réflexions sur la phrase', in *Language and Society. Essays A. M. Jensen*, Copenhagen 1961, 113–18 (reprinted in Id., *La linguistique synchronique* cit., 222–9); Id., 'De la variété des unités significatives', *Lingua*, 11, 1962, 280–8 (reprinted in Id., *La linguistique synchronique* cit., 168–79); Id., 'The Foundations of a Functional Syntax', *MSLL*, 17, 1964, 25–36; Id., 'L'autonomie syntaxique', *Méthodes de la grammaire*, Paris 1966, 49–64.

32 A. Martinet, *Elements of General Linguistics*, London 1964, is the translation of *Éléments de linguistique générale*, Paris 1960.

33 A. Martinet, *A Functional View of Language*, Oxford 1962.

34 Cf. P. L. Garvin, in Th. A. Sebeok, ed., *Current Trends* cit., 1, 499–522; and *L'école de Prague d'aujourd'hui*, *TLP*, 1, 1964.

35 I should like at least to mention here L. Tesnière, *Éléments de syntaxe structurale*, Paris 1959; G. Guillaume, *Langage et science du langage*, Paris 1964; E. Buyssens, *Les langages et le discours. Essai de linguistique fonctionnelle dans le cadre de la sémiologie*, Bruxelles 1943, now revised as *La communication et l'articulation linguistique*, Bruxelles 1967. Some further bibliographical references in G. C. Lepschy, *ASNP*, 34, 1965, 236–40.

36 But cf. G. Mounin, 'La notion de système chez A. Meillet', *Linguistique*, 1966: 1, 17–29.

37 See the series of books by É. Benveniste, devoted to comparative grammar, which started with his *Origines de la formation des noms en indo-européen*, Paris 1935; and the essays collected in Id., *Problèmes de linguistique générale*, Paris 1966.

38 Again a number of books of great importance also from a methodological point of view, was produced by J. Kuryłowicz, starting with his *Études indoeuropéennes*, Kraków 1935. See also the essays collected in Id., *Esquisses linguistiques*, Wrocław 1960.

39 Cf. L. V. Ščerba, *Izbrannye raboty po jazykoznaniju i fonetike*, I, Leningrad 1958.

40 Cf. A. A. Reformatskij, 'O sootnošenii fonetiki i grammatiki (morfologii)', in *Voprosy grammatičeskogo stroja*, Moskva 1955, 92–112.

41 Cf. R. I. Avanesov, 'O trex tipax naučno-lingvističeskix transkripcij', *Slavia*, 25, 1956, 347–71. For the three groups cf. M. Halle, in Th. A. Sebeok, ed., *Current trends* cit., 1, 5–21.

42 Cf. G. C. Lepschy, 'Nota sullo strutturalismo e sulla linguistica sovietica recente', *SSL*, 7, 1967, 1–22. See also the bibliographical surveys, B. A. Serebrennikov, ed., *Obščee jazykoznanie (1918–1962)*, Moskva 1965; A. A. Reformatskij, ed., *Strukturnoe i prikladnoe jazykoznanie (1918–1962)*, Moskva 1965.

43 Cf. S. K. Šaumjan, *Strukturnaja lingvistika*, Moskva 1965.

Chapter VII

1 Cf. W. F. Twaddell, in *LL*, 2: 1, 1949, 4–11; C. F. Voegelin, Th. A. Sebeok, in *IJAL*, 19: 2, Suppl. (Memoir 8), 1953, 56–61; C. C. Fries, in *Lg*, 30, 1954, 57–68; D. Gerhardt, in *ZPhon*, 8, 1954, 1–32; N. Chomsky,

Notes

in *MSLL*, 8, 1955, 141–50 (and discussion 150–8); T. De Mauro, in *WSLJb, Ergänzungsband* 6, 1967, 17–23; Id., *LeSt*, 2, 1967, 131–51.

2 Cf. R. Wells, 'Meaning and Use', *Word*, 10, 1954, 235–50.

3 S. Ullmann, *The Principles of Semantics*, Glasgow 1951, Oxford 1963³; Id., *Semantics. An Introduction to the Science of Meaning*, Oxford 1962; Id., *Language and Style. Collected Papers*, Oxford 1964.

4 Cf. B. L. Whorf, *Four Articles on Metalinguistics*, Washington 1949; Id., *Language, Thought and Reality. Selected Writings*, ed. J. B. Carroll, New York 1956.

5 Cf. A. Korzybski, *Science and Sanity*, Lakeville Conn. 1933, 1958⁴; S. Chase, *The Tyranny of Words*, New York 1938; S. I. Hayakawa, *Language in Thought and Action*, London 1952; and the anthology from the first ten years of *ETC*. (1943–53), ed. S. I. Hayakawa, *Language, Meaning and Maturity*, New York 1954.

6 Cf. J. Trier, *Der deutsche Wortschatz im Sinnbezirk des Verstandes. Die Geschichte eines sprachlichen Feldes*, I, Heidelberg 1931; and much information in S. Ullmann, *The Principles* cit.

7 Cf. C. E. Osgood, 'The Nature and Measurement of Meaning', *Psychol. Bull.*, 49, 1952, 197–237; C. E. Osgood, G. J. Suci, P. H. Tannenbaum, *The Measurement of Meaning*, Urbana Ill. 1957; J. G. Snider, C. E. Osgood, edd., *Semantic Differential Technique. A Sourcebook*, Chicago 1969.

8 Cf. Y. Bar-Hillel, R. Carnap, 'An Outline of a Theory of Semantic Information', in Y. Bar-Hillel, *Language and Information. Selected Essays in their Theory and Application*, Reading Mass. 1964, 221–74; Y. Bar-Hillel, 'Semantic Information and its Measures', *ib.*, 298–310; J. G. Kemeny, in *JSL*, 18, 1953, 289–308; R. S. Wells, in *PSAM*, 12, 1961, 237–44. On philosophical semantics cf. the anthology L. Linsky, ed., *Semantics and the Philosophy of Language*, Urbana Ill. 1952; see A. Tarski, *Logic, Semantics, Metamathematics*, Oxford 1956; H. Reichenbach, *Elements of Symbolic Logic*, New York 1947, 1956⁵; R. Carnap, *Introduction to Semantics*, Cambridge Mass. 1942, 1948³; Id., *Meaning and Necessity. A Study in Semantics and Modal Logic*, Chicago 1947, 1956²; L. Wittgenstein, *Philosophical Investigations*, Oxford 1953; W. v. O. Quine, *From a Logical Point of View*, Cambridge Mass. 1953; Id., *Word and Object*, New York 1960; J. L. Austin, *Philosophical Papers*, ed. by J. O. Urmson, G. J. Warnock, Oxford 1961. T. De Mauro, *Introduzione alla semantica*, Bari 1965 is mainly a discussion of the semantic conceptions of B. Croce, F. de Saussure, L. Wittgenstein.

9 Cf. for instance E. A. Nida, in *Word*, 7, 1951, 1–14; K. L. Pike, in *MSLL*, 8, 1955, 134–41; F. G. Lounsbury, *ib.*, 158–64; P. L. Garvin, in *Lg*, 34, 1958, 1–32; M. Joos, in *SIL*, 13, 1958, 53–70; L. Hjelmslev, in *8th Congr. Ling.*, 636–54; P. Ziff, *Semantic Analysis*, Ithaca New York 1960; L. Hjelmslev, in *Language and Society. Essays A. M. Jensen*, Copenhagen 1961, 55–63; R. B. Lees, in *MSLL*, 13, 1962, 5–20; M. Joos, *ib.*, 41–48; J. J. Katz, J. A. Fodor, in *Lg*, 39, 1963, 170–210; S. M. Lamb, in *AmA*, 66: 3, part 2, 1964, 57–78; L. J. Prieto, *Principes*

Notes

de noologie, The Hague 1964; G. C. Lepschy, in *Linguistics*, 15, 1965, 40–65; A. J. Greimas, *Sémantique structurale*, Paris 1966; Id., *Modelli semiologici*, Urbino 1967.

10 Z. S. Harris, 'Morpheme Alternants in Linguistic Analysis', *Lg*, 18, 1942, 169–80.

11 E. A. Nida, *Morphology*, Ann Arbor 1946, 1949². Cf. Id., in *Lg*, 24, 1948, 168–77, and 414–41.

12 C. F. Hockett, 'Problems of Morphemic Analysis', *Lg*, 23, 1947, (321–43) 322.

13 E. A. Nida, 'The Identification of Morphemes', *Lg*, 24, 1948, (414–41) 420.

14 C. F. Hockett, 'Linguistic Elements and their Relations', *Lg*, 37, 1961, 29–53.

15 Cf. C. E. Bazell, in *ArchL*, 1, 1949, 1–15; *Litera*, 1, 1954, 17–31; *Word*, 18, 1962, 132–42. Other interesting discussions: Z. S. Harris, in *IJAL*, 10, 1944, 196–211; D. L. Bolinger, in *Word*, 4, 1948, 18–23; S. Saporta, in *Word*, 12, 1956, 9–14; A. Koutsoudas, in *IJAL*, 29, 1963, 160–70 (and cf. *ib.*, 171–4); R. Fowler, in *Lingua*, 12, 1963, 165–76; W. Winter, in *Linguistics*, 3, 1964, 5–18; and the important contributions by P. H. Matthews, in *JL*, 1, 1965, 139–71; *FL*, 1, 1965, 268–89; R. H. Robins, 'Morphology and the Methods of Synchronic Linguistics', in *Methoden der Sprachwissenschaft* (*Enzyklopädie der geisteswissenschaftlichen Arbeitsmethoden*, 4), München 1968, 65–88.

16 On immediate constituent analysis cf. K. L. Pike, in *Lg*, 19, 1943, 65–82; R. S. Wells, in *Lg*, 23, 1947, 81–117; R. S. Pittman, in *Lg*, 24, 1948, 287–92; E. A. Nida, in *Lg*, 24, 1948, 168–77; S. Chatman, in *Word*, 11, 1955, 377–85; J. C. Street, in I. Rauch etc., edd., *Approaches in Linguistic Methodology*, Madison Wisc. 1967, 89–114.

17 M. Swadesh, 'The Phonemic Principle', *Lg*, 10, 1934, 117–29.

18 Cf. for instance C. Ebeling, in *Lingua*, 3, 1953, 309–21; B. Bloch, in *Lg*, 29, 1953, 59–61; W. Haas, in *Word*, 15, 1959, 1–18.

19 N. Chomsky, 'Semantic Considerations in Grammar', *MSLL*, 8, 1955, 141–50 and discussion 150–8.

20 Y. R. Chao, 'The Non-Uniqueness of Phonemic Solutions of Phonetic Systems', *BIHP*, 4: 4, 1934, 363–97; W. F. Twaddell, *On Defining the Phoneme*, Baltimore 1935; C. F. Hockett, 'A System of Descriptive Phonology', *Lg*, 18, 1942, 3–21; B. Bloch, 'A Set of Postulates for Phonemic Analysis', *Lg*, 24, 1948, 3–46 (on which cf. A. A. Hill, in *Lg*, 43, 1967, 203–7); B. Bloch, G. L. Trager, *Outline of Linguistic Analysis*, Baltimore 1942; G. L. Trager, H. L. Smith, Jr., *An Outline of English Structure* (SIL, Occasional Papers 3), Washington 1951.

21 C. F. Hockett, *The State of the Art*, The Hague 1968.

22 Bloomfield uses the expression 'rigid system' reviewing Saussure, in *MLJ*, 8, 1923, 317–19, and reviewing Jespersen's *Philosophy of Grammar*, in *JEGP*, 26, 1927, 444–6; both passages are reproduced in Hockett, *The State* cit., 11–12; on Chomsky and 'well definition' cf. *ib.*, 40 and passim. On the notion of 'computability' cf. M. Davis, *Computability and Unsolvability*, New York 1958.

Notes

23 C. F. Hockett, *The State* cit., 34, 76.

24 Cf. on B. Bloch the obituary by M. Joos, in *Lg*, 43, 1967, 3–18 (with Bloch's bibliography, *ib.*, 18–19). For Trager's thought cf. the volumes of *SIL*.

25 Cf. R. A. Hall, Jr., *Leave your Language Alone!*, Ithaca New York 1950 (revised edition with the title *Linguistics and your Language*, New York 1960); Id., *Introductory Linguistics*, Philadelphia 1964.

26 Cf. A. A. Hill, *Introduction to Linguistic Structures. From Sound to Sentence in English*, New York 1958.

27 Cf. Y. R. Chao, *Language and Symbolic Systems*, Cambridge 1968; J. H. Greenberg, *Essays in Linguistics*, Chicago 1957; D. Bolinger, *Aspects of Language*, New York 1968; P. L. Garvin, *On Linguistic Method. Selected Papers*, The Hague 1964.

28 Cf. Z. S. Harris, in *Lg*, 16, 1940, 216–31; *Lg*, 17, 1941, 345–9; *Lg*, 18, 1942, 169–80; *Lg*, 18, 1942, 238–45; *Lg*, 20, 1944, 181–205; *Lg*, 21, 1945, 121–7; *Lg*, 22, 1946, 161–83; *Lg*, 27, 1951, 288–333; *Word*, 10, 1954, 146–62; *IJAL*, 20, 1954, 259–70; *Lg*, 31, 1955, 190–222.

29 Z. S. Harris, *Methods in Structural Linguistics*, Chicago 1951 (with the title *Structural Linguistics*, Phoenix Books 1960).

30 Cf. Z. S. Harris, 'Discourse Analysis', *Lg*, 28, 1952, 1–30 and 474–94; Id., 'Co-occurrence and Transformation in Linguistic Structure', *Lg*, 33, 1957, 283–340; Id., 'Transformational Theory', *Lg*, 41, 1965, 363–401. See the books by Z. S. Harris, *String Analysis of Sentence Structure*, The Hague 1962; Id., *Discourse Analysis Reprints*, The Hague 1963; Id., *Mathematical Structures of Language*, New York 1968.

31 J. T. Waterman, *Perspectives in Linguistics*, Chicago 1963, 98.

32 J. P. Thorne, in *JL*, 1, 1965, 74.

33 Cf. C. F. Hockett, *A Manual of Phonology*, *IJAL*, 21: 4, part 1, 1955; Id., *A Course in Modern Linguistics*, New York 1958; Id., in *Lg*, 18, 1942, 3–21; *Lg*, 23, 1947, 321–43; *American Scientist*, 36, 1948, 558–72; *IJAL*, 14, 1948, 269–71; *SIL*, 7, 1949, 29–51; *SIL*, 8, 1950, 5–11; *SIL*, 10, 1952, 27–39; *Word*, 10, 1954, 210–34; *SIL*, 12, 1957, 57–73; *Human Biology*, 31, 1959, 32–9; *Scientific American*, 203: 3, 1960, 88–96; *PSAM*, 12, 1961, 220–36; *Lg*, 37, 1961, 29–53; *Lg*, 41, 1965, 185, 204.

34 Cf. C. F. Hockett, 'Two Models of Grammatical Description', *Word*, 10, 1954, 210–34; Id., *The State* cit., 24.

35 Cf. C. F. Hockett, 'Language, Mathematics, and Linguistics', in Th. A. Sebeok, ed., *Current Trends in Linguistics*, 3, The Hague 1966, 155–304 (also as a book, The Hague 1967), 156 note 3; Id., *The State* cit., 62 note 27.

36 Cf. S. M. Lamb, *Outline of Stratificational Grammar*, Washington 1966; see also H. A. Gleason, 'The Organization of Language: A Stratificational View', *MSLL*, 17, 1964, 75–95; S. M. Lamb, 'On Alternation, Transformation, Realization, and Stratification', *ib.*, 105–22.

37 Cf. K. L. Pike, in *Word*, 3, 1947, 155–72; *Word*, 8, 1952, 106–21; *8th Congr. Ling.*, 363–71.

Notes

38 Cf. K. L. Pike, *Phonetics. A Critical Analysis of Phonetic Theory and a Technique for the Practical Description of Sounds*, Ann Arbor 1943; Id., *Phonemics. A Technique for Reducing Languages to Writing*, Ann Arbor 1947.

39 Cf. K. L. Pike, *The Intonation of American English*, Ann Arbor 1945; Id., *Tone Languages*, Ann Arbor 1948; Id., in *5th Congr. Phon.*, 105–17.

40 K. L. Pike, *Language in Relation to a Unified Theory of the Structure of Human Behavior*, The Hague 1967² (prelim. ed. Glendale Calif. 1954 ff.).

41 Cf. K. L. Pike, 'Language as Particle, Wave, and Field', *The Texas Quarterly*, 2: 2, 1959, 37–54; Id., in *Lg*, 38, 1962, 242–4.

42 For the terminology cf. K. L. Pike, 'On Tagmemes Née Gramemes', *IJAL*, 24, 1958, 273–8. See also the survey Id., 'A Guide to Publications Related to Tagmemic Theory', in Th. A. Sebeok, ed., *Current Trends* cit., 3, 365–94.

43 Cf. K. L. Pike, in *Lg*, 38, 1962, 221–44; *Lg*, 39, 1963, 216–30.

44 K. L. Pike, *A Guide* cit., 367–8. Cf. also R. Longacre, in *Lg*, 36, 1960, 63–88; S. Belasco, in *Lingua*, 10, 1961, 375–90; Id., in *Linguistics*, 10, 1964, 5–15; R. Longacre, in *Lg*, 41, 1965, 65–76; and cf. *MSLL*, 20, 1967, 1–139.

45 Cf. D. Jones, *The Phoneme*, Cambridge 1950, 1967³.

46 Cf. J. R. Firth, *Papers in Linguistics 1934–51*, London 1957; F. R. Palmer, ed., *Selected Papers of J. R. Firth 1952–59*, London 1968; see also Id., *Speech*, London 1930; Id., *The Tongues of Men*, London 1937, both republished by P. Strevens, London 1964. Active in Britain are linguists with different interests and theoretical backgrounds such as L. R. Palmer (cf. *An Introduction to Modern Linguistics*, London 1936; a new edition is announced), C. E. Bazell (cf. *Linguistic Form*, Istanbul 1953), S. Ullmann (cf. his works on semantics, already quoted), W. Haas (cf. 'Zero in Linguistic Description', in *Studies in Linguistic Analysis*, Oxford 1957, 33–53), and others on whose work Firth's influence is more easily detectable, such as W. S. Allen (cf. 'Relationship in Comparative Linguistics', *TPhS*, 1953, 52–108), R. H. Robins (cf. *General Linguistics. An Introductory Survey*, London 1964), P. D. Strevens (cf. *Papers in Language and Language Teaching*, London 1965), F. R. Palmer (cf. *A Linguistic Study of the English Verb*, London 1965), J. Lyons (cf. *Structural Semantics*, Oxford 1963; *Introduction to Theoretical Linguistics*, Cambridge 1968).

47 Cf. the linguistic articles in *BSOAS*; interesting contributions in the quoted 'Special Publication of the Philological Society', *Studies in Linguistic Analysis*, Oxford 1957; and in the essays edited by C. E. Bazell, etc., *In Memory of J. R. Firth*, London 1966 (with Firth's bibliography, ix–xi) (on which cf. J.-M. Waaub, in *RPA*, 6, 1967, 43–72). See also J. Vachek, in *SFFBU*, 8 (A7), 1959, 106–13; G. L. Bursill-Hall, in *JCLA*, 6, 1960–1, 124–35 and 164–91; R. H. Robins, in C. Mohrmann etc., edd., *Trends in Modern Linguistics*, Utrecht 1963, 11–37; E. S. Kubrjakova, in M. M. Guxman, V. N. Jarceva, edd., *Osnovnye napravlenija strukturalizma*, Moskva 1964, 307–53; J. Cygan, in *KNf*, 11, 1964, 368–73; K. Kohler, in *Phonetica*, 17, 1967, 193–201;

a critique from a transformationalist viewpoint D. T. Langendoen, *The London School of Linguistics: A Study of the Linguistic Theories of B. Malinowski and J. R. Firth*, Cambridge Mass. 1968.

48 The exposition in the text is based mainly on M. A. K. Halliday, 'Categories of the Theory of Grammar', *Word*, 17, 1961, 241–92, and Id., A. McIntosh, P. Strevens, *The Linguistic Sciences and Language Teaching*, London 1964. See also M. A. K. Halliday, 'Grammatical Categories in Modern Chinese', *TPhS*, 1956, 177–224; Id., 'Some Aspects of Systematic Description and Comparison in Grammatical Analysis', in *Studies in Linguistic Analysis* cit., 54–67; Id., *The Language of the Chinese 'Secret History of the Mongols'*, Oxford 1959; Id., 'Class in Relation to the Axes of Chain and Choice in Language', *Linguistics*, 2, 1963, 5–15; Id., 'Syntax and the Consumer', *MSLL*, 17, 1964, 11–24; Id., 'Lexis as a Linguistic Level', *In Memory of J. R. Firth* cit., 148–62; Id., A. McIntosh, *Patterns of Language*, London 1966; Id., 'Some Notes on "Deep" Grammar', *JL*, 2, 1966, 57–67; Id., *Intonation and Grammar in British English*, The Hague 1967; Id., *Grammar, Society and the Noun*, London 1967; Id., 'Notes on Transitivity and Theme in English', *JL*, 3, 1967, 37–81, 199–244, and 4, 1968, 179–215. Cf. also R. M. W. Dixon, *Linguistic Science and Logic*, The Hague 1963; Id., *What is Language? A New Approach to Linguistic Description*, London 1965; and the discussion between P. H. Matthews, *JL*, 2, 1966, 101–10 and M. A. K. Halliday, *ib.*, 110–18.

Chapter VIII

1 F. de Saussure, *Cours de linguistique générale*, Paris 1949⁴, 317.

2 N. Chomsky, *Syntactic Structures*, 's-Gravenhage 1957.

3 Cf. also N. Chomsky, 'Three Models for the Description of Language', *IRE Trans. Inf. Theory*, IT2: 3, 1956, 113–24 (also in R. D. Luce etc., edd., *Readings in Mathematical Psychology*, II, New York 1965, 105–24).

4 N. Chomsky, *Syntactic Structures* cit., 80.

5 Cf. N. Chomsky, *Syntactic Structures* cit., 45; Id., *Current Issues in Linguistic Theory*, The Hague 1964, 62; Id., *Topics in the Theory of Generative Grammar*, The Hague 1966, 26, 52 (this last also in Th. A. Sebeok, ed., *Current Trends in Linguistics*, 3, The Hague 1966, 1–60).

6 N. Chomsky, *Aspects of the Theory of Syntax*, Cambridge Mass. 1965.

7 N. Chomsky, *Aspects* cit., 135–6.

8 N. Chomsky, *Aspects* cit., 141.

9 N. Chomsky, *Aspects* cit., 141.

10 N. Chomsky, *Three Models* cit., 123.

11 N. Chomsky, *Syntactic Structures* cit., 101 stated that 'not even the weakest semantic relation (factual equivalence) holds in general between active and passive'. This was based on examples like *everyone in the room knows at least two languages* and *at least two languages are known by everyone in the room*, the first of which would be true and the second false, if of the two persons in the room one knew only French and

Notes

German and the other knew only Spanish and Italian. That the example is not convincing has been noted, among others, by J. J. Katz, P. M. Postal, *An Integrated Theory of Linguistic Descriptions*, Cambridge Mass. 1964, 72.

12 N. Chomsky, *Aspects* cit., 132.

13 N. Chomsky, *Aspects* cit., 89 and cf. 99 ff.

14 N. Chomsky, *Aspects* cit., 141.

15 N. Chomsky, *Aspects* cit., 70.

16 N. Chomsky, *Aspects* cit., 162–3.

17 N. Chomsky, *Aspects* cit., 229.

18 N. Chomsky, *Aspects* cit., 163.

19 On this point are obviously relevant the positions of S. K. Šaumjan, *Strukturnaja lingvistika*, Moskva 1965 (and cf. N. Chomsky, *Aspects* cit., 124 ff.); more recent developments seem to point to a 'lexicalist' view of the base (which would make it more language-specific and less universal), and to the necessity of considering surface structures in the semantic interpretation. Cf. N. Chomsky, 'The Formal Nature of Language', in E. H. Lenneberg, *Biological Foundations of Language*, New York 1967 (397–442), 407; Id., 'Remarks on Nominalization', in R. Jacobs, P. Rosenbaum, edd., *Readings in English Transformational Grammar*, Waltham, Massachusetts 1970, 184–221.

20 Cf. M. Halle, *The Sound Pattern of Russian*, 's-Gravenhage 1959; Id., 'Phonology in Generative Grammar', *Word*, 18, 1962, 54–72; N. Chomsky, 'Some General Properties of Phonological Rules', *Lg*, 43, 1967, 102–28; N. Chomsky, M. Halle, *The Sound Pattern of English*, New York 1968; P. M. Postal, *Aspects of Phonological Theory*, New York 1968; R. T. Harms, *Introduction to Phonological Theory*, Englewood Cliffs 1968. See also the discussion between F. W. Householder (*JL*, 1, 1965, 13–34; 2, 1966, 99–100) and N. Chomsky, M. Halle (*JL*, 1, 1965, 97–138), on which cf. P. H. Matthews, in *JL*, 4, 1968, 275–83 with Halle's rejoinder, in *JL*, 5, 1969, 305–8.

21 Cf. J. J. Katz, J. A. Fodor, 'The Structure of a Semantic Theory', *Lg*, 39, 1963, 170–210; J. J. Katz, P. M. Postal, *An Integrated Theory* cit., 14.

22 N. Chomsky, 'The General Properties of Language', in F. L. Darley, ed., *Brain Mechanisms Underlying Speech and Language*, New York 1967 (73–88), 76.

23 E. H. Lenneberg, *Biological Foundations* cit., 220.

24 N. Chomsky, *The General Properties* cit., 84.

25 Cf. N. Chomsky, *Cartesian Linguistics*, New York 1966.

26 J. J. Katz, 'Mentalism in Linguistics', *Lg*, 40, 1964 (124–37), 130.

27 J. J. Katz, *The Philosophy of Language*, New York 1967, 181.

28 The bibliography of transformational grammar is already extensive; cf. W. Orr Dingwall, *Transformational Generative Grammar. A Bibliography*, Washington 1965; Id., in *Lingua*, 16, 1966, 292–316; G. C. Lepschy, 'La grammatica trasformazionale. Nota introduttiva e bibliografia', *SSL*, 4, 1964, 87–114; Id., 'La grammatica trasformazionale. Studi recenti', *SSL*, 6, 1966, 171–91; H. Krenn, K. Müllner,

Notes

Bibliographie zur Transformationsgrammatik, Heidelberg 1968. See also E. Bach, *An Introduction to Transformational Grammars*, New York 1964; A. Koutsoudas, *Writing Transformational Grammars: An introduction*, New York 1966; N. Ruwet, *Introduction à la grammaire générative*, Paris 1967. An important collection is J. A. Fodor, J. J. Katz, edd., *The Structure of Language. Readings in the Philosophy of Language*, Englewood Cliffs, New Jersey 1964. Several of Chomsky's works are collected in Italian translation in N. Chomsky, *Saggi linguistici*, Torino 1969 foll. (preface by G. Lepschy, vol. 1, 9–17).

Chapter IX

1 Cf. P. Guiraud, *Bibliographie critique de la statistique linguistique*, Utrecht 1954.
2 Cf. P. Guiraud, *Les caractères statistiques du vocabulaire*, Paris 1954; Id., *Problèmes et méthodes de la statistique linguistique*, Paris 1960; G. Herdan, *Language as Choice and Chance*, Groningen 1956; Id., *Type-Token Mathematics. A Handbook of Mathematical Linguistics*, 's-Gravenhage 1960; Id., *The Calculus of Linguistic Observations*, 's-Gravenhage 1962; Id., *Quantitative Linguistics*, London 1964; Id., *The Advanced Theory of Language as Choice and Chance*, Berlin 1966; Ch. Muller, *Initiation à la statistique linguistique*, Paris 1968.
3 Cf. G. Herdan, 'The Crisis in Modern General Linguistics', *Linguistique*, 1967: 1, 27–37 which is a violent criticism of Chomsky's theories.
4 G. K. Zipf, 'Relative Frequency as a Determinant of Phonetic Change', *HSPh*, 40, 1929, 1–95; Id., *Selected Studies of the Principle of Relative Frequency in Language*, Cambridge Mass. 1932; Id., *The Psycho-Biology of Language. An Introduction to Dynamic Philology*, Boston 1935 (cf. M. Joos, in *Lg*, 12, 1936, 196–210; G. K. Zipf, in *Lg*, 13, 1937, 60–70); Id., *Human Behavior and the Principle of Least Effort. An Introduction to Human Ecology*, Cambridge Mass. 1949.
5 Cf. N. S. Trubetzkoy, *Grundzüge der Phonologie*, Göttingen 1958², 230–41.
6 The examples in the text are taken from Guiraud's handbooks quoted above.
7 Cf. P. Guiraud, *Problèmes* cit., 86 ff.; G. Herdan, *Language* cit., 31 ff. See G. U. Yule, *The Statistical Study of Literary Vocabulary*, Cambridge 1944.
8 Cf. B. Mandelbrot, 'Structure formelle des textes et communication; deux études', *Word*, 10, 1954, 1–27 and 11, 1955, 424; P. Guiraud, *Problèmes* cit., 31 ff.
9 Cf. P. Guiraud, *Caractères* cit., 3.
10 Cf. P. Guiraud, *Problèmes* cit., 19.
11 Cf. M. Swadesh, in *PAPhilosS*, 96, 1952, 452–63; *AmA*, 55, 1953, 349–52; *IJAL*, 21, 1955, 121–37. See also A. L. Kroeber, C. D. Chrétien, in *Lg*, 13, 1937, 83–103; C. D. Chrétien, in *UCPL*, 1: 2, 1943, 11–20; A. L. Kroeber, in *Lg*, 36, 1960, 1–21. For a survey cf. D. Hymes, in *CAnthr*, 1, 1960, 3–44.

Notes

12 Cf. Y. Bar-Hillel, *Language and Information. Selected Essays on their Theory and Application*, Reading Mass. 1964, 288. For the present section I have made much use of the essays collected in this volume.

13 We say that *l* is the log of a number *n* (to the base *b*) if $b^l = n$. If in our formula the log is to the base 2, then the information is measured in *bits* (or binary digits).

14 Cf. H. Nyquist, in *Bell System Technical Journal*, 3, 1924, 324–46; R. V. L. Hartley, *ib.*, 7, 1928, 535–63; L. Szilard, in *Zeitschrift für Physik*, 53, 1929, 840–56.

15 Cf. C. E. Shannon, in *Bell System Technical Journal*, 27, 1948, 379–423 and 623–56; and as a volume Id., *The Mathematical Theory of Communication*, Urbana Ill. 1949, followed by W. Weaver, 'Recent Contributions to the Mathematical theory of Communication', *ib.*, 93–117. N. Wiener, *Cybernetics or Control and Communication in the Animal and the Machine*, New York 1948; Id., *The Human Use of Human Beings. Cybernetics and Society*, London 1950. Bibliographical information in F. L. Stumpers, *A Bibliography of Information Theory–Communication Theory–Cybernetics*, Cambridge Mass. 1953 ff. For the linguistic interest of this trend cf. G. A. Miller, *Language and Communication*, New York 1951; C. Cherry, *On Human Communication*, Cambridge Mass. 1957; I. M. Jaglom, R. L. Dobrušin, A. M. Jaglom, 'Teorija informacii i lingvistika', *VJa*, 9: 1, 1960, 100–10; R. Jakobson, 'Linguistics and Communication Theory', *PSAM*, 12, 1961, 245–52.

16 Cf. Y. Bar-Hillel, *Language and Information* cit., 283–97.

17 There are three journals devoted exclusively to this field: *MT*, from 1954, *MPiPL* from 1957, *TA* from 1960. Bibliographical information in É. and K. Delavenay, *Bibliography of Mechanical Translation*, 's-Gravenhage 1960; *Mašinnyj perevod 1949–60. Bibliografičeskij ukazatel' ITM i VT ANSSSR*, Moskva 1962. Simple introductions: É. Delavenay, *La machine à traduire*, Paris 1959 (and in English, *An Introduction to Machine Translation*, London 1960); D. Ju. Panov, *Avtomatičeskij perevod*, Moskva 1956 (1958², and in English, *Automatic Translation*, London 1960); G. Mounin, *La machine à traduire. Histoire des problèmes linguistiques*, The Hague 1964. Important works are W. N. Locke, A. D. Booth, edd., *Machine Translation of Languages. Fourteen essays*, New York 1955; A. D. Booth, L. Brandwood, J. P. Cleave, edd., *Mechanical Resolution of Linguistic Problems*, London 1958; A. G. Oettinger, *Automatic Language Translation*, Cambridge Mass. 1960; H. P. Edmundson, ed., *Proceedings of the National Symposium on Machine Translation* (1960), London 1961; National Physical Laboratory (Teddington), Symp. 13, *1961 International Conference on Machine Translation of Languages and Applied Language Analysis*, London 1962; A. Ghizzetti, ed., *Automatic Translation of Languages* (1962), Oxford 1966; A. D. Booth, ed., *Machine Translation*, Amsterdam 1967. On the use of computers in linguistics cf. S. M. Lamb, in *Lg*, 37, 1961, 382–412; P. L. Garvin, in *Lg*, 38, 1962, 385–9; Id., ed., *Natural Language and the Computer*

Notes

(1960–1), New York 1963; Id., B. Spolsky, edd., *Computation in Linguistics. A Case Book*, Bloomington 1966; D. G. Hays, ed., *Readings in Automatic Language Processing*, New York 1966; Id., *Introduction to Computational Linguistics*, London 1967. On algebraic linguistics cf. S. Marcus, *Algebraic Linguistics; Analytical Models*, New York 1967; Id., *Introduction mathématique à la linguistique structurale*, Paris 1967.

18 Cf. D. Ju. Panov, *Avtomatičeskij perevod*[2] cit., 7; Id. etc., *Perevodnaja mašina P. P. Trojanskogo*, Moskva 1959.

19 Cf. A. D. Booth etc., edd., *Mechanical Resolution* cit., 1 ff.; W. Weaver's *Translation* (1949) is printed in W. N. Locke etc., edd., *Machine Translation* cit., 15–23; the contribution by Booth and Richens, *ib.*, 24–46.

20 E. Reifler, *Studies in Mechanical Translation*, Washington 1950 ff.

21 V. A. Oswald, S. L. Fletcher, 'Proposals for the Mechanical Resolution of German Syntax Patterns', *MLF*, 36, 1951, 81–104.

22 Cf. Y. Bar-Hillel, *Language and Information* cit., 8–9.

23 Cf. D. Ju. Panov, *Avtomatičeskij perevod*[2] cit., 8; see L. Dostert, in W. N. Locke etc., edd., *Machine Translation* cit., 124–35; P. L. Garvin, in W. M. Austin, ed., *Papers in Linguistics in Honor of L. Dostert*, The Hague 1967, 46–56.

24 Cf. D. Ju. Panov, *Avtomatičeskij perevod*[2] cit., 41. The sentence quoted is the first one of the introduction of W. E. Milne, *Numerical Solution of Differential Equations*, New York 1953.

25 Cf. Y. Bar-Hillel, *Language and Information* cit., 185–218.

26 Cf. G. Mounin, *Les belles infidèles*, Paris 1955; E. Cary, *La traduction dans le monde moderne*, Genève 1956; A. V. Fedorov, *Vvedenie v teoriju perevoda*, Moskva 1958[2]; R. A. Brower, ed., *On Translation*, Cambridge Mass. 1959; G. Mounin, *Les problèmes théoriques de la traduction*, Paris 1963; I. I. Revzin, V. Ju. Rozencvejg, *Osnovy obščego i mašinnogo perevoda*, Moskva 1964.

27 Cf. M. Gross, 'On the Equivalence of Models of Language Used in the Fields of Mechanical Translation and Information Retrieval', a report presented at the 1962 Venice Conference (A. Ghizzetti, ed., *Automatic Translation* cit., 123–37) also in *Problems of Information Storage and Retrieval*, 2, 1964, 43–57. Cf. also P. Postal, *Constituent Structure. A Study of Contemporary Models of Syntactic Description*, The Hague 1964.

28 Cf. the journal *Methodos* (1949 ff.) and S. Ceccato, *Language and the Table of Ceccatieff*, Paris 1951; Id. etc., *Linguistic Analysis and Programming for Mechanical Translation* (*Mechanical Translation and Thought*), *Methodos*, 12: 45–7, 1960; and a collection of his works, Id., *Un tecnico fra i filosofi*, Padova 1964 ff. See also G. Mounin, in *TA*, 3, 1962, 92–5; V. A. Matveenko, in *VJa*, 13: 4, 1964, 120–9.

29 Y. Bar-Hillel, *Language and Information* cit., 9.

Select Bibliography

Only a few texts are given here, for a quick orientation. They have already been quoted in the relevant notes.

Chapter I J. Piaget, *Le structuralisme*, Paris 1968.

Chapter II F. de Saussure, *Cours de linguistique générale*, Lausanne 1916; in English trans. by W. Baskin, *Course in General Linguistics*, New York 1959, London 1960. There is an invaluable critical edition: F. de Saussure, *Cours de linguistique générale, édition critique par* R. Engler, Wiesbaden 1967 foll.

Chapter III N. S. Trubetzkoy, *Grundzüge der Phonologie*, Prague 1939; Göttingen 1958[2]; a useful anthology: J. Vachek, *A Prague School Reader in Linguistics*, Bloomington 1964.

Chapter IV L. Hjelmslev, *Omkring sprogteoriens grundlæggelse*, København 1943; in English trans. by F. J. Whitfield, *Prolegomena to a Theory of Language*, Baltimore 1953; Madison 1961[2]; Id., *Essais linguistiques*, Copenhague 1959.

Chapter V E. Sapir, *Language. An Introduction to the Study of Speech*, New York 1921; D. G. Mandelbaum, ed., *Selected Writings of Edward Sapir in Language, Culture, and Personality*, Berkeley 1949; L. Bloomfield, *Language*, New York 1933.

Chapter VI R. Jakobson, *Selected Writings*, The Hague 1962 foll.; A. Martinet, *Eléments de linguistique générale*, Paris 1960; in English trans. by E. Palmer, *Elements of General Linguistics*, London 1964.

Chapter VII Z. S. Harris, *Methods in Structural Linguistics*, Chicago 1951 (with the title *Structural Linguistics*, Chicago 1960); C. F. Hockett, *A Course in Modern Linguistics*, New York 1958; K. L. Pike, *Language in Relation to a Unified Theory of the Structure of Human Behavior*, Glendale 1954–60; The Hague 1967[2]; a useful anthology: M. Joos, ed., *Readings in Linguistics. The Development of Descriptive Linguistics in America since 1925*, Washington 1957; 1958[2]; J. R. Firth, *Papers in Linguistics 1934–1951*, London 1957; M. A. K. Halliday, A. McIntosh, P. Strevens, *The Linguistics Sciences and Language Teaching*, London 1964.

Chapter VIII N. Chomsky, *Syntactic Structures*, 's-Gravenhage 1957; Id., *Aspects of the Theory of Syntax*, Cambridge Mass. 1965; Id., M. Halle, *The Sound Pattern of English*, New York 1968; a useful anthology: J. A. Fodor, J. J. Katz, edd., *The Structure of Language*, Englewood Cliffs 1964.

Chapter IX Much information in G. A. Miller, *Language and Communication*, New York 1951; C. Cherry, *On Human Communication*, Cambridge Mass. 1957; Y. Bar-Hillel, *Language and Information. Selected Essays on their Theory and Application*, Reading Mass. 1964.

Appendix

𒀭𒀭𒀭𒀭𒀭𒀭

Chapter I Introductory Notions
For the history of linguistics: A. Varvaro, *Storia, problemi e metodi della linguistica romanza,* Napoli 1968; R. Posner's supplement, 'Thirty Years On', in the new edition of I. Iordan and J. Orr, *An Introduction to Romance Linguistics,* Oxford 1970; N. Drăganu, *Storia della sintassi generale,* Bologna 1970 (Italian trans. of *Istoria sintaxei,* Bucureşti 1945); H. Arens, *Sprachwissenschaft,* is available in a second enlarged edition, Freiburg-München 1969; so is M. Leroy, *Les grands courants de la linguistique moderne,* Bruxelles 1971; O. Szemerényi, *Richtungen der modernen Sprachwissenschaft, Teil I: Von Saussure bis Bloomfield 1916–1950,* Heidelberg 1971; G. Mounin, *La linguistique du XXe siècle,* Paris 1972; G. Helbig, *Geschichte der neueren Sprachwissenschaft,* Leipzig 1973; W. Motsch, *Zur Kritik des sprachwissenschaftlichen Strukturalismus,* Berlin 1974; D. Hymes, ed., *Studies in the History of Linguistics. Traditions and Paradigms,* Bloomington 1974; T. A. Amirova etc., *Očerki po istorii lingvistiki,* Moskva 1975 (German trans. *Abriss der Geschichte der Linguistik,* Leipzig 1980); L. Heilmann, E. Rigotti, edd., *La linguistica. Aspetti e problemi,* Bologna 1975; Th. A. Sebeok, ed., *Current Trends in Linguistics,* vol. 13, *Historiography of Linguistics,* The Hague 1975, includes E. F. K. Koerner, 'European Structuralism: Early Beginnings', 717–827; R. Engler, 'European Structuralism: Saussure', 829–86; G. C. Lepschy, 'European Structuralism: Post-Saussurean Schools', 887–902; D. Hymes, J. Fought, 'American Structuralism', 903–1176; E. Stankiewicz, 'Bibliography of the History of Linguistics', 1381–1446; H. Parret, ed., *History of Linguistic Thought and Contemporary Linguistics,* Berlin 1976; J.-P. Corneille, *La linguistique structurale. Sa portée, ses limites,* Paris 1976; E. F. K. Koerner, *Western Histories of Linguistic Thought. An Annotated Chronological Bibliography 1822–1976,* Amsterdam 1978; R.H. Robins, *A Short History of Linguistics,* London 1979 (second edition); G. Sampson, *Schools of Linguistics. Competition and Evolution,* London 1980 (to be used with caution). Since 1974 there is a journal devoted to the history of linguistics: *Historiographia Linguistica,* published by Benjamins in Amsterdam and edited by E. F. K. Koerner.

Useful collections of essays: A. A. Hill, ed., *Linguistics Today,* New York 1969; J. Lyons, ed., *New Horizons in Linguistics,* Harmondsworth 1970; N. Minnis, ed., *Linguistics at Large,* London 1971; W. O. Dingwall, ed., *A Survey of Linguistic Science,* University of Maryland 1971; T. Bolelli, ed., *Linguistica generale, strutturalismo, linguistica storica,* Pisa 1971; B. Malmberg, ed., *Readings in Modern Linguistics. An Anthology,* The Hague-Stockholm

Appendix

1972; F. W. Householder, ed., *Syntactic Theory, I: Structuralist*, Harmondsworth 1972. To the proceedings of the first nine congresses of linguists quoted on pp. 13–14 we can now add: *Actes du Xe congrès international des linguistes, Bucarest, 28 août – 2 septembre 1967*, Bucarest 1969–70; *Proceedings of the Eleventh International Congress of Linguists, Bologna-Florence, Aug. 28–Sept. 2, 1972*, Bologna 1974; *Proceedings of the Twelfth International Congress of Linguists, Vienna, August 28–September 2, 1977*, Innsbruck 1978. See also a selection of papers prepared for the 10th International Congress: M. Bierwisch, K. E. Heidolph, edd., *Progress in Linguistics*, The Hague 1970.

Among the monographs by individual authors: Ju. D. Apresjan, *Idei i metody sovremennoj strukturnoj lingvistiki (kratkij očerk)*, Moskva 1966 (trans. *Principles and Methods of Contemporary Structural Linguistics*, The Hague 1973, and cf. my review in *Lingua*, 47, 1979, 353–6); M. Bierwisch, *Strukturalismus* (1966, quot. p. 153 n. 9) is available in English: *Modern Linguistics. Its Development, Methods and Problems*, The Hague 1971 (cf. my review in *Journal of Literary Semantics*, 5:1, 1976, 46–7); G. Mounin, *Clefs pour la linguistique*, Paris 1968: F. R. Adrados, *Lingüística estructural*, Madrid 1969; R. Jakobson, 'Linguistics', in *Main Trends of Research in the Social and Human Sciences*, I, Paris 1970, 419–63 (also *Main Trends in the Science of Language*, London 1973); D. Crystal, *Linguistics*, Harmondsworth 1971; L. R. Palmer, *Descriptive and Comparative Linguistics. A Critical Introduction*, London 1972 (offers an interesting double discussion of structural linguistics and comparative philology, together with a vigorous critique of generative grammar).

Among dictionaries and encyclopaedias of linguistics, after the excellent, concise, pre-structuralist work by J. Marouzeau, *Lexique de la terminologie linguistique*, Paris 1951[3], I shall quote: J. Knobloch, *Sprachwissenschaftliches Wörterbuch*, Heidelberg 1961 foll. (last fascicule: 4, 1974, to 'deskriptive'); Ae. Springhetti, *Lexicon linguisticae et philologiae*, Romae 1962; M. Pei, *Glossary of Linguistic Terminology*, New York 1966; O. S. Axmanova, *Slovar' lingvističeskix terminov*, Moskva 1966; D. Steible, *Concise Handbook of Linguistics*, London 1967; F. Lázaro Carreter, *Diccionario de términos filológicos*, Madrid 1968[3]; R. Nash, *Multilingual Lexicon of Linguistics and Philology. English, Russian, German, French*, Coral Gables, Florida 1968 (only listing and translating terms; no definitions); G. R. Cardona, *Linguistica generale*, Roma 1969; R. Simone, *Piccolo dizionario della linguistica moderna*, Torino 1969; A. Martinet, ed., *La linguistique. Guide alphabétique*, Paris 1969; A. R. Meetham, ed., *Encyclopedia of Linguistics, Information and Control*, Oxford 1969; R. Simeon, ed., *Enciklopedijski rječnik lingvističkih naziva na 8 jezika*, Zagreb 1969; H. J. Vermeer, *Einführung in die linguistische Terminologie*, München 1971; R. R. K. Hartmann, F. C. Stork, *Dictionary of Language and Linguistics*, London 1972; W. Ulrich, *Wörterbuch. Linguistische Grundbegriffe*, Kiel 1972; O. Ducrot, T. Todorov, *Dictionnaire encyclopédique des sciences du langage*, Paris 1972 (trans. *Encyclopaedic Dictionary of the Sciences of Language*, Oxford 1981; particularly useful for the literary and critical sections; see also the Italian trans., with my preface, *Dizionario enciclopedico delle scienze del linguaggio*, Torino 1972); D. È. Rozental', M. A. Telenkova, *Spravočnik lingvističeskix terminov*, Moskva 1972; J. Dubois etc., *Dictionnaire de linguistique*, Paris 1973; Th. Lewandowski, *Linguistisches Wörterbuch*, Heidelberg 1973–75 (three vols); G. Mounin, *Dictionnaire de la linguistique*, Paris 1974; W. Welte, *Moderne Linguistik. Terminologie/*

Appendix

Bibliographie. Ein Handbuch und Nachschlagewerk auf der Basis der generativ-transformationnellen Sprachtheorie, München 1974; W. Abraham, *Terminologie zur neueren Linguistik*, Tübingen 1974; H. Stammerjohann, H. Janssen, *Handbuch der Linguistik*, München 1975; J.-F. Phelizon, *Vocabulaire de la linguistique*, Paris 1976; A.-J. Greimas, J. Courtès, *Sémiotique. Dictionnaire raisonné de la théorie du langage*, Paris 1979; D. Crystal, *A First Dictionary of Linguistics and Phonetics*, London 1980. Cf. the surveys by M.-E. Conte, 'Dizionari e glossari di terminologia linguistica', in *Studi di Grammatica Italiana*, 3, 1973, 273–87, and by S. C. Sgroi, 'A proposito dei dizionari di linguistica', in *Siculorum Gymnasium*, 27, 1974, 464–503.

Concerning non-linguistic structuralism, to the works mentioned on p. 153 n. 11 I shall add: Cl. Lévi-Strauss, the four volumes of *Mythologiques: Le cru et le cuit*, Paris 1964 (trans. *The Raw and the Cooked*, London 1970); *Du miel aux cendres*, Paris 1966 (trans. *From Honey to Ashes*, London 1973); *L'origine des manières de table*, Paris 1968 (trans. *The Origin of Table Manners*, London 1978); *L'homme nu*, Paris 1971; *La pensée sauvage*, Paris 1962 (trans. *The Savage Mind*, London 1966); the new edition of the 1947 fundamental *Les structures élémentaires de la parenté*, Paris 1967 (trans. *The Elementary Structures of Kinship*, London 1968); *Anthropologie structurale deux*, Paris 1973 (trans. *Structural Anthropology II*, London 1977; see also the trans. of the first collection: *Structural Anthropology*, London 1968). M. Foucault: see the trans. of *Les mots et les choses*, *The Order of Things*, London 1970; also *L'archéologie du savoir*, Paris 1969 (trans. *The Archaeology of Knowledge*, London 1972); *Surveiller et punir. Naissance de la prison*, Paris 1975 (trans. *Discipline and Punish. The Birth of the Prison*, London 1977); *Histoire de la sexualité. La volonté de savoir*, Paris 1976 (trans. *The History of Sexuality*, I, London 1979); important also his earlier *Histoire de la folie à l'âge classique*, Paris 1961 (new edition 1972) (trans. *Madness and Civilization. A History of Insanity in the Age of Reason*, London 1971); *Naissance de la clinique*, Paris 1963 (new edition 1972) (trans. *The Birth of the Clinic*, London 1973); see also the collection edited by D. F. Bouchard, *Language, Countermemory, Practice*, Oxford 1977, and C. Gordon, ed., *Power and Knowledge. Selected Interviews and Other Writings 1972–77*, Hassocks 1980. J. Lacan: see the trans. *Écrits. A Selection*, London 1977; and *Les quatre concepts fondamentaux de la psychanalyse*, Paris 1973 (trans. *The Four Fundamental Concepts of Psychoanalysis*, London 1977). J. Derrida: see the trans. *Of Grammatology*, Baltimore and London 1976; *La voix et le phénomène*, Paris 1967 (trans. *Speech and Phenomena*, Evanston Ill. 1973); *L'écriture et la différence*, Paris 1967 (trans. *Writing and Difference*, London 1978); *Marges de la philosophie*, Paris 1972; *La dissémination*, Paris 1972; *Positions*, Paris 1972; *La carte postale. De Socrate à Freud et au-delà*, Paris 1980. R. Barthes: see the trans. *Critical Essays*, Evanston Ill. 1972; *Le degré zéro de l'écriture*, Paris 1953 (*Writing Degree Zero*, London 1967); *Mythologies*, Paris 1957 (partial trans. *Mythologies*, London 1972); Éléments de sémiologie, Paris 1964 (trans. *Elements of Semiology*, London 1967); *Système de la mode*, Paris 1967; *S/Z*, Paris 1970 (trans. *S/Z*, London 1975); *Sade, Fourier, Loyola*, Paris 1971 (trans. *Sade, Fourier, Loyola*, London 1977); *Le plaisir du texte*, Paris 1973 (trans. *The Pleasure of the Text*, London 1976); *Roland Barthes*, Paris 1975 (trans. *Roland Barthes*, London 1977); *Fragments d'un discours amoureux*, Paris 1977 (trans. *A Lover's Discourse. Fragments*, London 1979); *Leçon*, Paris 1978; *La chambre claire. Note sur la photographie*, Paris 1980; a collection of essays ed. by S. Heath, *Image, Music, Text*, London 1977. J.

Appendix

Kristeva, Σημειωτική. *Recherches pour une sémanalyse,* Paris 1969; *Le texte du roman.* *Approche sémiologique d'une structure discursive transformationnelle,* The Hague 1970; *La révolution du langage poétique,* Paris 1974; *Polylogue,* Paris 1977; and a collection trans. mostly from *Polylogue: Desire in Language. A Semiotic Approach to Literature and Art,* Oxford 1981. More precise and penetrating are the analyses by G. Genette, *Figures,* Paris 1966; *Figures II,* Paris 1969; *Figures III,* Paris 1972 (trans. *Narrative Discourse,* Oxford 1980); *Mimologiques. Voyage en Cratylie,* Paris 1976; *Introduction à l'architexte,* Paris 1979; Ph. Sollers, *Logiques,* Paris 1968; Cl. Bremond, *Logique du recit,* Paris 1973. T. Todorov, *Introduction à la littérature fantastique,* Paris 1970; *Poétique de la prose,* Paris 1971 (trans. *The Poetics of Prose,* Oxford 1977); *Théories du symbole,* Paris 1977; *Les genres du discours,* Paris 1978; *Symbolisme et interprétation,* Paris 1978. For semiotics, see U. Eco, *Trattato di semiotica generale,* Milano 1975 (more legible than the English version *A Theory of Semiotics,* Bloomington 1976; see my review in *Lg,* 53, 1977, 711–14). There have been interesting developments in semiotic criticism around the Italian journal *Strumenti Critici* (Torino 1966 foll.): cf. M. Corti, *Metodi e fantasmi,* Milano 1969; *Principi della comunicazione letteraria,* Milano 1976 (trans. *An Introduction to Literary Semiotics,* Bloomington 1978); C. Segre, *I segni e la critica,* Torino 1969 (trans. *Semiotics and Literary Criticism,* The Hague 1973); *Le strutture e il tempo,* Torino 1974 (trans. *Structures and Time,* Chicago 1979); *Semiotica filologica,* Torino 1979; D'A. S. Avalle, *Tre saggi su Montale,* Torino 1970; *Modelli semiologici nella Commedia di Dante,* Milano 1975.

Of a different character are the studies which can be loosely grouped under the label 'text linguistics'; they try to define and analyse 'texts' rather than 'sentences', and have literary, semiotic and logical connexions; cf. H. Weinrich, *Tempus. Besprochene und erzählte Welt,* Stuttgart 1964 (second revised edition 1971); R. Harweg, *Pronomina und Textkonstitution,* München 1968; J. S. Petöfi, *Transformationsgrammatiken und eine ko-textuelle Texttheorie. Grundfragen und Konzeptionen,* Frankfurt a. M. 1971; W. Dressler, *Einführung in die Text-linguistik,* Tübingen 1971; W.-D. Stempel, ed., *Beiträge zur Textlinguistik,* München 1971; T. A. van Dijk, *Some Aspects of Text Grammars. A Study in Theoretical Linguistics and Poetics,* The Hague 1972; *Beiträge zur generativen Poetik,* München 1972; *Text and Context. Explorations in the Semantics and Pragmatics of Discourse,* London 1977; M.-E. Conte, ed., *La linguistica testuale,* Milano 1977.

Piaget's *Le structuralisme* (p. 153 n. 11) is available in English trans.: *Structuralism,* London 1971; see also F. Wahl etc., *Qu'est-ce que le structuralisme?,* Paris 1968, with chapters by O. Ducrot (linguistics), T. Todorov (poetics), D. Sperber (anthropology), M. Safouan (psychoanalysis), F. Wahl (philosophy). Other collections: *Yale French Studies,* 36–37, 1966, has been reprinted: J. Ehrmann, ed., *Structuralism,* Garden City, New York 1970; S. Chatman, S. R. Levin, edd., *Essays on the Language of Literature,* Boston 1967; M. Lane, ed., *Structuralism. A Reader,* London 1970; D. C. Freeman, ed., *Linguistics and Literary Style,* New York 1970; R. Macksey, E. Donato, edd., *The Languages of Criticism and the Sciences of Man. The Structuralist Controversy,* Baltimore 1970; A. J. Greimas, ed., *Essais de sémiotique poétique,* Paris 1972; D. Robey, ed., *Structuralism. An Introduction,* Oxford 1973; J. Sturrock, ed., *Structuralism and Since. From Lévi-Strauss to Derrida,* Oxford 1979; J. V. Harari, ed., *Textual Strategies. Perspectives in Post-Structuralist Criticism,* London 1980.

Monographic discussions: J.-M. Auzias, *Clefs pour le structuralisme,* Paris

184

Appendix

1967; P. Caws, 'What is Structuralism?', in *Partisan Review*, 35:1, 1968, 75–91 (and 'Structuralism', in *Dictionary of the History of Ideas*, vol. 4, New York 1973, 322–30); R. Boudon, *A Quoi sert la notion de 'structure'*, Paris 1968; N. Mouloud, *Langage et structures*, Paris 1969; an interesting discussion of the ideological implications of structuralism in S. Timpanaro, *Sul materialismo*, Pisa 1970, 123–221 (trans. *On Materialism*, London 1975, 135–219; revised and enlarged Italian edition, Pisa 1975); J. Martinet, *Clefs pour la sémiologie*, Paris 1973; J.-M. Benoist, *La révolution structurale*, Paris 1975; Ph. Pettit, *The Concept of Structuralism. A Critical Analysis*, Dublin 1975; J. Culler, *Structuralist Poetics*, London 1975; T. Hawkes, *Structuralism and Semiotics*, London 1977; R. Coward, J. Ellis, *Language and Materialism. Developments in Semiology and the Theory of the Subject*, London 1977; G. Strickland, *Structuralism or Criticism? Thoughts on How We Read*, Cambridge 1981; for a synthesis on structuralism, linguistic and non-linguistic, see my entry 'Strutturalismo' in *Enciclopedia del Novecento* (also in my *Mutamenti di prospettiva nella linguistica e altri saggi*, Bologna 1981).

Chapter II Saussure

On Saussure, cf. the systematic bibliography with over 2500 items by E. F. K. Koerner, *Bibliographia Saussureana 1870–1970. An Annotated, Classified Bibliography on the Background, Development and Actual Relevance of Ferdinand de Saussure's General Theory of Language*, Metuchen, N. J. 1972 (cf. also my review in *Linguistics*, 123, 1974, 95–102; H. Genaust, 'Compléments à la "Bibliographia Saussureana, 1916–1972" ', in *Historiographia Linguistica*, 3, 1976, 37–87). Useful bibliographical surveys are offered by R. Engler, in *CFS*, 30, 1976, 99–138; 31, 1977, 279–306; 33, 1979, 79–145. To quote only works published separately (not articles): N. Sljusareva, *Kritičeskij analiz problem vnutrennej lingvistiki v koncepcii F. de Sossjura*, Moskva 1970 (cf. my review in *CFS*, 28, 1973, 67–70); D'A. S. Avalle, *Corso di semiologia dei testi letterari (1971–1972)*, Torino 1972; E. F. K. Koerner, *Contribution au débat post-Saussurien sur le signe linguistique*, The Hague 1972; C. Vallini, *Linee generali del problema dell'analogia dal periodo schleicheriano a F. de Saussure*, Pisa 1972; D'A. S. Avalle, *L'ontologia del segno in Saussure*, Torino 1973; E. F. K. Koerner, *Ferdinand de Saussure. Origin and Development of his Linguistic Thought in Western Studies of Language. A Contribution to the History and Theory of Linguistics*, Braunschweig 1973 (cf. my review in *RomPh*, 30, 1977, 623–5); R. Amacker etc., *Studi saussuriani per Robert Godel*, Bologna 1974; *Les deux Saussures, Recherches/Sémiotext(e)*, 16, 1974; L.-J. Calvet, *Pour et contre Saussure*, Paris 1975; R. Amacker, *Linguistique saussurienne*, Genève 1975; J. Culler, *Saussure*, London 1976; N. A. Sljusareva, *Teorija F. de Sossjura v svete sovremennoj lingvistiki*, Moskva 1975 (cf. my review in *CFS*, 30, 1976, 182–85); R. Engler, *Saussure und die Romanistik*, Bern 1976; A. Elia, *Per Saussure, contro Saussure. Il 'sociale' nelle teorie linguistiche del Novecento*, Bologna 1978; C. Bierbach, *Sprache als 'Fait Social'. Die linguistische Theorie F. de Saussure's und ihr Verhältnis zu den positivistischen Sozialwissenschaften*, Tübingen 1978; C. Sanders, ed., *Cours de linguistique générale de Saussure*, Paris 1979; G. Dresselhaus, *Langue/Parole und Kompetenz/Performanz*, Frankfurt a. M. 1979; G. Lepschy, *Intorno a Saussure*, Torino 1979. For Saussure's work on the 'anagrams' cf. J. Starobinski, *Les mots sous les mots. Les*

Appendix

anagrammes de Ferdinand de Saussure, Paris 1971 (trans. *Words upon Words. The Anagrams of Ferdinand de Saussure,* New Haven 1979); P. Wunderli, *Ferdinand de Saussure und die Anagramme. Linguistik und Literatur,* Tübingen 1972.

The *Cours* has appeared in many new translations: Hungarian (1967), Serbo-croat (1969), Swedish (1970), Portuguese (1971), Japanese (revised 1972; new 1976), Vietnamese (1973), Korean (1975), Turkish (1976), Albanian (1977), Russian (revised 1977). De Mauro's commentary has been translated for the French edition, Paris 1972.

On the School of Geneva, see R. Godel, ed., *A Geneva School Reader in Linguistics,* Bloomington 1969 (cf. my review in *Linguistics,* 130, 1974, 113–16).

Chapter III   The Prague School

See the anthologies in Polish: M. R. Mayenowa, ed., *Praska szkoła strukturalna w latach 1926–1948,* Warszawa 1966; in Russian: N. A. Kondrašov, ed., *Pražskij lingvističeskij kružok,* Moskva 1967; and cf. J.-P. Faye, L. Robel, edd., *Le Cercle de Prague,* Paris 1969 (Change, 3); J. Fontaine, *Le Cercle linguistique de Prague,* Tours 1974; L. Matejka, I. R. Titunik, edd., *Semiotics of Art. Prague School Contributions,* Cambridge Mass. 1976; L. Matejka, ed., *Sound, Sign and Meaning. Quinquagenary of the Prague Linguistic Circle,* Ann Arbor 1977. There are influential trans. from J. Mukařovský, *Il significato dell'estetica,* Torino 1973; *The Word and Verbal Art,* New Haven 1977; *Structure, Sign and Function,* New Haven 1978.

On Russian Formalism, cf. K. Pomorska, *Russian Formalist Theory and Its Poetic Ambiance,* The Hague 1968; and good anthologies, in English: L. Matejka, K. Pomorska, edd., *Readings in Russian Poetics. Formalist and Structuralist Views,* Cambridge Mass. 1971; in French: T. Todorov, ed., *Théorie de la littérature,* Paris 1965; in the original Russian, with facing German trans.: J. Striedter, W.-D. Stempel, edd., *Texte der russischen Formalisten,* 2 vols, München 1969–72.

Essential for the knowledge of the development of Trubeckoj's thought is the edition, in the original Russian, prepared by R. Jakobson, *N. S. Trubetzkoy's Letters and Notes,* The Hague 1975 (cf. my review in *JL,* 12, 1976, 371–72). The *Grundzüge* (p. 160 n. 15) have appeared in English trans.: *Principles of Phonology,* Berkeley 1969.

For Baudouin de Courtenay: F. Häusler, *Das Problem Phonetik und Phonologie bei Baudouin de Courtenay und in seiner Nachfolge,* Halle (Saale) 1968; E. Stankiewicz, ed., *A Baudouin de Courtenay Anthology. The Beginnings of Structural Linguistics,* Bloomington 1972 (cf. my review in *Linguistics,* 178, 1976, 102–4); M. Di Salvo, *Il pensiero linguistico di Jan Baudouin de Courtenay,* Venezia-Padova 1975; T. S. Šaradzenidze, *Lingvističeskaja teorija I. A. Boduèna de Kurtenè i ee mesto v jazykoznanii XIX–XX vekov,* Moskva 1980.

Polivanov's *Stat'i* (p. 161 n. 32) have been trans. into English: *Selected Works. Articles on General Linguistics,* The Hague 1974 (cf. my review in *Linguistics,* 195, 1977, 67–70).

On the history of phonology, cf. F. M. Berezin, *Očerki po istorii jazykoznanija v Rossii (konec XIX–naçalo XX v.),* Moskva 1968; J. Krámský, *The Phoneme. Introduction to the History and Theories of a Concept,* München 1974; E. Fischer-Jørgensen, *Trends in Phonological Theory. A Historical Introduction,*

Appendix

Copenhagen 1975; J. Kilbury, *The Development of Morphophonemic Theory*, Amsterdam 1976; N. Davidsen-Nielsen, *Neutralization and Archiphoneme. Two Phonological Concepts and Their History*, Copenhagen 1978.

Chapter IV The Copenhagen School

There is an English trans. by F. J. Whitfield of a previously unpublished text: L. Hjelmslev, *Résumé of a Theory of Language*, Madison 1975. Hjelmslev's *Prolegomena* have been published in French by the Éditions de Minuit, in two different versions, one by a group of linguists, ed. by A. M. Léonard, in 1968, and the other, to supersede it, bu U. Canger, *Prolégomènes à une théorie du langage*, Paris 1971. *Sproget* (p. 162 n. 11) has appeared in English: *Language. An Introduction*, Madison 1970. There is also a second volume of L. Hjelmslev, *Essais linguistiques*, TCLC, 14, 1973 (cf. p. 162 n. 10). On his theory cf. G. Graffi, *Struttura, forma e sostanza in Hjelmslev*, Bologna 1974.

Chapter V The Beginnings of American Structuralism

There are two important collections: M. Silverstein, ed., *Whitney on Language. Selected Writings of William Dwight Whitney*, Cambridge Mass. 1971 (with an introduction by R. Jakobson, 'The World Response to Whitney's Principles of Linguistic Science', xxv–xlv); C. F. Hockett, ed., *A Leonard Bloomfield Anthology*, Bloomington 1970 (cf. my review in *Linguistics*, 108, 1973, 120–28). See also H. M. Hoenigswald, ed., *The European Background of American Linguistics*, Dordrecht 1979.

Chapter VI Functional Linguistics

Of R. Jakobson's *SW* (cf. p. 167 n. 1) the vols published include: 1. *Phonological Studies*, 1962; 2. *Word and Language*, 1971; 4. *Slavic Epic Studies*, 1966; 5. *On Verse, Its Masters and Explorers*, 1979. Cf. *R. Jakobson, A Bibliography of His Writings*, The Hague 1971; among his main recent publications see a large collection of essays in French: *Questions de poétique*, Paris 1973; *Coup d'oeil sur le développement de la sémiotique*, Bloomington 1975; *Six leçons sur le son et le sens*, Paris 1976 (trans. *Six Lectures on Sound and Meaning*, Hassocks 1978); with L. Waugh, *The Sound Shape of Language*, Bloomington 1979; *Brain and Language. Cerebral Hemispheres and Linguistic Structure in Mutual Light*, Columbus, Ohio 1980; *Dialogues* (with K. Pomorska), Paris 1980. Cf. also E. Holenstein, *Jakobson ou le structuralisme phénoménologique*, Paris 1974 (trans. *Roman Jakobson's Approach to Language. Phenomenological Structuralism*, Bloomington 1977); L. R. Waugh, *Roman Jakobson's Science of Language*, Lisse 1976; D. Armstrong, C. H. van Schoneveld, edd., *Roman Jakobson. Echoes of His Scholarship*, Lisse 1977.

Among Martinet's works, cf. *Évolution des langues et reconstruction*, Paris 1975; *Studies in Functional Syntax. Études de syntaxe fonctionnelle*, München

Appendix

1975; and the descriptive analysis edited by him, *Grammaire fonctionnelle du français,* Paris 1979.

The influence of Benveniste's work keeps growing (he died in 1976 after a tragic period of incapacitation), not only in the field of comparative philology, but also in theoretical linguistics and semiotics. See a second collection *Problèmes de linguistique générale,* II, Paris 1974 (and the trans. of the first, *Problems in General Linguistics,* Miami 1971); *Le vocabulaire des institutions indo-européennes,* Paris 1969 (trans. *Indo-European Language and Society,* London 1973). Cf. the two collections devoted to him: *Mélanges linguistiques offerts à Émile Benveniste,* Paris 1975; J. Kristeva etc., edd., *Langue, discours, société. Pour Émile Benveniste,* Paris 1975. See the obituaries by T. Bolelli, *Émile Benveniste,* Roma 1978; Y. Malkiel, in *RomPh,* 34, 1980, 160–94.

Among Kuryłowicz's works, cf. *Esquisses lingistiques,* II, München 1975 (cf. p. 170 n. 38).

For Šaumjan (now at Yale), cf. the English trans. of *Strukturnaja lingvistika* (cf. p. 170 n. 43), *Principles of Structural Linguistics,* The Hague 1971; *Applikativnaja grammatika kak semantičeskaja teorija estestvennyx jazykov,* Moskva 1974 (in English *Applicational Grammar as a Semantic Theory of Natural Languages,* Edinburgh 1977).

Important developments in semiotics have been produced in the School of Tartu; cf. Ju. M. Lotman, *Struktura xudožestvennogo teksta,* Moskva 1970 (Italian trans. *La struttura del testo poetico,* Milano 1972); *Analiz poetičeskogo teksta. Struktura stixa,* Leningrad 1972 (trans. *Analysis of the Poetic Text,* Ann Arbor 1976); and see A. Shukman, *Literature and Semiotics. A Study of the Writings of Yu. M. Lotman,* Amsterdam 1977. There are useful anthologies: Ju. M. Lotman, B. A. Uspenskij, edd., *Ricerche semiotiche. Nuove tendenze delle scienze umane nell'URSS,* Torino 1973; Id., id., edd., *Semiotica e cultura,* Milano-Napoli 1976; D. P. Lucid, ed., *Soviet Semiotics. An Anthology,* Baltimore 1977; C. Prevignano, ed., *La semiotica nei paesi slavi,* Milano 1979; and the series ed. by L. M. O'Toole and A. Shukman, *Russian Poetics in Translation,* University of Essex 1971 foll.

Chapter VII   Structural Linguistics

Among other works by some of the linguists mentioned in this chapter, see D. L. Bolinger, *The Phrasal Verb in English,* Cambridge Mass. 1971; *Degree Words,* The Hague 1972 (cf. my review in *RomPh,* 32, 1979, 411–15); an enlarged second edition of *Aspects of Language,* New York 1975, and a streamlined third edition, with D. A. Sears, New York 1981; J. H. Greenberg, *Language, Culture and Communication,* ed. by A. S. Dil, Stanford 1971; *A New Invitation to Linguistics,* Garden City, New York 1977; Z. S. Harris, *Papers in Structural and Transformational Linguistics,* Dordrecht 1970; *Notes du cours de syntaxe,* Paris 1976; and cf. S. Plötz, ed., *Transformational Analysis. The Transformational Theory of Zellig Harris and Its Development,* Frankfurt a. M. 1972; C. F. Hockett, *The View from Language. Selected Essays, 1948–1974,* Athens, Georgia 1977; W. P. Lehmann, *Descriptive Linguistics. An Introduction,* New York 1972; E. A. Nida, *Exploring Semantic Structures,* München 1975; *Language Structure and Translation.* Essays ed. by A. S. Dil, Stanford 1975; on Pike cf. R. M. Brend, ed., *Selected Writings to Commemorate the 60th Birthday of K. L. Pike,* The Hague 1972; M. Swadesh, *The Origin and*

Appendix

Diversification of Language, ed. by J. Sherzer, London 1972; G. L. Trager, *Language and Languages,* San Francisco 1972. In general cf. R. Austerlitz, *The Scope of American Linguistics,* Lisse 1975.

Interesting developments in the field of sociolinguistics, with W. Labov, *Sociolinguistic Patterns,* Philadelphia 1972; *Language in the Inner City. Studies in the Black English Vernacular,* Philadelphia 1972; and cf. in Britain P. Trudgill, *The Social Differentiation of English in Norwich,* Cambridge 1974; Id., *Sociolinguistics. An Introduction,* Harmondsworth 1974.

For British linguistics, cf. the collection ed. by F. R. Palmer, *Prosodic Analysis,* London 1970; M. A. K. Halliday (now at the University of Sydney), *Explorations in the Functions of Language,* London 1973; *Learning how to Mean. Explorations in the Development of Language,* London 1975; *Language as Social Semiotic. The Social Interpretation of Language and Meaning,* London 1978; and the collection ed. by G. R. Kress, *Halliday: System and Function in Language,* London 1976; J. Lyons, *Semantics,* Cambridge 1977; *Language and Linguistics. An Introduction,* Cambridge 1981; P. H. Matthews, *Inflectional Morphology. A Theoretical Study Based on Aspects of Latin Verb Conjugation,* London 1972; *Morphology,* London 1974; *Generative Grammar and Linguistic Competence,* London 1979 (cf. my review in *The Cambridge Quarterly,* 9:1, 1979, 77–85); F. Palmer, *Grammar,* Harmondsworth 1971; *The English Verb,* London 1974 (second revised edition); *Semantics. A New Outline,* Cambridge 1976; R. H. Robins, *Diversions of Bloomsbury. Selected Writings on Linguistics,* Amsterdam 1970; D. Crystal, *The English Tone of Voice. Essays in Intonation, Prosody and Paralanguage,* London 1975. An important descriptive work: R. Quirk etc., *A Grammar of Contemporary English,* London 1972. There is an anthology by W. Kühlwein, *Linguistics in Great Britain,* vol. I: *History of Linguistics,* Tübingen 1971, vol. II, *Contemporary Linguistics,* ib. 1970.

Chapter VIII   Transformational Grammar

This is the framework which has become dominant in theoretical linguistics. There have been many developments, such as generative semantics, associated with the names of G. Lakoff, J. R. Ross, J. D. McCawley, etc. (cf. G. Cinque, ed., *La semantica generativa,* Torino 1979), case theory (Ch. J. Fillmore), relational grammar (P. M. Postal and D. Perlmutter), etc. But the innovations which are, in my opinion, more original and interesting, have come from Chomsky himself in the elaboration of what is known as the extended theory and its revisions.

In the first period of transformational theory the main effort was directed in overcoming the descriptive inadequacies of traditional structural linguistics (which was presented, in generative terms, as an instance of phrase structure grammar), through the introduction of new operations called transformations. But it was realized that transformations were too powerful a device, and work over the last dozen years has concentrated on the attempt to constrain this device, by imposing *conditions* on transformations. Linguistic theory must be constrained, in such a way that it accounts only for natural languages (and not for other semiotic systems), and that it allows for explanations of possible variations between one language and another, both in the way they define variable parameters, and in the way they depart from invariant principles along a scale of *markedness.*

Appendix

The drift of the research has been towards the elaboration of a more abstract, explanatory model, with few general principles from which rules are deduced on which constraints are then imposed. The most recent view of the organization of grammar assumes that there are: (1) a *phonetic representation*, derived from surface structure, and (2) a *logical form* of the sentence, also derived from surface structure; (semantic representation is derived from logical form and from representations on other cognitive systems). These two levels are connected by means of the syntactic structure of the sentence, which consists of (3) a *deep structure*, indicating the basic relations between elements of simple sentences, in terms of *thematic role* (agent, patient, etc.) and *grammatical function* (subject, object, etc.); and (4) a *surface structure*, which is an extension of the deep structure, obtained via transformations.

The different movement rules previously used in transformational grammar are reduced to one simple rule 'Move α', constrained by certain *conditions*. The main notions used are: *government*, which is related to the traditional view of the governing of complements (in generative theory, A governs B if the first node which immediately dominates A also immediately dominates B); a nominal complement is assigned a *case* by the category which governs it; *binding* concerns the relations of co-reference between nominal elements: anaphors, pronominal NPs, full NPs (an anaphor must have its antecedent in its governing category, i.e., in a sentence or NP in which it is governed). The rule 'Move α' moves a category from B to A, and leaves in the position B a *trace* (an *empty category*) co-indexed to the moved category. The trace may be an anaphor or a full NP, and so behave differently according to binding conditions. This seems to account economically for data which otherwise would require *ad hoc* explanations, and for the different behaviour of different languages (cf. the synthetic exposition by G. Cinque, *Il generativismo e i suoi sviluppi*, xerox, 1980, to appear in C. Segre, ed., *La linguistica oggi*; and, for a detailed, systematic presentation, A. Radford, *TG. A Beginner's Guide to Chomsky's Extended Standard Theory (E.S.T.)*, Bangor 1980, duplicated, to be published by Cambridge University Press).

Among Chomsky's works I shall quote: *Language and Mind*, New York 1972 (a new edition which includes, besides the three chapters of the 1968 edition, 'Form and Meaning in Natural Languages' (1969), 'The Formal Nature of Language' (1967), 'Linguistics and Philosophy' (1969)); *Studies on Semantics in Generative Grammar*, The Hague 1972 (which includes 'Remarks on Nominalization' (1970), 'Deep Structure, Surface Structure and Semantic Interpretation' (1970), 'Some Empirical Issues in the Theory of Transformational Grammar' (1972)); *Reflections on Language*, London 1976; *Essays on Form and Interpretation*, New York 1977 (which includes, besides an Introduction, 'Questions of Form and Interpretation' (1975), 'On the Nature of Language' (1975), 'Conditions on Transformations' (1973), 'Conditions on Rules of Grammar' (1976)); *Language and Responsibility*, Hassocks 1979; *Rules and Representations*, Oxford 1980 (the first four chapters based on lectures given at Columbia University in 1978 and at Stanford in 1979; chapter 5 'On the Biological Basis of Language Capacities'; chapter 6 'Language and Unconscious Knowledge' (1976)); *Lectures on Government and Binding*, Dordrecht 1981. Important earlier works recently made available are: *The Logical Structure of Linguistic Theory*, New York 1975 (in the version which goes back to 1955–56, with an interesting introduction of 1973); *Morphophonemics of Modern Hebrew*, New York 1979 (December 1951 revision of the University of Pennsylvania M.A. thesis).

Appendix

On Chomsky, cf. J. Lyons, *Chomsky*, London 1970 (enlarged edition 1977); G. Harman, ed., *On Noam Chomsky. Critical Essays*, Garden City, New York 1974; B. D. Den Ouden, *Language and Creativity. An Interdisciplinary Essay in Chomskyan Humanism*, Lisse 1975; J. Leiber, *Noam Chomsky. A Philosophical Overview*, Boston 1975.

General introductions to transformational grammar: M. K. Burt, *From Deep Structure to Surface Structure. An Introduction to Transformational Syntax*, New York 1971; J. T. Grinder, S. H. Elgin, *Guide to Transformational Grammar. History, Theory, Practice*, New York 1973; E. Bach, *Syntactic Theory*, New York 1974; A. Akmajian, F. Heny, *An Introduction to the Principles of Transformational Syntax*, Cambridge Mass. 1975; R. L. Whitman, *English and English Linguistics*, New York 1975; P. Culicover, *Syntax*, New York 1976; R. Huddleston, *An Introduction to English Transformational Syntax*, London 1976; S. J. Keyser, P. M. Postal, *Beginning English Grammar*, New York 1976; B. Jacobsen, *Transformational Generative Grammar. An Introductory Survey of Its Genesis and Development*, Amsterdam 1977; R. P. Stockwell, *Foundations of Syntactic Theory*, Englewood Cliffs 1977; C. L. Baker, *Introduction to Generative-Transformational Syntax*, Englewood Cliffs 1978; N. Smith, D. Wilson, *Modern Linguistics. The Results of Chomsky's Revolution*, Harmondsworth 1979; S. Soames, D. M. Perlmutter, *Syntactic Argumentation and the Structure of English*, Berkeley 1979; F. J. Newmeyer, *Linguistic Theory in America. The First Quarter-Century of Transformational Generative Grammar*, New York 1980.

On various theoretical developments, cf. E. Bach, R. T. Harms, edd., *Universals in Linguistic Theory*, New York 1968 (with contributions by Ch. J. Fillmore, E. Bach, J. D. McCawley, P. Kiparsky); W. L. Chafe, *Meaning and the Structure of Language*, Chicago 1970; G. Lakoff, *Irregularity in Syntax*, New York 1970; Ch. J. Fillmore, D. T. Langendoen, edd., *Studies in English Semantics*, New York 1971; P. M. Postal, *Cross-Over Phenomena*, New York 1971; P. M. Postal, *On Raising. One Rule of English Grammar and Its Theoretical Implications*, Cambridge Mass. 1974; R. A. Hudson, *Arguments for a Non-Transformational Grammar*, Chicago 1976; J. E. Emonds, *A Transformational Approach to English Syntax. Root, Structure-Preserving, and Local Transformations*, New York 1976; R. Jackendoff, $\bar{X}$ *Syntax: A Study of Phrase Structure*, Cambridge Mass. 1977; R. W. Cole, ed., *Current Issues in Linguistic Theory*, Bloomington 1977; P. W. Culicover, Th. Wasow, A. Akmajian, edd., *Formal Syntax*, New York 1977; D. E. Johnson, P. M. Postal, *Arc Pair Grammar*, Princeton 1980.

For phonology: F. Dell, *Les règles et les sons. Introduction à la phonologie générative*, Paris 1973 (trans. *Generative Phonology*, Cambridge 1980); S. A. Schane, *Generative Phonology*, Englewood Cliffs 1973; S. R. Anderson, *The Organization of Phonology*, New York 1974; L. M. Hyman, *Phonology. Theory and Analysis*, New York 1975; D. L. Goyvaerts, G. K. Pullum, edd., *Essays on the Sound Pattern of English*, Ghent 1975.

For aspects of morphology: M. Aronoff, *Word Formation in Generative Grammar*, Cambridge Mass. 1976.

Chapter IX Mathematical Linguistics and Machine Translation
In this field the main drift of research has been away from statistical computation

191

and machine translation, and towards the study of artificial intelligence, formal grammars (in connexion with generative theory), and the relationship between logic and linguistics.

I shall quote: M. Davis, ed., *The Undecidable. Basic Papers on Undecidable Propositions, Unsolvable Problems and Computable Functions,* New York 1965 (cf. p. 172 n. 22); M. Minsky, *Computation. Finite and Infinite Machines,* Englewood Cliffs 1967; Id., ed., *Semantic Information Processing,* Cambridge Mass. 1968; Id., S. Papert, *Perceptrons. An Introduction to Computational Geometry,* Cambridge Mass. 1969; beside the one quoted on p. 178 n. 12, there is another volume of collected papers by Y. Bar-Hillel, *Aspects of Language. Essays and Lectures on Philosophy of Language, Linguistic Philosophy, and Methodology of Linguistics,* Jerusalem 1970. Some interesting contributions appear in the proceedings of a 1968 Olivetti conference: *Linguaggi nella società e nella tecnica,* Milano 1970; G. Miller, E. Galanter, K. H. Pribram, *Plans and Structure of Behavior,* London 1970 (USA edition 1960); T. Winograd, *Understanding Natural Language,* Edinburgh 1972.

On formal linguistics: S. Ginsburg, *The Mathematical Theory of Context-Free Languages,* New York 1966; M. Gross, A. Lentin, *Notions sur les grammaires formelles,* Paris 1967 (trans. *Introduction to Formal Grammars,* Heidelberg 1970); J. E. Hopcroft, J. D. Ullman, edd., *Formal Languages and their Relation to Automata,* Reading Mass. 1969; B. Brainerd, *Introduction to the Mathematics of Language Study,* New York 1971; R. Wall, *Introduction to Mathematical Linguistics,* Englewood Cliffs 1971; M. Gross, *Mathematical Models in Linguistics,* Englewood Cliffs 1972; J. P. Kimball, *The Formal Theory of Grammar,* Englewood Cliffs 1973; A. Kasher, *Linguistics and Logic. Conspectus and Prospects,* Kronberg/Ts. 1975; B. Hall Partee, *Fundamentals of Mathematics for Linguistics,* Dordrecht 1978; J. D. McCawley, *Everything that Linguists have Always Wanted to Know about Logic* *but Were Ashamed to Ask,* Oxford 1981.

The contact between logic and grammar has always been important and fruitful, from Aristotle to the Stoics, the Modistae, Port Royal, Leibniz, Frege, Wittgenstein, etc. But it is fair to add that, particularly from the beginning of the nineteenth century, linguistics has developed a closer link with historical disciplines and with psychology and has been reducing its traditional connexion with logic. One of the main logicians of our century, Rudolf Carnap, wrote an influential work called *Logische Syntax der Sprache,* Wien 1934 (trans. *The Logical Syntax of Language,* London 1937), but in it he dealt with the formation and transformation rules of artificially constructed symbolic languages, not natural ones. He felt that 'in consequence of the unsystematic and logically imperfect structure of the natural word-languages (such as German or Latin), the statement of their formal rules of formation and transformation would be so complicated that it would hardly be feasible in practice' (*Logical Syntax,* p. 2).

Other philosophers took a more optimistic view of the possibility of a logical analysis of natural languages; particularly inspiring and stimulating proved the observations by Hans Reichenbach in his *Elements of Symbolic Logic,* New York 1947, which was animated by 'the desire to connect logic with the actual use of language' (p. vi). Generative grammar took a view of language which, to some more traditional linguists, appeared to be too abstract and algebraic to be able to deal with the syntactic vagaries, semantic idiosyncrasies, emotive colouring and unconscious implications of natural languages; and in any case there developed a branch of mathematical study of formal languages in connexion

Appendix

with generative grammar. But some logicians thought, on the contrary, that the use made of logical notions and notations in generative grammar was not rigorous enough and not as thorough-going as it should have been.

The most influential defender of this view was the philosopher Richard Montague, who died tragically in 1971. His work has been adapted and developed, in connexion with generative grammar, by Barbara Hall Partee and other linguists over the last ten years. Montague states: 'There is in my opinion no important theoretical difference between natural languages and the artificial languages of logicians; indeed, I consider it possible to comprehend the syntax and semantics of both kinds of languages within a single natural and mathematically precise theory' (Thomason, quoted below, p. 222).

For Montague, syntactic study is subordinated to semantics, i.e. to the study of meaning. In the tradition of Alfred Tarski, meaning is assumed to determine the truth-value of a sentence, that is the conditions under which the sentence is true or false, in different circumstances. The *extension* (i.e., the set of things indicated by a noun, or the truth-value of a sentence) depends on the meaning, and on other relevant facts about the use of the sentence; the meaning can be considered, at least in part, as 'a function which yields as output an appropriate extension when given as input a package of the various factors on which the extension may depend. We will call such an input package of relevant factors an *index*; and we will call any function from indices to appropriate extensions for a sentence, name, or common noun an *intension*' (D. Lewis, in Partee 1976, quoted below, p. 6).

In Montague grammar we find a *syntax* based on *categories* (with some transformational elements, to deal with quantifiers; but basically it is a kind of context-free phrase structure grammar called 'categorial grammar', in the tradition of K. Ajdukiewicz, 'Die syntaktische Konnexität', in *Studia Philosophica*, 1, 1935, 1–27, trans. in S. McCall, ed., *Polish Logic,* Oxford 1967, 207–31); a *lexicon* which lists lexical items with their syntactic category; and a *semantics* with translation rules into intensional logic (in the tradition of R. Carnap, *Meaning and Necessity. A Study in Semantics and Modal Logic*, Chicago 1947). The translation of any sentence is derived from the translation of its constituents.

The work of Montague, and studies in the framework of Montague grammar in general, are highly technical and impenetrable to readers not versed in symbolic logic. But some of the basic points can be made informally; for instance, Barbara Hall Partee stresses the importance of the connexion between syntax and semantics in Montague grammar, as the specification of the whole on the basis of its constituent parts should be the same in both: 'the syntactic analysis should build up larger units from (or equivalently, analyse them into) just those parts on the basis of which the meaning of the larger unit can be determined' (Partee 1976, quoted below, p. 52). For instance, for the expression *the boy who lives in the park* three different underlying structures have been suggested:

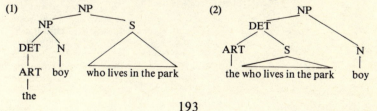

Appendix

(3)

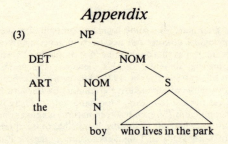

In singular phrases of the form *the a*, the class denoted by *a* has one and only one member. In structure (3) the class of boys and the class of those who live in the park are combined, and the superordinate NOM denotes their intersection (the class of those who both live in the park and are boys); the use of *the* indicates, correctly, that this class has only one member. This interpretation is not applicable to structure (1), where the relative clause would have to be nonrestrictive (there is only one boy, and he lives in the park), nor to structure (2), which suggests that there is only one person who lives in the park. It is clear that semantically (3) is preferable to (1) and (2), but this would not be appreciated in a different grammatical approach which did not aim to connect syntax and semantics (cf. Partee 1976, pp. 53–5).

There is a growing literature on Montague grammar. The main articles by Montague have been collected posthumously: R. H. Thomason, ed., *Formal Philosophy. Selected Papers of Richard Montague*, New Haven 1974; see also B. Hall Partee, 'Montague Grammar and Transformational Grammar', in *Linguistic Inquiry*, 6, 1975, 203–300; Ead., ed., *Montague Grammar*, New York 1976; S. Davis, M. Mithun, edd., *Linguistics, Philosophy, and Montague Grammar*, Austin 1979; D. R. Dowty, *Word Meaning and Montague Grammar. The Semantics of Verbs and Times in Generative Semantics and in Montague's PTQ*, Dordrecht 1979; D. R. Dowty, R. E. Wall, S. Peters, *Introduction to Montague Semantics*, Dordrecht 1981.

Terminological Index

🀰🀰🀰🀰🀰🀰

The same terms may be used by different authors with different values, or different terms with the same values. As in the text so in this index no attempt at standardization has been made but the terminologies of the different authors have been preserved.

Terminological Index

Index of Names

ⓢⓢⓢⓢⓢⓢ

Variant spellings of proper names have been preserved in the notes. In this index the variants are listed but all page references will be found under one form only for each name.

199

Index of Names

Index of Names

201

Index of Names

202

Index of Names

203

Index of Names

Montague, R., 193–4
Morse, S. F. B., 30
Motsch, W., 181
Mouloud, N., 185
Moulton, W. G., 164
Mounin, G., 151, 154–5, 170, 178–9, 181, 182
Mukařovský, B., 53, 159, 186
Muller, Ch., 177
Müller, H., 164
Müller, M., 74
Müllner, K., 176
Munot, Ph., 161
Murat, V. P., 164

Nagel, E., 153
Nash, R., 182
Nava, G., 155
Neurath, O., 166
Newman, S. S., 165
Newmeyer, F. J., 191
Nida, E. A., 75, 114, 171–2, 188
Niederhäusern, I. von, 155
Nitsch, K., 160
Noreen, A., 60, 65, 160
Nyquist, H., 146, 178

Oettinger, A. G., 178
Oltramare, A., 154
Orr, J., 157, 181
Osgood, C. E., 113, 171
Oswald, V. A., 148, 179
O'Toole, L. M., 188

Palmer, F. R., 174, 189
Palmer, L. R., 11, 174, 182
Panov, D. Ju., 178–9
Papert, S., 192
Parret, H., 181
Passy, P., 160
Pavel, T., 155
Pedersen, H., 151, 162
Pei, M., 182
Peirce, C. S., 30
Perlmutter, D., 189, 191
Peters, S., 194
Petöfi, J. S., 184
Petrova, G. V., 157

Pettit, Ph., 185
Phelizon, J.-F., 183
Piaget, J., 153, 180, 184
Pike, K. L., 75, 102, 122–4, 164–5, 171–4, 189
Pipping, R., 154
Pittman, R. S., 172
Plötz, S., 188
Polivanov, E. D., 62, 161, 186
Pomorska, K., 186–7
Posner, R., 181
Pospelov, N. S., 158
Postal, P. M., 176, 179, 189, 191
Pott, A. F., 21
Potter, R. K., 168
Preston, R. J., 165
Preusler, W., 163
Prevignano, C., 188
Pribram, K. H., 192
Prieto, L. J., 113, 169, 171
Pulgram, E., 168
Pullum, G. K., 191

Quine, W. v. O., 171
Quirk, R., 189

Radford, A., 190
Rask, R., 65, 162
Rauch, J., 172
Reformatskij, A. A., 170
Reichenbach, H., 171, 192
Reifler, E., 147, 179
Rensch, K. H., 154–5
Revzin, I. I., 153, 179
Rice, S. A., 166
Richens, R. H., 147, 179
Riedlinger, A., 154
Ries, J., 166
Rigotti, E., 181
Robel, L., 186
Robey, D., 184
Robins, R. H., 151, 172, 174, 181, 189
Rogger, K., 154, 157
Ronjat, J., 154
Rosenbaum, P., 176
Rosetti, A., 164
Ross, J. R., 189

Index of Names

Index of Names